Great American Journeys

This Centennial Edition belongs to

JOHN POOL

Name   1888   NATIONAL   Date
            1988   GEOGRAPHIC
                 SOCIETY

The Free Trade Deal

The Free Trade Deal

Edited by Duncan Cameron

James Lorimer & Company, Publishers
Toronto, 1988

To the memory of Bishop Adolphe Proulx

Cover photos: Canapress Photo Service

Canadian Cataloguing in Publication Data
Main entry under title:
The Free trade deal
ISBN 1-55028-076-7 (bound) ISBN 1-55028-074-0 (pbk.)
1. Canada — Commercial treaties. 2. United States — Commercial
treaties. 3. Canada — Commerce — United States. 4. United States —
Commerce — Canada. 5. Free trade and protection. 6. Canada —
Economic conditions — 1971- .* I. Cameron, Duncan, 1944- .
HF1766.F73 1988   382.9'71'073   C88-0973674-6

James Lorimer & Company, Publishers
Egerton Ryerson Memorial Building
35 Britain Street
Toronto, Ontario M5A 1R7
Printed and bound in Canada
6 5 4 3 2 1 88 89 90 91 92 93

Contributors

John Calvert is a senior researcher with the Canadian Union of Public Employees and author of *Government Ltd..*

Duncan Cameron is a professor of political economy at the University of Ottawa and co-author of *Ethics and Economics*, co-editor of *The Other Macdonald Report* and editor of *The Free Trade Papers*.

Stephen Clarkson is a professor of political science at the University of Toronto and author of *Canada and the Reagan Challenge*.

Michael Clow is a professor of political science at Saint Thomas University in Fredericton.

Marjorie Griffin Cohen is a professor at the Ontario Institute for Studies in Education and author of *Free Trade and the Future of Women's Work* and *Women, Markets and Economic Development in Nineteenth Century Ontario*.

Deborah Coyne is a professor of constitutional law at the University of Toronto.

Susan Crean is an editor of *This Magazine*, author of *Newsworthy* and *Who's Afraid of Canadian Culture?*, and co-author of *Two Nations*.

Donna Dasko, Ph.D., is vice-president of Environics Research Group and co-author of the Globe-Environics Poll.

John Dillon is a researcher with GATT-fly, a project of the Canadian churches for global economic justice.

Daniel Drache is a professor of political science at Atkinson College, York University and co-editor of *The Other Macdonald Report* and *The New Practical Guide to Canadian Political Economy*.

Kirk Falconer served as a researcher with the Standing Committee on Finance and Economic Affairs of the House of Commons.

Giles Gherson is the Washington correspondent of the *Financial Post*.

Andrew Jackson is with the labour resources branch of the Canadian Labour Market and Productivity Centre.

Patricia Lane is a lawyer in Vancouver.

Hugh Mackenzie is research director for the United Steelworkers of America (Canada).

Riel Miller holds a Ph.D. in economics from the New School for Social Research in New York City.

Mary Beth Montcalm is a professor of political studies at the University of Manitoba.

Scott Sinclair, a graduate of the University of Prince Edward Island, is a doctoral candidate at York University.

Frank James Tester is a professor of environmental studies at York University.

John W. Warnock teaches political economy at the universities of Victoria and Regina and is the author of *Free Trade and the New Right Agenda*.

Mel Watkins is a professor of economics at the University of Toronto. An editor of *This Magazine*, he is perhaps best known as author of "The Watkins Report," done when he chaired the Task Force on the Structure of Canadian Industry.

Contents

Acknowledgments

In preparing this book I received much appreciated counsel and assistance from the authors of individual chapters. Daniel Drache, Stephen Clarkson, John Calvert and Mel Watkins merit particular thanks for their advice and support. Curtis Fahey of James Lorimer and Company lent not only his editorial skills but also provided encouragement beyond any reasonable call of duty. The special contribution of the publisher, Jim Lorimer, at a time when the editor was struggling with the conception of this project, is gratefully acknowleged, as is the skill exhibited by Dave Hogan in dealing with authors in the new world of electronic publishing. The copy-editing skills of Catherine Marjoribanks were much appreciated.

At the University of Ottawa, my colleagues are a constant source of support, moral as well as intellectual. By according me a research leave stipend, the Social Sciences and Humanities Research Council of Canada made it possible for me to devote time to this project.

A group of friends and colleagues produced this work. But others, though they bear less responsibility for the result, made it possible as well. Special thanks to Tony Clarke and also to Gil Levine and Ed Finn. Finally, this volume is dedicated to the memory of Adolphe Proulx who served as Bishop for the region of Gatineau-Hull. It was a great privilege to have known him. His teachings about social justice are overshadowed only by his work on behalf of those in need. Those who knew him were struck by his goodness. His life was about making a better world and, as his religion professes, it seemed to make him a better person. He is missed. What he accomplished is not forgotten.

Introduction

On January 2, 1988, Prime Minister Mulroney and President Reagan signed an agreement to join Canada and the United States in a new free-trade area. The separate ceremonies took place 462 days after the prime minister announced to the House of Commons his intention to seek a comprehensive trade arrangement with the U.S. Scheduled to come into force on January 1, 1989, the accord is officially described as *The Canada-U.S. Free Trade Agreement*. It is both less, and more, than that. Less, because not all trade restrictions between the two countries have been eliminated; notably for Canada, American protectionist trade laws remain in effect. More, because in important respects, namely energy and other natural resources, services and investment, it goes well beyond what is generally understood by free trade. In fact, what has been agreed upon between the two countries is a continental economic treaty with important political implications, especially for Canada.

For the Conservative government, the free-trade agreement represents the centrepiece of its economic strategy for Canada. The accord is intended to enhance Canada's competitive position, using the American market as a springboard for reaching other international markets. The Tories argue that Canadian industry needs tariff-free access to the North American market with its 250 million consumers. In other words, Canada's economic future lies in rationalizing industry on a North American basis so as to better serve the world market. The government denies that Canada's political future will in any way be compromised as a result of forging closer economic links with the U.S.

For the U.S., the economic impact of the pact is small, but not insignificant. A report prepared for the U.S. Trade Representative by the American International Trade Commission showed that U.S. industry had little to gain, or lose, from tariff reductions. But the accord is important for the Americans. It offers the U.S. non-discriminatory access to Canadian natural resources, a significant long-term advantage. At a time when the U.S. is running short of key raw materials, including petroleum, Canada has agreed not to favour Canadian resource users over American users.

For Canada, the agreement is by any measure an historic document. The preliminary agreement, reached shortly before midnight on October 3, 1987, was heralded by the American president as a "new economic constitution for North America." In Canada the entente has provoked strong reaction, both for and against. "Economic rape," "a magnificent achievement," "an unprecedented abandonment of national powers and massive transfers of authority and decision-making from Canada to the U.S.," "will secure jobs and better standards of living for Canadians to the end of the century and into the next" — these comments indicate the extent of controversy over free trade.

Within Canada there is good reason for the wide interest in the issues raised by the deal. Canadians have begun the most important political debate of this generation, perhaps of this century. Yet many people remain uncertain about what it all means. This book has been prepared to allow them to judge the agreement: to identify and understand the issues it raises. Expert commentary on the various articles of the accord should help the reader see what lies behind the complexities of the legal text. *The Free-Trade Deal* looks at the issues arising from the agreement as well as the text of the agreement itself. The perspective is critical but not unbalanced. While rhetoric and emotion are very much part of the debate over free trade, and legitimately so because of what is at stake, this book aims at improving the quality of that debate by providing information and informed comment that goes beyond the official interpretation of the text.

Buying the Deal

For many Canadians opposed to the free-trade deal, the accord represents a threat to our national existence. This is a serious charge. It is made by serious people. And it deserves to be considered carefully, not just dismissed as overstatement. Fierce opposition to free trade reflects the concern, not so much that Canada will disappear, but that if the deal goes ahead, Canadians will lose control over their destiny and that of their country. As this book will show, in addition to the far-reaching concessions made as part of this deal, the ability of elected representatives to introduce new policies has been reduced as part of an undertaking to a foreign government. In a very real sense, a significant measure of national control over the economy has been handed over to the North American private sector. For many Canadians, including both opposition parties in the House of Commons and the provincial governments of Ontario and Prince Edward Island, this makes the agreement unacceptable.

It should be clearly understood that free trade is not a *fait accompli*. Since both the Liberals and New Democrats have pledged, if elected, to renounce the deal, only the re-election of a majority Conservative government will ensure that the agreement does not die before being implemented, or is not abrogated once it becomes law. For the deal to take effect on January 1, 1989, passage of legislative amendments to implement the agreement must first take place. The required amendments to existing legislation need the approval of the House of Commons and Canadian Senate before the end of 1988 in order to meet the implementation date. Therefore, an election will be called (or forced) if the legislative amendments get bogged down in parliament. Moreover, constitutionally, the Conservatives must call an election before the fall of 1989 at the latest. Given that the agreement contains a six-month abrogation clause, a new Canadian government could still withdraw from the deal, even if the Conservatives manage to implement it. And, of course, the American Congress must pass ratifying legislation as well, which raises additional uncertainties about the future of the accord.

Thus, barring failure to ratify in the U.S., the future of free trade will be resolved politically within Canada. Simply put, if in a 1988 election the Canadian people reject the Conservative government, they reject the agreement. Neither the Liberals nor the New Democrats are prepared to proceed on implementation. A letter from the new prime minister to the American ambassador would suffice to kill the accord before it comes into effect. A Conservative defeat in a 1989 election would likely have the same effect, though this is somewhat more problematic. Once an international agreement like this deal takes force there would be pressure on a new government not to pull out. Unless public opinion in Canada has clearly rejected free trade, this pressure might have some effect, particularly on a Liberal majority government.

It is clear, however, that an NDP government or one that needed NDP support would abrogate the agreement. Thus either a Liberal or NDP minority administration would withdraw from the deal. And a Conservative minority would be unlikely to survive in the House of Commons.

The Mulroney government is well aware of the hazards that lie ahead. As the prime minister said of the free-trade initiative on June 6, 1986, "of course my neck is on the line." Speaking at the University of Brandon in September 1986, Mulroney promised that the Canadian people would be consulted about free trade. Given the importance attached to the deal by all three parties, the public debate over the meaning of free trade for Canada will frame the impending election contest. The government and its supporters have already indicated on what grounds they expect to fight. Indeed, the government has been making its position clear since the bilateral initiative was launched and it is unlikely to change its basic message.

Selling the Deal

What does the government say to sell this deal? What is the official interpretation of the text? First, the government trumpets the creation of a binding dispute-settlement mechanism as a breakthrough for Canada. The U.S., it says, has agreed to relinquish some of its sovereignty, since the entente replaces U.S. judicial review of trade disputes with binational panels where Canada will be represented. This establishes an important historical precedent for joint management of the North American economy. From now on, trade harassment of successful Canadian exporters will be reduced. American companies will be deterred from acting against Canadian companies by the prospect of having favourable decisions under U.S. law overturned by a binational panel. In addition, it is held that the U.S. trade-remedy process will be less political under the accord. Decisions by U.S. authorities — the International Trade Commission and the Department of Commerce — will be more impartial with the new disputes agency in place than they were when faced only with judicial review by U.S. courts. The disputes agency can be thought of as a deterrent to politically inspired decisions in the U.S against Canadian industry.

Second, the government insists that the deal has limited scope: it is about tariff reductions and trade disputes, matters of commercial policy. Under the accord, Canada only continues the policy of increased trade liberalization that was begun through the seven successive GATT (General Agreement on Tariffs and Trade) negotiations since the second World War. The bilateral nature of the agreement is downplayed as well. Canada and the United States are simply setting out together on a path that will be followed by other nations within the current eighth GATT round. By acting now, Canada gets a headstart in making the economic adjustments necessary to compete in a tougher, more competitive international environment.

Third, the government believes that there is no better economic strategy alternative for Canada than a bilateral trade deal with the U.S. Since the U.S. is Canada's best customer, taking nearly 80 per cent of all exports, it makes sense from the point of view of trade policy to enhance Canadian access to the American market. At the same time, the deal opens the Canadian economy to American competition, and in so doing it should reduce the productivity gap between the two nations in the all-important manufacturing sector. The creation of a North American capital market, by removing restrictions on flows of investment and assuring national treatment to foreign investment in each other's economies, helps to increase the efficiency of spending on new plants and equipment. Further, a wider market, combined with more freedom for capital investors, points towards a more prosperous North America. Increased competition will lower prices, raise the Gross National Product (GNP) per capita and create jobs. For the government, this is a win-win agreement. Both Canada and the U.S. gain overall. A stronger Canadian economy makes for a more independent foreign policy. A richer Canada can be more generous with social programmes.

Finally, the Conservatives point to their record on economic issues and claim that they have justified the confidence placed in them by the Canadian people. Lower rates of unemployment and of inflation show that the objectives laid out in the 1984 election campaign are being met. When they elected more members to the House of Commons than any other party has ever elected, Canadians expected good government and they have got it from the Conservatives. The free-trade deal will produce more jobs and prosperity. Canadians can trust the government on this score.

These arguments are made by Conservative ministers and members of parliament in defence of the accord. Since they will be heard over and over again, they require close examination. Do the arguments stand up to close scrutiny? At the very least it can be said that an alternative interpretation of the Conservative claims about the deal can be made. And it is clear that those concerned about the consequences of the agreement for Canada want to consider alternative views. As is to be expected, the official interpretation of the deal puts the agreement in the best possible light. In its public campaign in favour of the agreement, the government rarely considers arguments critical of the deal. Nevertheless, such arguments also merit attention. As the chapters in this book show, the government's case can be refuted.

Trade Politics

Though presented by the government as a Canadian undertaking, it is important that the negotiations be assessed from the American perspective. In chapter one, Giles Gherson sets out the American objectives in the bilateral talks. He demonstrates that the U.S. was able to achieve its main goals and that U.S. negotiators found the negotiations particularly useful for resolving specific trade grievances against Canada. Politically, the deal is part of the American strategy for dealing with a back-breaking trade deficit. It shows other U.S. trading partners that the Americans are serious about prying open markets abroad. If international negotiations under GATT fail to meet American demands, the U.S. is prepared to negotiate separate agreements with major trading partners. The pact with Canada is proof of its intention in this regard. Other U.S. trading partners, including Japan, Korea, Hong Kong, Taiwan and Singapore, are now reportedly prepared to risk bilateral talks in order to forestall unilateral American legislative or administrative action aimed at reducing the U.S. trade deficit. The conclusion is clear: by taking the world's largest trading relationship and putting it under a bilateral treaty, the U.S. and Canada are in effect weakening the multilateral trading system established under GATT.

While Canada has negotiated an agreement that liberalizes North American commerce, chapter two shows that the deal also has important implications for Canadian political practices. Bilateralism in trade represents a significant shift in Canadian foreign policy, since Canada has always championed international economic institutions. Also, provincial powers under the Constitution are restricted by the accord. Thus, Canada's ability to establish public goals is set into a new North American framework. The deal, then, constitutes a major undertaking, going beyond a normal political initiative. Whatever the benefits that may accrue to Canada from the free-trade deal, it must be evaluated in the larger context of changes to Canadian political life.

According to the government, it was all-important to eliminate the threat of American protectionism. A bilateral treaty that brought the rule of law to bear on trade relations was needed to restrain political actions on either side of the border. Indeed, if Canada could forego normal political channels, and deal with its superpower neighbour through a neutral mechanism, this would be attractive. Unfortunately, as Stephen Clarkson points out in chapter three, this seems highly unlikely to occur as a result of the agreement.

Under the terms of the deal, Canada's bilateral political dealings with the U.S. will increase substantially. The countries have institutionalized their economic relationship in the Canada-U.S. Trade Commission (CUSTER), but this body can be expected to reproduce the power dynamics of the bilateral relationship, where all the influence of the American government can be brought to bear directly on Canada's representatives. Canada is head to head with the U.S. within the commission, and, in contrast to our position in multilateral institutions, no allies are available to help out. At its heart, this is a deal based on goodwill, not on law as law is generally understood. If either party decides to ignore the wishes of the other it can do so. Nothing in the treaty prevents it. The only options available to an unhappy party are to retaliate against its partner or to scrap the deal altogether.

Free-trade supporters see the trade-disputes procedures as the key provision of the treaty. For Canada, they represent the major concession by the United States. Indeed, under the agreement, the creation of new dispute-settlement procedures for trade in goods is the best possible argument for justifying claims that Canada comes out ahead in the deal. But when the elaborate provisions set out in the treaty are stripped down to essentials, they amount to very little gain for Canada. Most claims made by supporters are exaggerated. When measured against what Canada sought in negotiations — guarantees concerning market access — the trade dispute provisions are a disappointment. In brief, if the case for the agreement rests on the disputes provisions, it has to be judged severely, and indeed it has been judged on this basis and found wanting by free-trade supporters as well as critics.

Though the government is unwilling to admit it, Canada failed to achieve its principal objective in talks with the U.S.: secure access to the U.S. market. There is no reason for confusion on this point, as chapter four outlines. What Canada wanted from the U.S. was clearly stated by the government. As Brian Mulroney himself said: "U.S. trade laws can't apply to Canada, period." Yet U.S. trade laws still apply to Canada under the accord. Worse, the key U.S. protectionist measures — its countervailing duty and anti-dumping laws — are actually incorporated into Chapter 19 of the agreement! The intended outcome of the talks from the Canadian perspective was a *new* set of trade laws to govern commercial relations between the two countries, and a court of *first* resort to resolve disputes. Canada achieved neither.

The government argues that lower tariffs will expand trade. This creates wealth, and the increased competition in the larger market ensures that benefits will be distributed to the population in the form of lower prices. This argument is the basis on which many Canadians find free trade economically attractive. Riel Miller scrutinizes this argument in chapter five and finds it wanting. Though many have been led to believe that, as a result of free trade, all goods available in the U.S. will be made available in Canada, duty-free, this is hardly the whole story. It is correct that by 1998 all American-made goods could be imported into Canada duty-free, and that tariff reductions could eventually lower prices on those goods, but individual Canadians will pay Canadian sales taxes on American goods even if they bring them back themselves from the U.S. And, of course, duty will be paid on all goods purchased in the U.S. but made elsewhere. Under free trade, a Japanese video recorder purchased in New York would be subject to both a duty and a Canadian sales tax. Rules of origin will be in effect, and someone will still have to check where a good was made in order to determine if duty must be paid.

But there is a larger economic argument concerning consumer prices that is also addressed in chapter five. It is that lower prices will put more money in the hands of Canadians, which will then be spent to create new wealth. This new wealth could then be used as Canadians see fit — for example, new social programmes could be created as a result of the larger tax revenues accruing from the increased wealth. Such arguments rest on the premise that a wider North American market would promote greater efficiency in production, increase competition and thus lower prices. Yet, as Riel Miller shows, it is hard to believe that the removal of the few remaining tariffs in North America could have such an impact. The more likely effect would be to enhance the trend towards fewer, larger producers. Large firms could take advantage of national treatment provisions to buy out competitors, or drive them out of business by lowering prices initially, then raising prices once competition has been eliminated. Efficient small firms are always takeover targets; it is cheaper and easier to buy success than create it. Price competition is more properly understood as a tool of corporate expansion than as the natural result of a larger market. Though there is no doubt that large firms do compete, there is no convincing evidence to suggest that they do so primarily through price reductions that benefit the consumer. This may occur, but it is more often the case that companies try to secure advantages over competitors by various strategic methods, including advertising, marketing, new product research and development, and other measures that increase costs and thus, eventually, prices.

A New Economic Constitution for North America

Despite government assertions, the entente is much broader than a trade deal. Daniel Drache makes it clear in chapter six that the text deals with matters that go beyond anything ever signed by Canada in the trade field. Fully ten of the twenty-one chapters in the agreement cover matters other than trade in goods. These include technical standards, energy, services, movement of people for business purposes, investment and financial services, as well as the creation of joint institutions and the application of trade law. And provisions with respect to trade in goods go further than any trade agreement ever

signed by Canada. The deal opens negotiations to set common standards for tradeable goods, for instance. Under this agreement Canada
agrees not just to treat American goods like Canadian goods for purposes of trade; Canada also agrees not to discriminate against
American purchasers of Canadian goods by imposing higher prices,
restricting supplies, or otherwise disrupting American access to
Canadian goods and resources.

The deal introduces new North American economic rules that are
based on the concept of national treatment. They bind governments,
particularly the Canadian government, in many specific respects, and
indeed justify the comment made by President Reagan that the deal offers "a new economic constitution for North America." The implications of these rules are stunning, so much so that critics believe that
once they are well known the deal will likely be rejected by Canadians.
But until the new rules are fully understood, the major difficulty is getting people to believe what Canada has in fact given away in this agreement.

The agreement extends the right of national treatment across the
border to U.S.-based suppliers of the Canadian market. As Mel Watkins demonstrates in chapter seven, the deal allows American investors to purchase virtually anything in Canada that has a value of less
than $150 million, no questions asked. And if a Canadian company is
already owned by Americans, the limit is waived. Large acquisitions
face nominal review and so-called cultural industries are excluded
from this "up for sale" policy. Of course, some Canadian businesses
welcome the deal because it allows them investment rights in the U.S.
These new rights of national treatment do compensate for the lack of
secure access to the American market for Canadian exports. Under the
deal, a Canadian firm could forestall the threat of American protectionism and gain access to U.S. government contracts by moving to
the United States. Therefore, the deal actually encourages what it was
supposed to prevent: new investment by Canadian-based firms will
now be more likely to take place in the U.S. rather than in Canada. For
major Canadian firms, free trade means they get American citizenship.

Chapter eight focuses on resources. In this sector, Americans are
guaranteed a share of whatever is commercially available in Canada
without any discrimination allowed on the basis of nationality; the only
qualifier is the provision that, for resources in short supply, Americans

cannot claim more than their proportionate share, based on historical precedent. Looked at from any perspective, this part of the agreement means that the larger American economy gains, permanently, rights of control over the resources of the smaller Canadian economy, unless they are in short supply, in which case Canada has still given up its right to control export levels. Furthermore, Canada can no longer require that American owners undertake to upgrade resources before they are exported. As chapter nine explains, a new common market for energy means that a made-in-Canada price for energy is gone forever. Thus Canadian decisions concerning resource extraction and energy pricing are divorced from our own industrial policy decisions.

Resource sharing in the energy field has dramatic consequences for Canada. For each three barrels of oil produced in Canada, one barrel is now exported to the United States. Canada can no longer choose to conserve diminishing supplies of petroleum by cutting off exports to the U.S., though conventional supplies of crude oil are only sufficient to meet Canadian needs for eleven years at current rates of consumption. Incredibly, under the deal, Canada in effect gives the U.S. ownership rights over one-third of these reserves. And yet Canadian reserves cannot even begin to meet American needs, since they only amount to a fraction of U.S. consumption. The only way Canada could forego shipping oil to the U.S. in times of short supply would be either to stop producing oil, or to set the domestic price so high that the Americans would no longer buy it. As if this were not enough, the inability to supply domestic customers at prices other than those prevailing in North America means that Canada gives up its comparative advantage in energy and simultaneously puts itself at a cost *disadvantage* with respect to American competitors. This is the case because Canada's climate leads it to use more energy than Americans. At equal prices, everything Canadians produce will be more expensive than what Americans produce, simply because Canadians use more energy. That Canada could agree to make Canadian products less competitive just as Canada moves towards free trade makes no sense whatever. But that is exactly what Canada agrees to in the energy chapter of the deal.

Chapter ten outlines the implications of the deal for the manufacturing sector. The government has argued that, just as the Auto Pact brought increased prosperity to southern Ontario, free trade will have a similar impact on the manufacturing industry as a whole. But measures like those that made the Auto Pact a success are ruled out in the future for other manufacturing sectors by the deal itself! Canada cannot, for instance, introduce performance requirements for new American investments. With the new rules in place, Canada can no longer require of American companies that they undertake research and development activities in Canada. If, instead, Canada decides to subsidize such undertakings, the incentives must be offered to U.S. firms as if they were Canadian firms.

Without the undertaking by the big three auto makers to assemble one car in Canada for every car sold in Canada, there would be no Auto Pact. Yet under free trade Canada can no longer oblige an American manufacturer to do anything of this nature. Similarly, there would not be an Auto Pact without a commitment from American auto makers that 60 per cent of the value added in manufacturing automobiles in Canada be from Canadian-made materials. Under the terms of the free-trade deal, Canada can no longer require domestic sourcing by American companies.

Indeed the Auto Pact itself — and this point is made clearly in chapter eleven — may be significantly weaker as a result of the accord. Since the performance requirements in the pact (assembly and content rules) are enforced by withdrawing duty-free privileges from auto makers who fail to meet these safeguards, the elimination of duties under free trade simultaneously eliminates the enforcement mechanism of the Auto Pact. Under free-trade rules, about all Canada can do is offer an American company cheap labour, a cheap dollar and a pledge to maintain low costs across the board — minimal environmental restrictions and social benefits for workers, reduced taxes and so on — and hope for the best. Canada has always been able to negotiate favourably with American investors because it has the seventh-largest market in the world for automobiles. This rich domestic market, though small in comparison to the American market, gives Canada a good bargaining position with respect to any investor. In the free-trade agreement, Canada has given up this leverage with respect to American companies, not just in autos but in all sectors.

The new trade rules make it difficult, if not impossible, for Canada to introduce public policies to promote national industrial development. They have important implications for any industrial strategy that would tie public purchasing policy to job creation, for example, as John

Calvert shows in chapter twelve. Interestingly, what has been given away to the U.S. with respect to performance requirements under the treaty has, by extension, been given away for Canadian business as well. National treatment is a two-edged sword. Eliminating performance requirements for American investors eliminates them for Canadian investors also. What, under the terms of the deal, Canada cannot require of American companies, it can hardly turn around and require of Canadian companies.

Marjorie Cohen explains in chapter thirteen that the agreement allows national treatment for American sellers of certain commercial services and offers the right of establishment and commercial presence to all others. In international trade negotiations this represents an unprecedented concession to the strong American services sector. Unlike other nations that have resisted American attempts to include services in trade agreements, Canada has agreed to open its domestic market to American service firms. There is no evidence that sufficient thought has been given to the consequences of this action for Canada's economic future. Services account for nearly 70 per cent of GNP and are growing faster than any other sector in the economy. Yet no studies of the potential impact of the deal on this sector have been made by the government. In addition to specific concerns raised for the future of data processing, telecommunications and other service industries, Marjorie Cohen shows that the agreement creates a major obstacle for the future development of public services in Canada.

Under the deal, the creation of any new social programme would have to meet the requirements of Article 2010, the "public monopolies" clause and Article 2011, the "nullification and impairment" clause. Taken together, these clauses imply that, if Canada were to create a public sector programme for, say, day-care, American day-care firms would have to be compensated for the loss of any potential commercial benefits they could expect in the absence of the public sector programme. These provisions of the accord make the costs of such a social programme significantly higher than they would otherwise be. In fact, the cost of compensating American firms for their potential losses could be so high as to rule out the creation of new programmes in all areas where American firms already provide services. These would include auto and other insurance schemes. As well, compensation would have to be paid in the event that a Canadian government decided to create a Crown corporation in any sector.

By requiring compensation, these provisions of the deal effectively redefine the role of the public sector in Canada. Indeed, they make it conform to the American idea of government services — something better left to private producers. And yet Canadians should know that in the area of health care, for example, Canada's public medicare scheme costs about one-third less than American private health care (as a percentage of GNP). The publicly financed Canadian programme brings health care to every citizen at less cost than the private American system; moreover, the American health system simply does not cover those 35 million people who cannot afford a private health plan. Given these facts, the American model hardly seems an appropriate one to imitate, but under the trade deal Canada has little choice. The nullification and impairment clause could force Canada to compensate expensive private producers in the U.S. before introducing a less expensive public sector programme with better coverage. For public services, and in other sectors as well, the free-trade deal would thus thwart any government intent on creating what Canadians now take for granted: not only medicare, but a public broadcasting system, a national railway or a provincial hydro company.

Chapter fourteen looks at financial services. Here, too, Canada gave up much more than it got. When combined with domestic deregulation, the financial services provisions of the deal may well erode national control over the one sector that has been Canadian-owned: banking and finance. Canadian industry needs a safe, solid, domestic financial structure in order to take advantage of lower American tariffs. Yet it appears that the deal actually weakens the national commitment to a strong financial sector that serves Canadian needs. For instance, American firms may now come in and buy up Canadian trust companies and investment dealers. The deal removes the distinction between Americans and Canadians with respect to ownership of Canadian banks. In return Canada gets nothing more concrete than a promise to be accorded national treatment if and when the U.S. lifts national restrictions on banking practices.

In agriculture, as John Warnock outlines in chapter fifteen, Canada makes concessions that threaten farm production in some sectors — such as seasonal fruit and vegetables — and will weaken its competitive position in others — such as egg, poultry and turkey production. Moreover, Canada has agreed to negotiate agricultural issues internationally in concert with the U.S. Since the U.S. wants to eliminate GATT provisions that provide the basis in international law for domestic marketing boards, it would appear that the government reassurances made to farmers that marketing boards will not be affected by the trade deal are suspect to say the least. The elimination of tariffs puts Canada's food processing industry, employing some 250,000 people, at serious risk and could well kill many farms as well. Without the tariff, food producers and processors will struggle against each other and feel increased pressure from American competitors. The likely result is that food processing will be "rationalized" (that is, move to the U.S.), leaving Canadian farmers no choice but to ship production south and compete against American producers who have a competitive advantage because of a more favourable climate.

Under the deal, Canada closes off all its economic strategy options with the exception of the North American market option. This is a high risk strategy to say the least, particularly when the deal does not assure secure access to the American market for Canadian exports. It seems that the fixation on the size of the American market has persuaded the government that the removal of remaining American tariffs amounts to the best economic strategy available to Canada, bar none. Worse, by accepting this deal, the government does bar, by treaty, any future adoption of a domestic industrial strategy. Canada not only gives up this option willingly, it does so in the form of a treaty that takes away the option for as long as the treaty remains in force. No other interpretation of the agreement can be admitted. Rather than constituting an alternative policy for Canada, free trade eliminates all other alternatives.

Beyond Trade

Because free trade is an economic strategy it has implications for Canada that go well beyond the specific provisions of the deal. As Mary Beth Montcalm shows in chapter sixteen, the drift towards contintentalism in Canadian economic life explains much of the support and opposition to the deal. In addition, chapter seventeen leaves no doubt that

xvi The Free Trade Deal

free trade will accelerate a trend that has led to regional divisions within Canada. Indeed, Canada as a whole could well suffer a fate similar to that of the Maritime provinces at the beginning of this century when increased industrial concentration led industry and finance to migrate to more populous centres.

That the physical appearance of Canada could well change as a result of the workings of the free-trade deal is the conclusion of chapter eighteen on the environment. Frank Tester shows that the provisions of the agreement dealing with energy, forestry, and agriculture will act to encourage environmentally destructive mega-project developments.

The way Canadians deal with issues in the workplace is likely to be affected by the deal as well. In chapter nineteen, Patricia Lane argues convincingly that the ability to set national and provincial standards on issues like maternity leave, part-time work and job training will all be influenced by the need to compete on the "level playing field" with American companies. The role of unions in Canadian society and also the outcome of specific contract negotiations can hardly be separated from the new competitive conditions introduced by the trade deal.

In chapter twenty, Susan Crean discusses Canadian culture, noting that it is neither excluded nor exempted from the deal. In fact, any new initiatives in the cultural field will be subject to a blanket retaliation clause that allows the Americans to take measures of "equivalent commercial effect" if Canada introduces a programme that American firms feel impinges on their ability to make money in the cultural marketplace. By the terms of the deal, Canada has accepted the American definition of culture: a commodity to be bought and sold for profit.

Deborah Coyne argues in chapter twenty-one that the most unwelcome result of the free-trade deal may be that the capacity of the federal government to exercise national leadership in the public interest is imperilled. Taken together with the Meech Lake agreement, the trade deal opens a new constitutional era. While major international economic transformations call out for national initiatives, neither the federal, nor the provincial level of government will be able to respond. The balance of power between the two jurisdictions is altered in favour of the provinces by the Meech Lake Accord, while the ability of both the provinces and the federal government to respond to new challenges in social policy, energy or finance is tied down by the continental economic framework of the bilateral deal with the United States.

Canadian public opinion has evolved with the free-trade debate. In chapter twenty-two, Donna Dasko explains how the issue has been perceived over time. Since it was first raised in a general way by business groups, public opinion has shifted. According to Dasko, Canadians still tend to support free trade in the abstract. However, opposition to this deal is growing as Canadians learn more about the specific concessions made to the U.S. by the Mulroney government.

A Matter of Trust

Initial foreign reaction to the pact is revealing. Clayton Yeutter, the top U.S. trade negotiator, is reported to have said, while selling the deal to Congress, that Canada does not know what it signed, and that, within twenty years, it will be sucked into the American economy. Israel's senior trade official, the man who negotiated a bilateral deal for his country with the U.S. earlier in the decade, suggested that Canadian negotiators gave up one hundred times more than was necessary to get the deal. Mexican authorities have said that, unlike Canada, they have no intention of signing an agreement with the U.S. that hands control over natural resources to the Americans. Such reactions abroad only stiffen the resolve of critics at home.

And there are many critics of the trade deal. Not only do many people not trust the government's interpretation of the agreement, they do not trust the government. For them, the process of negotiating free trade is revealing of the government's unwillingness to be frank and honest with the Canadian public. From the outset, the Conservative government was intent on maintaining secrecy with respect to what was being negotiated. Canadians were kept unaware of the progress of the talks. According to the government, this was largely because of the need to conceal Canada's hand from the Americans. And for the same reason the government was not prepared to discuss or debate openly with opponents of the bilateral strategy, except in the most general way. Organizations like the Canadian Labour Congress, the most important labour body in Canada, representing more than 2 million workers, were not a part of the process. Consultations were undertaken, however, with representatives of Canadian industry through the Sectoral Advisory Groups on International Trade (SAGITs).

Labour leaders are strongly opposed to the deal and they are joined in their opposition by such grass-roots organizations as the national Pro-Canada network. This group has brought together churches, women's organizations, social agencies, farmers, seniors, teachers, nurses, environmentalists, academics and the Business Council for Fair Trade, as well as labour, in opposition to free trade. Coalitions to fight the deal have been formed in every province. Their message is simple. In a parliamentary democracy an important departure from usual practice requires either that the government seek an electoral mandate, or that the policy have all-party support in the House of Commons. Since the Liberals and New Democrats oppose free trade, constitutional tradition suggests that the government should seek the approval of the Canadian public before implementing the deal.

PART I

Trade Politics

1

Washington's Agenda

Giles Gherson

In the Reagan administration and on Capitol Hill, the idea of free trade with Canada was always appealing but never well defined. At best, it was ambivalently regarded in Washington's corridors of power as a benign adventure that held out the possibility of economic benefit, and at little cost. Moreover, in an administration obsessed by the ideology of economic market forces and the practice of political imagery, free trade with the U.S.'s northern neighbour struck just the right chords. In the abstract, at least, it presented a powerful symbol of retreating government intervention and supremacy of the free market.

As part of the policy agenda for Ronald Reagan's second term, a U.S.-Canada free-trade agreement floated in and out of the consciousness of key administration planners. Its accomplishment was regarded largely as a luxury — the necessities were such core political programmes as tax reform, the Strategic Defense Initiative and bolstering Nicaraguan contras.

In retrospect, it is clear that when President Reagan and Prime Minister Mulroney first committed themselves to exploring freer trade between the two countries at the March 1985 Shamrock Summit in Quebec City, the American side had only the vaguest notion of what it had in mind.

Indeed, even over a year later in July 1986, when the free-trade negotiations had officially been launched, Douglas McMinn, the Assistant Secretary of State for Commercial Affairs and one of the administration's senior trade policy officials, remarked: "We have no clear sense at the outset what will happen. We think a comprehensive free-trade agreement would be in our interest politically, but economically the objectives simply aren't so clear yet — we just have to let the negotiations evolve."

Given this more or less extemporaneous approach to the venture, it was not surprising that the two negotiating teams did little more than spin their wheels for the first ten months. Yet ad hocery alone does not satisfactorily explain how it happened that the two sides diverged so sharply as the negotiations proceeded that ten days before the negotiating deadline of October 3, 1987, the entire venture was at the point of collapse.

There were some basic policy themes at the root of the American response to Prime Minister Mulroney's initiative. In fact, in substantive policy terms the idea of a Canadian free-trade agreement had three quite separate objectives, each with its own set of advocates: a model for the eighth round of negotiations (the so-called Uruguay Round) under the auspices of the Geneva-based General Agreement on Tariffs and Trade (GATT); a North American accord; and an effective solution to Canada-U.S. trade irritants.

The first, and the most vaguely expressed, call for a trade agreement with Canada emanated from the 1980 Reagan presidential election campaign. Repeatedly, Reagan advocated the establishment of a North American accord that would embrace the U.S., Canada and Mexico. To many, it simply smacked of campaign rhetoric, but apparently Reagan's interest in the idea was deep-seated and persistent. On the other hand, the accord idea was not fleshed out much beyond the level of slogans and campaign speeches. And certainly, it was not grounded in any practical assessment of joint Mexican, Canadian and American economic and security interests. Rather, in the aftermath of the second OPEC (Organization of Petroleum Exporting Countries) oil shock, a North American accord evoked the possibilities of secure access to Canadian and Mexican resources, and over time, a larger, single North American market for American manufacturers. Interestingly, the call for a North American accord resurfaced as a theme in President Reagan's 1988 State of the Union Address.

At the same time, within the outward-looking trade policy bureaucracy in Washington a Canada-U.S. free-trade agreement was always viewed primarily as a testing ground for the ambitious American agenda being formulated for the next round of multilateral trade negotiations. In the mid-1980s, pressures were building in the U.S. for a fresh set of trade liberalizing negotiations under GATT. Multilateral negotiations of this nature had been held on an ad hoc basis by the world's trading nations seven times since the creation of GATT. But instead of focusing on tariff cutting, as had the most recent negotiating rounds of the 1960s (Dillon, Kennedy) and 1970s (Tokyo) the Americans now wanted to establish a firm set of rules to constrain a host of non-tariff barriers that were springing up around the globe in the guise of national industrial policies. American economic officials, pondering the rise of the first American trade deficit in fifty years, saw four decades of tariff-centered GATT trade liberalization being undermined by a foreign barrage of industrial subsidies, investment restrictions, import barriers and domestic sourcing preferences for government purchases. The American agenda consisted not only of tougher codes on subsidies and government procurement but also extension of the GATT system of trade rules to cover agricultural goods and internationally traded services, including investment and intellectual property (to protect against international trademark, patent and copyright infringement).

The problem for American trade officials was not simply the complexity of their agenda at a time when international consensus on most of these issues was scant. It was also that, while the Americans had a clear idea of the international practices they believed impeded the free flow overseas of American goods, services and capital, they had done astonishingly little work defining plausible internationally workable solutions. Consequently, for trade officials at the office of the United States Trade Representative (USTR), and the Departments of Commerce and State, a bilateral Canada-U.S. trade negotiation offered a rare chance to test ideas and possible solutions. Then, when the Uruguay Round negotiations moved into full gear in 1988, the American team could get off to a fast start — and not alone but with the backing of an important ally, Canada.

The third, and arguably dominant, strain in the American policy towards the Canadian free-trade initiative was rooted in the special interest politics of Capitol Hill. Quiescent until aroused by the hearings held by the Senate Finance committee in April 1986 — the committee's job was to authorize the special "fast-track" negotiating authority needed by the administration in order for talks with Canada to begin — the special interests and their Senate interlocutors swiftly became the most vocal force in defining the American approach to the negotiations.

Just as the American trade establishment hoped to use the free-trade negotiations with Canada as an instrument to fulfil a broader purpose, so too the Senate "fair traders" wanted to send a signal to the rest of the world. They insisted the administration abandon what was characterized as an overly relaxed, even spineless posture towards foreign unfair trade practices. A start could be made by using the free-trade negotiations to get tough with Canada, the U.S.'s biggest trading partner. Articulating the very philosophy that underlay the congressional push to strengthen American trade laws in a major legislative package, the Finance Committee demanded that improved Canadian access to the American market be made explicitly contingent on liberalized access to the Canadian market.

Although Canada regards itself as essentially a free trader, and, more than that, one of the most open economies in the industrialized world, such was not the view held by the Finance Committee senators. Woefully ignorant of the enormous penetration American investment and goods have historically enjoyed in Canada, the senators instead focused on a handful of specific complaints. For Canadians watching the proceedings, and only too aware of the steps the Mulroney government had already taken to reduce bilateral irritants — terminating the National Energy Program and sharply curbing foreign investment review — the senators' litany of unfair Canadian trade practices painted an entirely unrecognizable picture.

At their meeting on April 11, 1986, widely viewed by the administration and Canadian authorities as a pro forma gathering to ratify the fast-track negotiating process, the Senate Finance committee members balked. Senator after senator trotted out a pet irritant of concern to constituents. The list was long, including below-market Canadian softwood lumber stumpage fees, agricultural subsidies, regional development subsidies, cheap natural gas export prices, the long-festering border broadcasting dispute, alleged Canadian telecommunications import restrictions, then unchanged compulsory licensing of foreign pharmaceutical patents, and discriminatory provincial liquor board listing policies.

"I've told Ambassador Yeutter [the U.S. trade representative] this morning we could very well vote to turn down fast-track," Oregon Republican and Finance Committee chairman Robert Packwood told a startled gallery as he opened his remarks to the committee and the day's chief witness, Clayton Yeutter. "We have gotten no satisfactory response from the Canadian government that they want to end their subsidies and practice fair trade," he added. Later on he told Yeutter: "Maybe the best thing I can do for you, Mr. Ambassador, is turn this down so you can go back to the Canadians and say, Folks, this deal is over for the next ten years unless you loosen up on some of these issues."

Thirteen days later, the committee met again. After receiving personal assurances from President Reagan that the negotiations would seek to fix senators' trade concerns, with a separate effort to resolve the lumber dispute, the senators eked out a 10-10 vote, which was enough to constitute approval of fast track. It was a close call, indeed.

The Washington Trade Environment

When the Mulroney government launched its free-trade initiative in 1985, the primary trade policy objective was to neutralize what Canada's Washington ambassador, Allan Gotlieb, forcefully argued was a secular trend towards increased American protectionism. The protectionist upsurge, which was a symptom of the mushrooming American trade deficit, manifested itself in the rising incidence of U.S. industry-sponsored trade-remedy actions against allegedly unfairly priced or subsidized imports. Increasingly, Canadian products were becoming either the principal target of these actions, or simply lumped in with a group of imports from a variety of countries. Worse, there were a growing number of cases being pursued that had questionable merit, but served as effective tools for harassment of foreign producers.

A second symptom of the growing American frustration with the apparently ever worsening pattern of soaring imports and atrophying exports was the politicization of trade. Reflecting the angry mood spreading across the American manufacturing, agricultural and energy belts, Congress began to see trade as perhaps the most important political issue of the day. In 1985 work began in both the Republican-controlled Senate and the Democratic House of Representatives to fashion omnibus trade bills — essentially catch-alls incorporating the growing heap of industry-specific legislation aimed at curbing imports and ending what was perceived in the U.S. as unfair trading practices used by foreign nations to damage American industry.

It was not hard to see Canada's enormous vulnerability to the American protectionist threat, with some 75 per cent of her exports (representing 25 per cent of GNP) destined for the huge market south of the border. For Gotlieb, a distinguished international lawyer — but no trade expert, as he readily acknowledges — the answer seemed to lie in replacing the existing lack of structure in U.S.-Canada trade relations with a formal legal framework. Optimally, of course, the framework would protect Canadian industry from ill-founded harassment cases, and from the potentially damaging extension of American trade law.

Curiously, despite the Canadian embassy's concerns about the bitter protectionist mood brewing on Capitol Hill — and, in certain cases, direct legislative attacks against Canadian imports — there was little anticipation of the cool reception in store for the free-trade negotiations in the Senate Finance committee. Whereas the Canadian government, and the Reagan administration, too, persisted in viewing the bilateral trade negotiations as part of American foreign policy towards Canada, and therefore deserving of friendly sympathy, in fact senators placed the issue squarely in the troubled realm of trade policy.

"I think we have to send a strong signal to the administration that we ought to have someone standing up and fighting for the economic interests of this country. We need to end the trade deficit," declared Texas Democratic Senator Lloyd Bentsen, now the chairman of the Finance committee, "We've been stiffed by the administration refusing to deal with us on trade and I'm fed up with it." Added Republican committee member Jack Danforth of Missouri, "I think it's necessary for Congress, and especially this Finance committee, to re-establish some sort of relationship with the administration where we are again players in trade policy. We're not now. We've had several trade bills in this committee, but the administration stonewalls us and says, We're not interested in trade legislation this year. At some point Congress has to be assertive on trade, or we'll lose all credibility."

As it happens, the confrontation over trade between the administration and Congress had been building for some time. The White House request for fast-track negotiating authority simply provided the senators with their first major opportunity to force the Reagan administration into a show-down that could force some real concessions over the conduct of trade policy.

What Ottawa failed to appreciate was just how controversial the fast-track process had become in Washington. In fact, it never was particularly popular in Congress. It was instituted originally in the 1974 trade bill as a practical device to enable the executive branch to negotiate international trade agreements, an area falling under congressional jurisdiction. The problem was that American trade partners were justifiably reluctant to spend several years negotiating a highly technical treaty with an American administration, only to see Congress unravel the effort by insisting on changes as the price for ratification. As a result, Congress set up the fast-track procedure: the administration could apply for Congressional authority to negotiate a foreign trade agreement that could not be altered during ratification — only accepted or rejected.

Rejecting a trade agreement after it had been laboriously negotiated was inevitably a politically extreme act. As a consequence, the entire fast-track edifice rested — usually rather precariously — on a foundation of congressional trust and confidence in the administration of the day. In April 1986, those were two ingredients that were conspicuously absent in Congress's appraisal of White House trade policy.

In 1985 the American trade deficit passed a record $150 billion, and all signs (accurately, as it turned out) pointed to an even larger shortfall in 1986. Even as the American economy was moving into its fifth straight year of fairly robust recovery, entire portions of the U.S. industrial midwest and northeast seemed mired in recession-like conditions. With once-giant industrial employers in the steel, automotive parts, machine tool, agricultural implements and consumer goods sectors hobbled by import penetration and the loss of foreign markets, wave after wave of layoffs were wrecking large cities and small towns. With congressional elections looming in November 1986, Congress

increasingly felt compelled to demonstrate an ability to act. As Senator
Bentsen later told his first press conference as Finance committee
chairman later that year, after the Democrats had won control over the
Senate: "We can't afford to be a Taco Belle economy." He was referring to the ever-growing chain of fast food outlets in the South,
emblematic of the new low-wage service sector that was soaking up
employment across the nation.

The acuteness of the American trade problem certainly had plenty to do with the policies of the Reagan administration. But the culprit
was far less an unwillingness to tackle foreign trade barriers than a mis-
guided dollar policy during the president's first term. Under then
Treasury Secretary Donald Regan, a former chairman of Wall Street
financial services giant Merrill Lynch, the American dollar was allowed to soar to record post-war highs. The non-interventionist policy
was unpopular all around, since it forced up interest rates in Europe
and Japan, while in the U.S. it laid the groundwork for what later became known as "the hollowing of American industry." American
goods, from agricultural products to electronics — two areas where
Americans considered themselves pre-eminent — were being priced
out of foreign markets, while exchange rate advantages unleashed a
flood of low-priced imports. But to Regan and his undersecretary for
monetary affairs Berryl Sprinkel, (later chief of Reagan's Council of
Economic Advisors when Regan moved to the White House as chief
of staff in 1985), a soaring dollar was a sign of economic strength, and
was not to be tampered with.

By 1985, a new and politically astute treasury secretary, James
Baker, was in the midst of orchestrating a dollar devaluation. But even
half a year later, in April 1986, it still had the appearance of too little
too late. The high dollar had persisted for too long — import penetration had grown too entrenched, while American manufacturers had
retrenched too far — for a sudden about-face. The result was a growing sense of urgency on Capitol Hill for some form of blunt instrument
to deal with the trade crisis. The answer seemed to lie in tougher administrative action against unfair trade. At the most basic level, it
seemed not only patently unfair, but also a growing threat to the
American economy, that the colossal American market should be targeted by export subsidizing foreign governments, which themselves

placed enormous tariff and bureaucratic barriers in the way of American exports.

By 1986, the Reagan administration had received the message and was itself hardening its posture on trade. In a presidential trade statement in September 1985, Reagan promised to pursue vigorously complaints about foreign unfair trade practices, using the discretionary authority available to him under Section 301 of the Trade Act. As well, the administration made a commitment to impose emergency import restraints available under Section 201 of the same act where there was evidence of injurious surges of imported product.

But Congress had largely given up on the administration, with both the Senate and the House working on different versions of a sweeping trade reform bill. A key turning point had been Reagan's antagonizing of the powerful (and protectionist) textile, clothing and footwear lobbies. In the summer of 1985, Reagan turned back a recommendation from the International Trade Commission that the imposition of textile quotas was warranted to counteract damage to the domestic industry caused by rising imports. Around the same time, Agriculture Secretary John Block promised Congress Section 301 retaliation against subsidized imports of wheat-flour from Europe. But the administration dropped the promise, apparently in response to Department of Defense pleas that it would only result in loss of defense industry orders from Europe.

This was the tempestuous atmosphere surrounding trade policy questions in Washington, little understood in Ottawa, that by mischance came to a boil just as the Canada-U.S. free-trade negotiations were due to start.

The Negotiations

When 39-year-old Ambassador Peter Murphy returned home from his position with the U.S. delegation to GATT to lead the U.S.-Canada free-trade negotiations, plenty of eyebrows were raised. Trade experts in Washington, and particularly the capital's select group of "Canada-hands," were flabbergasted by the choice. It was already clear that the administration had not thought terribly deeply about what its objectives were, and indeed, appeared not to be assigning much importance to them.

Canada had already picked out of retirement one of Ottawa's most tough-minded and intellectually formidable senior policy-makers to lead its team. Simon Reisman was 66, a former deputy finance minister in the early 1970s, and a blunt-spoken and wily trade negotiator who had led Canada's side in the U.S.-Canada Auto Pact negotiations of 1964-1965. Reisman's association with the Auto Pact was symbolic on both sides of the border, since that agreement — and Canada's flexible interpretation of its provisions — has been widely considered one of the greatest economic victories ever perpetrated on the U.S. by its northern neighbour.

As well as the enormous differences in age and outlook, the two men came to the bargaining table with vastly unequal experience. Reisman had been a top Canadian policy-maker since the mid-1960s, and was steeped in the economic and political history of Canadian-American relations. Murphy, while unquestionably a rising star until illness forced him to cut short his tour in Geneva, had no real policy-making experience to speak of; he was a successful bureaucrat. And while his talents as a trade negotiator were widely praised, he had made his mark in the narrow sphere of textile negotiations as deputy chief, then chief U.S. textile negotiator.

Murphy also had to grapple with several other shortcomings. First, he knew very little about Canada, the intertwining of the American and Canadian economies, or the depth and breadth of the bilateral relationship. More than that, when he arrived in Washington he found little formal preparation for the negotiations at a policy level within the administration.

These factors alone were enough to warn Canadian observers and other Washington free-trade watchers that hopes were fast dimming for a collegial negotiation between two teams searching for novel approaches to bilateral trade problems. What was not clear just yet was how much of an adversarial game the negotiations were about to get into.

Murphy is primarily a gifted tactician, not a thinker. He didn't enter his new job as chief negotiator for the free-trade negotiations with many preconceptions, but he certainly understood the import of the Senate Finance committee 10-10 vote that came so close to killing the whole exercise. That embarrassing episode, both for the administration and, more personally, Murphy's boss Clayton Yeutter, turned Congress's special interest concerns into the centrepiece of American objectives at the bargaining table.

Murphy's instructions from Congress were undeniably clear. In a sense, they had been written into the Senate resolution sponsored by then Senate majority leader Robert Dole, and passed by the Senate just after the April 24, 1986, 10-10 vote allowing fast-track to proceed. The list contained nine tough negotiating demands reflecting the expressed concerns of the Finance committee. In a nutshell, the resolution demanded that Canada be made to open up its market for American goods and services; curb its seemingly enormous array of industrial, energy and agricultural subsidies, all of which were incompatible with the American free market philosophy; scrap its foreign investment controls; live up to American-style rules on patents, trademark and copyright; ensure that its provinces implement the relevant terms of the agreement (for example, by eliminating liquor board discrimination against American wines and spirits); and ensure that federal and provincial governments open up their purchases to American suppliers. The kicker in the Dole list of demands, however, was the most ominous, since it appeared to deal a blow to Canada's principal objective in the free-trade negotiations. The free-trade agreement, it said, must "ensure that United States persons retain full access to United States trade remedies affecting imports from Canada."

This detailed list of demands instantly became the core of Murphy's negotiating objectives. His so-called "accounting-ledger" approach to the negotiations was reinforced by the highly decentralised structure of the negotiating team Murphy assembled during the summer of 1986. It was in sharp contrast to the very centralized "mini-bureaucracy" Simon Reisman hand picked for his own separate agency, the Trade Negotiator's Office (TNO), which was installed away from the rest of the government in a spanking new Ottawa office tower.

For his part, Murphy had neither sufficient seniority to attract the movers and shakers in Washington's trade bureaucracy to his team; nor did he have the mandate to conscript them. The best he could hope for was to recruit senior officials from his own agency, USTR, and the other trade-related departments of Commerce, Agriculture, State and so on, on a part-time, as-needed basis. Officials such as Ann Hughes, the deputy assistant secretary for North America in the Commerce Department, or Ralph Johnston, the State Department's deputy assistant secretary for trade, or even Richard Self, USTR's deputy assistant trade representative for services trade, had plenty of other matters to attend to. For the most part, these senior officials operated as part of Murphy's core negotiating team, but continued to report through their direct superiors to their own departmental cabinet secretaries. As for the Treasury Department, senior officials there refused, for the most part, to accede any authority to Murphy and insisted on negotiating issues such as investment and financial services rules directly with the Canadians. Within the Washington trade community, word quickly spread that Murphy was having difficulty attracting resources.

In Ottawa, Reisman's closely-knit group, numbering nearly one hundred, had been formulating a comprehensive approach to the negotiations for six months before the first sessions in June 1986. Indeed, largely unbeknownst to the Canadian public and much of the government, the TNO's group of economists and trade policy technocrats had devised a sweeping vision of a North American free-trade area.

The TNO's rigorous preparation for the negotiations and its carefully constructed game-plan created an understandable urge to take control of the negotiations right from the start and keep them focused on Canada's agenda. But the scheme backfired. From the first meeting, the small American team, still feeling its way, felt patronized by the large, well-organized Canadian contingent. At the first session in Reisman's Ottawa boardroom, American officials found themselves facing a wall on which there hung a large photograph of a child with its arm around an elephant, symbolizing Canada's friendship with, yet vulnerability to, the American colossus. The photograph — combined with the aggressive Canadian tone in the discussions — caused the Americans to wonder suspiciously whether they were being set up for demands that would produce a lop-sided arrangement.

At the heart of the TNO free-trade vision was a binding dispute-settlement procedure that would establish a special bilateral set of rules to govern Canada-U.S. trade disputes. In its purest form, it entailed the substitution of anti-trust rules for both countries' existing anti-dumping trade laws, and, as well, the drawing up of a "subsidies code" that would clearly state what sorts of government subsidies were to be illegal in a free-trade agreement. The regulations would be administered by a series of bilateral consultative and arbitrative bodies.

To the American team, as hard-headed trade negotiators and also as bureaucrats all too aware of Congress's prickly mood, all this sounded far too exotic to fly in Washington. They wanted to concentrate on the more prosaic agenda of eliminating bilateral trade irritants and drawing up joint frameworks for dealing with the new areas of trade in services and intellectual property. Combined with the elimination of all bilateral import tariffs over a specified period — the core of any free-trade agreement in the Americans' eyes — the Dole list, it was thought, would add up to an eminently respectable trade deal.

To the Canadians, the American side's emphasis on tactical manoeuvres designed to address the issue of irritants seemed nothing more than nickel-and-diming in the face of an historic opportunity to develop a broad set of bilateral trade rules. But at the same time, the Americans were becoming increasingly frustrated with Reisman's inflexibility. "Simon has in mind a complete structure called free trade, in which all the elements must fit exactly as he has them carefully arranged in his mind, or the entire thing comes tumbling down," commented one senior American trade negotiator at a May 1987 cocktail reception. "Instead of negotiating, he's constantly telling us why he's right."

To some degree, the American complaint seemed valid. There was an understandable reluctance to set up elaborate binational — and therefore supranational — institutions to govern an integrated North American economic zone. For one thing, it went far beyond anything authorized by Congress at the start of the negotiations. The Canadian team seemed to be proposing an institutional structure more akin to a common market than a free-trade area. And that concept had implications for U.S. sovereignty which the Americans were just not prepared to deal with.

Looking back on the negotiations, an unnamed member of the American team recalled a greater American sensitivity to the question of Canadian sovereignty than sometimes seemed to exist on the Canadian side: "Sometimes we laughed among ourselves that we were the ones protecting Canada from its own negotiating team's attempts to integrate the two economies far more than most people realized."

But there was another reason why the Canadian proposal to create a new bilateral set of trade rules essentially failed: the American team early on made the establishment of a clear set of rules on subsidies the *sine qua non* of any bilateral dispute settlement procedure. What the Americans had in mind was a Canadian commitment to curtail an array of subsidy programmes deemed to distort trade. After all, in the Americans' eyes, industrial subsidy programmes were somehow a distinctly Canadian practice, emblematic of a more interventionist economy. If Canadians wanted to circumvent the full force of American trade law, they would have to agree to behave more like Americans.

The flaw in the reasoning, as the Canadian negotiators quickly pointed out, was that there were no shortage of industrial subsidies south of the border — primarily at the state and municipal level, but also taking the form of generous federal tax breaks. You must agree to the same subsidy code you want us to accept, the Canadians told the Americans. However, during the course of the negotiations, the American negotiators were unable to secure agreement from the U.S. National Governors' Association (representing state governments) to limit subsidies. Their argument was that Canadian subsidies directly affected Canadian companies' ability to penetrate the American market, whereas forsaking subsidies in the U.S.would simply weaken American firms' ability to compete against corporate competitors from many other countries.

The stalemate over dispute settlement dogged much of the negotiations. Murphy was unwilling to offer even a hint of movement on a binding dispute-settlement procedure until he had secured some important Canadian concessions on subsidy programmes, and on tighter Auto Pact rules. On the other side, Reisman was unwilling to move very far on these items until he had an indication Murphy was willing to deal on an automatic trade-dispute process. The stalemate was fortified by an unmistakable aura of mistrust, and at times acrimony, that had steadily built up between the two chief negotiators over fifteen months of talks.

In the end, it took political intervention at the eleventh hour to salvage an agreement that at least minimally met the two sides' basic political needs. As Yeutter told Congress's first open hearing on the agreement, held by the House Ways and Means trade sub-committee on February 6, 1988, the deal was mostly crafted during the final ten days — and much of it in the last seventy-two hours — before the fast-track bargaining deadline of midnight, October 3.

The Deal

In the final analysis, it was the American business view of the free-trade agreement that largely prevailed. The core of the agreement is the elimination of cross-border tariffs over ten years. This was always the top American objective in the negotiations, and it was this element that was seen to hold the most tangible economic benefits for American industry. As soon as a (still-classified) U.S. International Trade Commission study (completed at the end of 1986) showed there were barely any American industries that would actually suffer from the elimination of tariffs on Canadian imports, the American team pressed for complete lifting of all bilateral tariffs and along the fastest possible timetable. Given Canada's relatively high level of tariffs — on average, twice the level of those in the U.S. — the move to duty-free treatment eliminates obstacles to cracking the Canadian market for many American industries.

In addition, despite fiercely resisting Canada's top demand for a dispute-settlement process, there are signs that the compromise formula eked out during the negotiation's final hours could in the end serve American industry's needs. Bearing in mind the litigious nature of American business, it would not be surprising to see swift recourse to the bilateral dispute-settlement provisions whenever Ottawa or a province introduces a policy considered detrimental to American interests. If that is the case, a proposal designed to limit the scope of U.S. protectionism towards Canada could also serve as a bulwark against future Canadian industrial policy initiatives.

2

Striking a Deal

Duncan Cameron

The *Canada-U.S. Free Trade Agreement* is an instrument of international law. As such it binds the two parties. For Canada, the entente has the status of an international treaty and, in Canada, the treaty-making power is a prerogative of the executive branch of government, that is to say the Cabinet. For the United States, it constitutes an executive agreement. While the authority to negotiate was provided by an act of Congress, the agreement is not subject to the normal treaty-making procedures provided for under the U.S. Constitution; for instance, it does not require passage by a two-thirds majority of the Senate. However, it is usually held that an executive agreement has the status of an informal treaty in the U.S. and that, as such, it becomes a part of "the supreme law of the land" just as if it had been negotiated under Article 2 of the U.S. Constitution.

Although, in both countries, the treaty-making power comes under federal jurisdiction, there are important differences with respect to procedures for implementing treaties. It should be remembered that it is not the treaty as such that has legal standing before Canadian courts; rather it is the domestic legislation implementing the accord that gives the international agreement legal force. In Canada, where the treaty deals with matters which the Constitution designates as federal, no problems arise. The Parliament of Canada is simply asked to approve new laws, or amendments to existing laws, and the treaty can then take effect on the prescribed date, January 1, 1989. But where the treaty covers matters within the legislative competence of the provinces, this requires that the provinces also implement legislation to give effect to the treaty. This is so because, constitutionally, it is held that the federal government cannot acquire additional legislative powers simply by entering into a treaty.

In the U.S., legislation implementing the trade deal requires majority approval in both the Senate and House of Representatives. A treaty, at the time it is enacted into law, takes precedence over any other laws, federal or state, that may be in conflict with it, though it may require court action to establish the validity of a claim arising from a treaty. But at the same time, federal laws adopted after the treaty has taken force have precedence over the treaty laws. In the U.S., in other words, where there may be an inconsistency between a law arising from a treaty obligation and an Act of Congress, the inconsistency is resolved in favour of the more recently enacted of the two. Thus, future changes to U.S. laws may modify the trade deal. Of course, in such an instance, the U.S. would be in default of its obligations to Canada and presumably Canada could invoke the provisions of the agreement and ask that the U.S. bring its laws into conformity with the accord.

Ultimately, then, though treaty obligations are spelled out in domestic law in both countries, the basis of an international agreement, like any agreement for that matter, is goodwill. Canada expects the U.S. to abide by the terms of the trade accord, and the U.S. expects Canada to do likewise. This is important because, though provisions of the treaty are given effect in both countries through domestic law, it is only the two governments that are bound by the treaty itself. It is the mutual undertakings of the two parties to the agreement that give it meaning.

The agreement was negotiated so as to be consistent with world trade rules as laid down by the General Agreement on Tariffs and Trade (GATT). Article XXIV of the GATT treaty sets out the requirements any such agreement must meet in order to qualify as a free-trade area under international law. The Canada-U.S. accord seems to meet the provisions of GATT, though the GATT council may yet object to certain provisions. Article XXIV is clear about the objectives of a free-trade area. Paragraph 4 of that article says that members of GATT "recognize the desirability of increasing freedom of trade by the development, through voluntary agreements, of *closer integration between the economies of the countries* party to such agreements [emphasis added]."

The provisions in the treaty establishing GATT that allow for free-trade areas and customs unions (a free-trade area plus a common external tariff) are set out in some detail because such undertakings represent major exceptions to the general rules that govern world trade. The basis of GATT is that nations agree to non-discrimination as the basis for trade policy. Nations agree to offer access to their own market on equal terms to all GATT members. This is known as the "most favoured nation" or MFN principle. It means that nations do not favour imports from one country over imports from other countries. Of course, the basis of a free-trade area is precisely to discriminate against goods that come from outside the area by providing for tariff-free trade within the area. Thus, though the accord may meet the formal requirements of GATT, it is in fact a major departure from normal GATT practice. Free trade lowers tariffs in North America while maintaining them against the rest of the world. In the process, some trade with other countries will be diverted to North America. Instead of purchasing from previously lower cost suppliers in Third World countries, for instance, Canada will buy from the U.S. because of the new lower tariff. Rather than being seen as furthering international trade liberalization, the agreement can also, and more properly, be understood as continental protectionism.

Liberalizing North American Trade

If the deal is judged only by the number of published pages alloted to each subject, the most important issues would seem to be those concerning tariffs between the two countries. They will be phased out gradually; over ten years, from January 1, 1989 to December 31, 1998, all tariffs will be reduced to zero. Some tariff reductions occur immediately, others are phased in over five years, and most are phased in over ten years. Two documents listing the scheduled tariff changes for Canada and the U.S. were released with the text of the agreement. Taken together they cover every item traded between the two countries. It takes over one thousand pages to list both countries' tariffs. But, of course, all cross border commerce is not affected by the tariff changes, since most trade was tariff-free before the agreement. About 85 per cent of Canadian goods entered the U.S. tariff-free, and 95 per cent faced a tariff of less than 5 per cent, before the agreement was signed.

What is affected is the classification of goods. Under the agreement Canada and the U.S. adopt a new tariff nomenclature — a new method for naming traded goods — the "harmonized system" (HS). Both countries had decided to implement this new system once the tariff changes resulting from the seventh round of GATT negotiations were concluded. Thus, the new tariff schedule would have been set without the bilateral agreement. Until now both Canada and the U.S. had in place systems which differed from the one that is used internationally. A common international system like the HS facilitates commercial understanding, trade, and tariff adminstration. Presumably, it should prove beneficial in harmonizing Canadian tariff administration to international standards. But the release of the two huge tariff schedules should not confuse people. Though tariffs are important, remaining tariffs were small, particularly on the U.S. side, where they averaged 4.2 per cent on the few goods still subject to tariff. This deal is not principally about tariff reduction, for either country.

In producing for commercial exchange, what counts is not just the final product; how it is produced is also important. But most trade rules treat only tradeable goods, and only as final products. Not only is this deal the first to cover traded services, it also affects how final products are produced, and goes on to specify who can have access to resources and under what conditions. The general rule governing the deal is that national treatment is accorded to sellers of goods and services, producers of goods and services and, with a few exceptions, investors. This means that unless otherwise provided, economic agents on either side of the border are equally at home to operate in both countries. In Canada, American companies have all the rights of Canadian companies: rights to buy and sell, and the right to be treated like Canadian companies under the law. In fact, the law cannot discriminate between Canadian and American companies for any purposes except those expressly set out in the treaty, and there are few such special cases. Normally, national treatment means that foreign sellers in a domestic market must be treated on an equal footing with domestic producers. But in standard practice this treatment applies only once the goods have been authorized for sale in that domestic market. In other words, foreign sellers must first meet national specifications, standards and health regulations; clear customs; and pay duty charges, before they receive national treatment. Also, governments reserve the right to deny foreign suppliers certain privileges. For instance, they may not be able to tender for all government contracts.

This agreement extends the right of national treatment across the border to U.S.-based suppliers of the Canadian market. While there are a few large Canadian companies that stand to benefit in the U.S. from this agreement, most Canadian firms will face new competition from American firms. It is no exaggeration to say that, under the new rules, for American firms, Canada becomes a part of the U.S. economy.

The Preamble

The intentions of the partners to the agreement are specified in its preamble. In what amounts to a joint resolution agreed to by the two governments, the preamble announces nine common principles that underlie the accord. Matters referred to are friendship, economic welfare, a wider market, new trade rules, security for investment, international competitiveness, reduction of trade distortions by governments, conformity to GATT and promotion of international trade. In each instance, the language is general, bordering on vague, and leaves room for wide interpretation. Nevertheless, the preamble does touch on specific concerns and provides a useful guide to what follows in the agreement itself.

What is clear is that in framing the preamble both governments have attempted to build support for the accord. By casting the intentions of the framers in a favourable light, the preamble expresses political leadership. It represents the vision of the two governments — a shared vision. While the Canadian government says that "the Preamble establishes from the outset that this is a trade agreement," it really does more than that. At the outset, it establishes the resolve of the parties "to strengthen the unique and enduring friendship between their two nations; to promote productivity, full employment and a steady improvement of living standards in their respective countries." The third point in the preamble is the first that deals with trade. Of the nine points in the preamble, only two deal with trade as such and one of those (point three) includes trade in services which, in itself, denotes much wider coverage than anything ever undertaken by any other trade agreement.

Point five of the preamble refers to predictability "for business planning and investment" in a "commercial environment." This, it can be argued, indicates that investor rights take priority over other rights, since investor rights are singled out for mention whereas other rights (human, environmental, labour, etc.) are not. This interpretation is certainly consistent with the rest of the agreement. Point six talks about strengthening competitiveness in global markets, which implies that policies to reduce the costs of doing business around the world will be favoured. This can be interpreted to mean that labour costs, or the cost of social programmes, or the cost of programmes to protect the environment, will have to be restrained. While talk of increasing international competitiveness is necessarily vague, it does indicate the two governments' priorities. The preamble does not state, for instance, that government programmes are needed to protect the environment. What the preamble does do, in point seven, is single out "government-created trade distortions" as something to be reduced while preserving "the Parties' flexibility to safeguard the public welfare."

Point eight of the preamble refers to "mutual rights and obligations under GATT and other multilateral and bilateral instruments of co-operation." The important matter of the relationship between the bilateral trade deal and other foreign policy practices is presented here very narrowly. The preamble says the deal is part of the resolve of the two countries "to build" on GATT. Similarly, in point nine, the preamble refers to "the harmonious development and expansion of world trade" and to the deal as "a catalyst to broaden international co-operation." As in the first two points in the preamble, this language has a reassuring effect. Talk of friendship in point one reassures Congress that this treaty is mostly about friendship with Canada and point two reassures Canadians that national economic goals are not being subverted by the deal. As well, the pact is to be understood as preserving and enhancing the status quo internationally.

That is rhetoric; the reality is quite different. What is clearly established by reading between the lines of the preamble is that this is more than a simple trade agreement between two countries. The deal is also about the role of governments in relation to the economy in today's world.

Objectives and Issues

Chapter 1 of the accord outlines its objectives and scope while Chapter 2 provides definitions to be used for purposes of interpreting the agreement. Taken together, these two chapters reveal the extent to which the deal goes beyond bilateral trade and raises fundamental political issues. As the Canadian government says in introducing Chapter 1, it "moves beyond other free-trade agreements negotiated under GATT." This is, in fact, a significant understatement. Article 102 outlines the objectives of the deal. Subsection (a) deals with the trade aspects and the other four subsections cover matters that go beyond trade. Of significant interest is (e), which says that the deal is to "lay the foundation for further bilateral and multilateral co-operation" between Canada and the United States.

The objectives of the deal raise major political issues involving Canadian foreign policy, national independence and constitutional practice in the Canadian state. Of course, these three issues are the perennial ones of Canadian political life. What is unacceptable, however, is that they be given new meaning as a result of what is supposed to be a trade deal. Yet this is no doubt what has been done.

As a result of the deal, Canada commits itself to joining a sort of North American trading bloc. This is certainly contrary to everything Canada has worked for since World War II. In almost every sphere — political, economic, social, environmental, work, health, transport, telecommunications, postal service, education, science, child welfare, international development and culture — Canada has favoured international institutions rather than discriminatory bilateral arrangements. While Canada has signed continental agreements which cover many important matters (defence, auto trade, fisheries, boundaries, the environment), and would no doubt benefit from others, (an acid rain treaty with teeth, for example), such bilateral undertakings have never been considered to take precedence over international agreements. Even the Auto Pact was ratified by Canada in a way consistent with broad GATT principles; until this deal closed it off to include only existing North American participants, it was always open on a multi-lateral basis to others who could meet its requirements. Yet Article 104 (2) states that the bilateral deal "shall prevail" in the event of conflict with other obligations. The accord therefore sets Canadian foreign policy in a North American context.

Given the disproportionate power advantage conferred on the U.S. by virtue of its size, economic strength and superpower status, Canada has sought to deal with the Americans using internationally agreed rules as the reference point. Particularly in economic negotiations, it has been a cardinal principle that Canada join with other nations to increase its bargaining advantage vis à vis the United States. While bilateral agreements are a necessary feature of Canadian-American relations, Canada has always tried to avoid being caught in a situation where the U.S could wield its power advantage directly.

Under the deal, Canada has agreed to negotiate internationally in concert with the U.S. on issues about which Canada and the U.S. have divergent interests and have disagreed in the past. These issues include agriculture, where we are competitors, investment, where Canada has large stocks of foreign investment in place and the U.S. does not, and services, where Canada is a net importer and the U.S. a large exporter. In allying itself in this way with American interests, Canada, for the first time in peacetime history, has accepted that its national negotiating stance in international affairs is a matter to be decided by provisions of a bilateral treaty. Thus, in the foreign policy field, the implications for Canadian independence are much greater than the government has led people to believe. Can it be doubted that an overwhelming desire to sign a deal overcame the usual concern for preserving Canadian independence?

Under Article 105, Canada makes a commitment "to accord national treatment with respect to investment" as well as "to trade in goods and services." Extending national treatment to investment goes far beyond what is normally considered to be part of an agreement to set up a free-trade area. Agreement on movement of capital or of people (which is also in part covered by the deal) is usually restricted to common market arrangements, not free-trade areas. This implies that the Canada-U.S. free-trade agreement is a half-way house to a North American common market.

In the case of a bilateral common market, where one partner is ten times the size of the other, the question arises of which partner is going to be dominant. Or, to put it another way, perhaps the question does not arise. Canada's undertakings to the U.S. on investment and services restrict, by treaty, its capacity to make future laws in these areas. Such undertakings constrain national independence more directly than does membership in GATT, or the UN, or even NATO. And yet, these undertakings do not have all-party agreement in the House of Commons. Both the Liberals and New Democrats are opposed to the deal, in part on the grounds that it unduly limits Canadian and parliamentary sovereignty.

The impact of the deal on the Canadian Constitution also requires careful consideration. The federal government's powers in the area of external relations do not allow it to amend unilaterally the Constitution, or to ignore the provinces on matters that come under exclusive provincial jurisdiction. This principle was put forward to the Ontario Select Committee on Economic Affairs, which spent nearly a year studying the implications of free-trade negotiations, by Professor Richard Simeon in his April 1986 presentation, and it is soundly based in constitutional law. In addition, the recent Meech Lake Accord provides for provincial consensus on matters affecting the Canadian Constitution.

As drafted, the trade agreement would appear to limit the provinces' powers to act in areas of their own jurisdiction. Article 103 states that "the Parties to this Agreement shall ensure that all necessary measures are taken in order to give effect to its provisions, including their observance, except as specifically provided elsewhere in this agreement, by state, provincial and local government." It appears quite clear that the intent of this clause is to say that, unless expressly exempted, matters falling under provincial jurisdiction are included in this agreement. As a minimum, these would include financial institutions, investment, energy, services, norms and standards for labelling and packaging of goods. Eventually, too, they would include those issues that arise from the continuing negotiations on the use of government policies to promote economic development and the implications of such so-called subsidies for the application of countervailing and anti-dumping duties. Therefore, it appears that the provinces have the constitutional right, not just to be consulted and informed about the agreement, but to approve or disapprove of those provisions which affect provincial powers in matters under provincial jurisdiction.

Finally, as is widely recognized, the Government of Canada had no direct mandate from the Canadian people to negotiate a free-trade area with the United States, since the issue was not discussed in the 1984 election. Moreover, in a parliamentary democracy, there is a constitutional convention that when a government undertakes a major departure in public policy, one that does not command all-party support in the House of Commons, it should, at a moment of its choosing, go to the people on the issue. Given the objectives of the agreement, there is no doubt that this is such a major undertaking. Politically speaking, then, the federal government should carry out the promise made by Prime Minister Mulroney in Brandon in 1986 to consult the Canadian people, before proceeding to implement free trade on January 1, 1989. The workings of parliamentary democracy and the magnitude of the agreement allow no other interpretation of the government's responsibilities.

3

The Canada-United States Trade Commission[1]

Stephen Clarkson

It has long been the hope of many professionals in the field of Canadian-American relations that the most complicated bilateral relationship in the world be simplified into a rational system. Economists have pined for fair trade laws to replace the arbitrary trade actions taken by less efficient American businesses seeking protection against Canadian exports. Lawyers have proposed supranational tribunals that could end the extra-territorial application of American laws and court practices to sovereign Canadian courts and companies. Diplomats, dismayed by the many other disputes that bedevil relations between Canada and the United States, have argued that these interminable spats be dealt with by some more coherent process than reeling out the hoses every time some parochially ignited fire breaks out in Congress.[2]

If only the management of conflict in the Canadian-American relationship could be taken out of the hands of politicians and handed over to impartial, objective bodies made up of officials, judges or experts — so goes this rationalist logic — then economic decisions on such matters as investment location and industrial development could be made on their merits to the presumed benefit of both partners, and Canada would be spared the periodic crises with the United States that have punctuated the history of English-speaking North America. The

Macdonald Royal Commission's call for bilateral free trade with a Canadian exemption from American trade-remedy laws and a "standing arbitral tribunal" was but the most recent and influential in a long line of rationalist appeals for a sanitization of the messy realities of Canada's dealings with the world's most powerful economy and most fragmented political system.[3]

When Prime Minister Mulroney took the Macdonald Report for his own agenda and launched his government's free-trade initiative in October, 1985, he apparently believed that a trade treaty could extricate Canada from the skeins of America's trade protectionism. Unfortunately, the journey to the prime minister's apolitical nirvana was strewn with political booby traps. As predicted by those sceptical about the prospects of trade liberalization during a time of high protectionism, the United States refused to grant its biggest trading partner immunity, either from its trade-remedy legislation or from its trade tribunal system. Canada won no significant exemption from the American non-tariff barriers, and had to settle for a palliative (if much trumpeted) appeal procedure that was fastened uncomfortably onto the existing American trade-remedy process (see chapter four).

It may have come as no surprise to White House watchers that the Americans brought their own agenda to the bargaining table, but it seems to have come as a shock to most interested Canadians to discover in late 1987 that a much vaunted *trade* agreement should have incorporated such American demands as virtually unrestricted "national treatment" for American firms in Canada's energy, service and banking sectors (see chapters nine, thirteen and fourteen), as well as commitments to "harmonize" the way the two countries set their technical and production standards. Canada had proposed, but the U.S. had disposed. Prime Minister Mulroney made meagre progress towards his free-trade dream, while the United States moved a long way towards President Reagan's own vision of a "North American accord" — the economic integration of Canada and Mexico in a U.S.-dominated continental market.

The government's preface to Chapter 18 of the free-trade agreement tells us that the deal establishes institutions "to provide for the joint management of the Agreement and to avoid and settle any disputes between the Parties respecting the interpretation or application of any element of the Agreement." What it does not tell us is that these insitutions incorporate elements of both the Canadian and American agendas. On the one hand, there is the placebo of a convoluted dispute-settlement mechanism (misleadingly described as "binding") that was put in place to disguise the Canadian negotiators' failure to gain their treasured exemptions. On the other hand, there is a vague but portentous reference to "*joint* management of the Agreement" and to settling "*any* disputes" arising from "the interpretation *or* application of *any* element of the Agreement [emphasis added]."

This chapter will examine the significance of the procedures to be established for managing the economic integration established by the agreement. The principal instrument created to manage the agreement is the Canada-United States Trade Commission (CUSTER). To understand the implications of this institution we must first grasp the full range of activities for which CUSTER will be responsible in implementing and managing the agreement. We can then ask how CUSTER is supposed to operate in order to meet its many responsibilities. The next step will be to consider those aspects of managing the deal that are kept out of CUSTER. This will allow us to assess how much the management of the Mulroney-Reagan deal will achieve the objective of depoliticizing conflict in the bilateral relationship.

CUSTER's Management Mandate

Chapter 18 of the agreement specifies a number of responsibilities that CUSTER will have, but one has to read the whole text, clause by legal clause, to understand the full scope of what CUSTER will have to do to turn this agreement into reality. Five main functions have been assigned to the new institution: notification, consultation, dispute settlement, continuing negotiations and executive decision-making.

Notification

Essential for "predictability" in making the agreement work is giving each side advance information about what changes the other country proposes to make in its laws and regulations that might affect the other's rights under the deal. Article 1803 specifies that each party "shall provide written notice to the other Party of any proposed or actual measure that it considers might materially affect the operation of this Agreement." Such notification shall explain the rationale for the measure and be given "as far in advance as possible." In addition to this self-reporting, a party "shall promptly provide information and respond to questions pertaining to any actual or proposed measure" whether or not it has notified its partner about it. This presumably would include such questions as the American concern in 1988 about Canada's proposed tariff remissions for textiles.

Other references in the text confirm that mutual notification is to be a substantial responsibility.

- On border measures each side is to notify the other about any "major proposed changes in customs administration," defined to include such minor administrative changes as changing the hours of service of a customs office. (Annex 406 D.9.b)
- On technical standards each party must provide the other with full texts of proposed federal-level measures on standards and procedures for approving new products. Each side shall also explain when one of its federal bodies doesn't accept test results coming from the other (607.1). This responsibility extends to notification of proposed provincial/state measures and those of "major national private organizations" such as the Canadian Standards Association. (607.3)
- If either side decides to impose import restrictions as emergency ("safeguard") actions against surges of imports it must notify its partner— whether the action is aimed bilaterally at the partner (1101.2) or globally oriented towards third countries (1102.3).
- In the wide field of services, each party must notify the other whenever it intends not giving national treatment to the other. (1402.3)
- In the field of investment measures, each party must notify the other whenever it intends not giving national treatment to an investor of the other side. (1602.8)

Since the two federal governments are continuously altering their laws, since provincial and state legislatures are constantly passing legislation and since national, private-sector associations are continually modifying their professions' regulations, CUSTER's notification function will be substantial.

Consultation

Notification is but the informational prelude to serious diplomatic pressure being applied. Beyond providing notification, each side must take part in "consultations" when requested by the other "regarding any actual or proposed measure or *any other matter* that it considers affects the operation of this Agreement, *whether or not* the matter has been notified in accordance with Article 1803" (1804.1). These consultations are clearly meant to be more than quiet chats between officials over coffee. The idea of consultation is to achieve "mutually satisfactory resolution" before disagreements reach the intensity of actual bilateral conflicts.

The importance of consultations as a tool for one government to take its complaints for resolution to the other is demonstrated by the number of specific cases in the agreement for which consultations are anticipated:

- On the rules of origin of goods (for the purpose of duty-free passage across the border), the parties are to consult to ensure that provisions "are administered effectively, uniformly and consistently with the spirit and intent of this Agreement." (303)
- On border measures, each side is to consult the other about any "major proposed changes in customs administration that would affect the flow of bilateral trade." (Annex 406 D.9)
- Before imposing any quantitative import restrictions arising from action against third countries on meat goods, each side is to provide, beyond mere notification, an opportunity for consultation. (704.2)
- Before imposing any quantitative import restrictions arising from action on energy from third countries, each side is to provide an opportunity for consultation to avoid "undue interference with or distortion of [its] pricing, marketing or distribution arrangements." (902.4)

- In emergency actions, consultations are to follow notification, whether the intended measures are to be bilateral or global actions. (1101.2 or 1102.4)
- A party is to engage in notification and consultation before denying the other a benefit in services on the grounds that they are provided by a third country. (1406.1)

The heavy emphasis on notification and consultation throughout the agreement has significant implications for Canada's political institutions and the role that the U.S. will now be able to play within them. Notification will require an unprecedented reporting capability far beyond what any subdivision in the existing Department of External Affairs (or the Department of State) could currently manage as part of its regular tasks. Canada is committing itself to establishing a new notification procedure to which all departments, Crown corporations and related agencies would have to report on a continuing basis. One can conceive a duplication and expansion of the present Treasury Board, lodged in a large wing of CUSTER's Canadian headquarters. If such lobbyists for bilateral free trade as the Business Council on National Issues were hoping that trade liberalization through bilateral free trade would "downsize" government, the Kafkaesque procedures that CUSTER will be forced to develop may prove disheartening.

CUSTER's notification function will necessarily play a centralizing role within each country's federal system. The Canadian provinces will have to accept monitoring by their federal government that they would, until now, have strenuously resisted, jealous as they are of their constitutional rights. Finally, the application of notification requirements are more likely to constrain Canadian than American government processes. This is not just because of Canada's smaller size and greater vulnerability; it is because notification is a more effective constraint over a parliamentary than a congressional system. Since the legislative process in Canada's federal and provincial governments is more orderly — and so more susceptible to monitoring — than the far more unpredictable congressional procedures in the American federal and state systems, it is likely that this notification obligation will give the U.S. considerably more diplomatic leverage over Canada's political processes than Canada will receive over American policy-making.

The emphasis on consultations in the agreement indicates that CUSTER is to take on important functions previously filled by the diplomats in the Department of External Affairs. In this sense, CUSTER will assume the diplomatic job of resolving each partner's complaints by making assurances, or even commitments, on behalf of its governments, federal or provincial, so as to satisfy the partner's concern about some established measure, current move or proposed action. In order for this mechanism to work, Ottawa will have to create a substantial communications network reaching all parts of government in Canada. This would require high levels of federal-provincial trust so that, for instance, the Canadian representation in CUSTER could assure the United States that the Saskatchewan agriculture department's ban on certain pesticides will not diminish American exports. Given the demonstrated weaknesses of External Affairs in federal-provincial communications and the failure of the Department of Regional and Industrial Expansion to rectify prior failures in federal-provincial co-operation, Ottawa will be hard put to develop a bureaucratic structure sufficiently capable for CUSTER's needs.

It is assumed, though not established, that CUSTER will enjoy the constitutional power necessary to negotiate legislative corrections by the provinces so that it can give assurances to the United States that a dispute panel's report requiring a change in a provincial programme will be acceded to. Given the impressive de-centralization achieved by Canada's political system in the 1970s and 1980s, it is highly doubtful that such an overbearing federal agency could be tolerated by provincial premiers who have so recently gained the prerogatives of nominations to the Senate and the Supreme Court.

The enshrinement of consultation in the agreement seems destined to raise, not lower, the level of politicization of Canadian-American differences. This paradoxical effect is suggested by the all-purpose nullification article. Article 2011 calls for consultations whenever one side objects to an action by the other side which, "*whether or not* such measure conflicts with the provisions of this Agreement, causes nullification or impairment of any benefit reasonably expected to accrue [emphasis added]" from the agreement. This means that *any* measure, even one in accord with the agreement, that reduces benefits that the other party "reasonably" expected to achieve, may be sent to consultation. If, for instance, Edmonton was pricing its natural gas feedstocks for the Alberta petrochemical industry lower than the North American market level, the U.S. could demand consultations about this "impairment" of the benefits its petrochemical industry was expecting from the continental energy agreement. Far from depoliticizing conflicts between the countries, the agreement drastically increases the range of issues over which disagreement can legitimately arise.

More ominous for Canada, an increased level of politicization does nothing to reduce the United States' predominance in deciding how these matters are resolved. As Denis Stairs of Dalhousie University has recently written: "Ironically, this may work in the end to Canada's disadvantage. That is, the Canadian side in the commission will usually be in a position to compromise, whereas, because of the division of power between Congress and the Executive branch of government, the American side often will not. Heads, they win; tails, we lose."[4] The recent debacle over softwood lumber (now entrenched in the Mulroney-Reagan deal) showed that the American goal in trade issues is the permanent power to veto any potentially threatening federal or provincial government actions.

The United States' interest in bilateral free trade has been to use Canada as an instrument in its multilateral trade negotiating strategy in the Uruguay Round of the General Agreement on Tariffs and Trade (GATT) negotiations. By "levelling its playing field" and "harmonizing" its policies on American models, Canada has become a valuable example for the United States. CUSTER's consultation function will mark a significant step beyond what the U.S. could have managed under previous standards of arm's-length diplomacy in defending its beleaguered hegemony.

Dispute Settlement

CUSTER oversees the trade-disputes mechanism (see chapter four). Its role includes establishing rosters of eligible panelists, selecting the members for each dispute panel and deciding to accept or reject the dispute panel's final report. In addition, CUSTER has responsibility for other kinds of dispute settlement. If negotiations (1803) and consultations (1804) fail to resolve an issue within thirty days, the complaining party can call on CUSTER to hold a meeting to initiate procedures to resolve the dispute (1805). This CUSTER is to do within ten days. If within another thirty days it has not been able to resolve the dispute under Article 1805, CUSTER may set up binding arbitration (1806.1) or a dispute panel, the selection and timetables for which are spelled out in Article 1807. When a panel submits its final report the buck passes back to CUSTER, which has then to decide whether to accept the panel's findings.

Apart from arbitration or dispute panels as the end of the notification and consultation process, CUSTER's dispute-settlement role is specifically mentioned in three other matters.

- In cases of emergency ("safeguard") actions CUSTER has no discretion: it must refer actions unresolved by consultation to arbitration under Article 1806. (1103 and 1806.1.a)
- It is to institute arbitration procedures in case of disagreement concerning the level of government support for wheat, oats and barley. (Annex 705.4.16)
- A party may invoke Articles 1806 (arbitration) or 1807 (dispute settlement) after "available administrative remedies have been exhausted" concerning the temporary entry for business persons. (1504.2)

CUSTER's clout appears to be entirely based on moral suasion. It is assumed that, once the arbitration or dispute panels have produced their reports, the offending government measure will be changed to conform to these judgments. Although Article 1806 talks of "binding arbitration" it does acknowledge that one side might "fail to implement" the panel's allegedly binding ruling. If this occurs, and if CUSTER can't make up its mind on one of its dispute panel's final reports, a party which "considers that its fundamental rights...or benefits" under this agreement "would be impaired by the implementation or maintenance of the measure at issue" will be "free to suspend the application to the other Party of *benefits of equivalent effect* [emphasis added]" until the issue is resolved (1807.4).

Translated, this legalese means that, if CUSTER doesn't come up with a mutually satisfactory solution to a dispute, the aggrieved party can take things into its own hands and retaliate. The agreement doesn't specify *who* would decide *what* retaliation would be justified or *how* "equivalent effect" would be calculated. Obviously these would be highly contentious decisions. If the other side felt the retaliation excessive, would it be free to retaliate in turn? CUSTER will be the obvious institution expected to decide whether the measures taken were appropriate to the injury received. (Since all observers agree that retaliation by either side ends up by hurting Canada more than the United States, this means that retaliation as a sanction in the conflict-resolution process is a credible weapon only for the United States.) Although the agreement is an elaborate effort to take Canadian-American trade tensions out of politics, it could easily achieve the opposite and accentuate political tensions by multiplying dangerously strained situations.

Continuing Negotiations

Since some of the details that have been written into the deal may prove unworkable, and since both sides have affirmed they want to make the agreement still more comprehensive, there are several provisions for a second phase of negotiations. While Chapter 19 sets up a separate institution to negotiate a new subsidy code, it is CUSTER that will be expected to carry out these further discussions in most other cases. The second phase of negotiations will cover issues of far-reaching importance.

- The annual quantity limitations on the exports of textiles are to be renegotiated before 1998. (Rules of Origin, Section XI, rule 17)
- At the request of either party, an acceleration of the rate of general tariff elimination, spelled out in Chapter 4, can be negotiated. (401.5)
- The parties are to undertake additional negotiations to harmonize non-agricultural technical standards and product approval procedures. (608)
- In agricultural goods, the agreement anticipates further co-operation to eliminate or reduce import barriers. (703) (Since tariffs are being eliminated in any case, this presumably refers to the United States's expressed desire to eliminate Canada's marketing boards and quotas on specific products like poultry and eggs.)

- On government procurement, the agreement specifies that new negotiations shall take place to expand the agreement's provisions further. (1307)
- In architectural services, negotiations are to develop common professional standards. (Annex 1404.A.2)
- On services, the agreement anticipates new negotiations further to expand the agreement's provisions. (1405.1/2)

These references in the text imply that CUSTER is to carry on in phase two what Simon Reisman's Trade Negotiator's Office and the office of Clayton Yeutter, the U.S. Trade Representative, did in phase one: undertake top level trade-liberalization talks. Even if these negotiations are carried on directly between other departments of the two governments, they will require teams of top-level officials having a close rapport with CUSTER.

Decision-making

CUSTER is to do more than monitor, consult, arbitrate and negotiate. To fulfil its part in the application of the agreement, CUSTER will also have to take executive action on a number of issues.

- CUSTER will receive the annual progress reports of the working groups on harmonization of technical standards in food and agriculture. (708.4.c)
- In cases of emergency action, the two sides are to attempt to agree on the compensation that the import-restricting country should offer the exporting country. (1102.5)
- In government procurement, the two sides are to co-operate in monitoring the implementation, administration and enforcement of the obligations they entered into. They are to collect and exchange detailed annual statistics on their government's purchases, classifying them by category of goods, country of origin and criteria of tendering. (1306.1/2)
- The agreement has other open-ended features that are likely to dump very hot potatoes onto CUSTER's lap. The United States has won a blank cheque (the "notwithstanding" clause in Article 2005) that lets it retaliate or seek compensation for claimed los-

ses that Canadian *cultural policies* may be thought to cause American business. Whenever the U.S. exercises this right of cultural counterattack, CUSTER will presumably be called in to discuss — if not pass judgment on — whether this action is fair or foul.

It should by now be clear that, while the imprecision of much of the agreement could have some of the functions apparently designated for CUSTER taken over by other government departments, CUSTER is no institutional pussycat. The agreement has set it up with wide-ranging administrative, judicial and executive responsibilities that will require it to make decisions on behalf of the two governments. CUSTER's management responsibilities — described vaguely as "to supervise the implementation of this Agreement...to oversee its further elaboration, and to consider *any other matter* that may affect its operation" (1802.1) — are quite simply enormous.

In its institutional dimension, the free-trade agreement is being packaged as an ambitious attempt to codify and transform the entire range of the world's largest, though still largely informal, economic relationship. In this light, CUSTER plays the role of watchdog. This massive exercise in rationalization could be jeopardized if CUSTER turns out to be unworkable. Since CUSTER's performance will be crucial to the deal's success, we need to look beyond its responsibilities to find out what the agreement says about this super-institution's proposed mechanisms.

CUSTER's Institutional Structure

What exactly CUSTER will look like and how it will work is pretty hard to tell from the text of the agreement. The document only gives us five clues:

- CUSTER "shall be composed of representatives of both Parties. The principal representative of each Party shall be the... Minister primarily responsible for international trade." (1802.1)
- CUSTER "shall convene at least once a year in regular session to review the functioning of this Agreement." (1802.3)

- CUSTER's "regular sessions...shall be held alternately in the two countries." (1802.3)
- CUSTER shall "establish its [own] rules and procedures." (1802.5)
- "All decisions of the Commission shall be taken by consensus." (1802.5)

These five clues give us some indicators that help us check whether CUSTER's capabilities can meet its responsibilities.

Clue 1 is crucial. If it is to be staffed by "representatives" of the two governments, then CUSTER cannot possibly be an autonomous judge insulated from the political pressures coming from the two partners. CUSTER, in other words, will *not* be a *supranational* body manned by career bureaucrats who are independent of either country, as is the Commission of the European Community. CUSTER is apparently going to be a *binational* institution. Some may be pleased by this since neither partner is apparently giving up sovereignty by setting up a supranational authority. But if being binational is another way of saying it will be two-headed, we may come to find that the two governments have given birth to an institutional freak having as much chance of survival as unseparated Siamese twins.

Take, for instance, the simple question of who will pay and pension these pipers. If CUSTER's personnel are to be like any other Canadian or American bureaucrats, they will owe their jobs, their salaries and their prospects for promotion and retirement to the politicians in Ottawa and Washington who hired them and who, presumably, will still be able to fire them. Since the principal representative of the Canadian government is identified as the minister responsible for international trade, it will be just as difficult for the Canadian representatives to make decisions that differ from Ottawa's wishes as it will be for American representatives to act in defiance of Washington's interests. Far from being a body acting as umpire controlling the game played by the competing teams, it is going to have active members of the teams making calls on the plays. Far from providing us with a more rational way of coping with conflict, CUSTER is going to be inescapably politicized whenever it deals with cases over which the two governments have differing positions.

Clue 2 seems to be a complete non-starter. If CUSTER "convenes" periodically, this implies that it is not to be a permanent body but rather a grouping of "representatives" who come together on an ad hoc basis. Such an impermanent institution could not begin to shoulder the heavy responsibilities it has been assigned.

If it holds meetings alternately in the two countries, then CUSTER is apparently a character with two addresses and two headquarters like the International Joint Commission. This confirms that it is to be binational, with no supranational personnel to do the technical research needed to decide the contentious issues that will come before it. By implication, there is to be no common secretariat to keep the files, prepare agendas for meetings, follow up on decisions and, more important still, generate a devotion to the process of continental conflict-solving. Only the secretariat for the trade subsidies negotiation is indicated as a possible bureaucratic "support" — and only if CUSTER so directs (1909.7). Instead, each side will do its own administration and monitoring, field its own teams for consultations and negotiations and have its own decision-making procedures. This arrangement works well enough for the International Joint Commission, often the model for the rationalist dream of continental harmony. But the International Joint Commission succeeds because it avoids highly contentious and politically sensitive issues. By contrast, CUSTER's terms of reference explicitly load it down with myriad conflicts that are necessarily going to be highly politicized. While some issues are already anticipated, most will come to it as complaints from one aggrieved party or the other. The separation of administrations could generate even more conflict when there is disagreement between the two agencies, say, in the assessment of a panelist's impartiality or expertise.

Clue 4 seems flatly to contradict Clue 1. If it determines its own rules and procedures, CUSTER will be a self-governing institution independent of its parent governments. It defies common sense to think that CUSTER could decide that its Canadian representatives weren't accountable to Parliament through the minister for international trade, or answerable to questions posed by the Auditor General. Could it somehow vote its own budget or levy fees to pay for its costs? It is hard to believe Parliament would tolerate such autonomy for CUSTER's Canadian component. Since some of the most important decisions affecting Canadian society in the future will neither be in the hands of

Parliament nor the Supreme Court but of CUSTER — its acceptance of a panel's report is meant to lead to "removal of a measure not conforming with this Agreement" — Canadian citizens will want to know far more about the many notifications, consultations and decisions that CUSTER will be continuously engaged in than they were ever told about the fateful negotiations misleadingly developed in Simon Reisman's Trade Negotiator's Office. According to the text, publication of information on disputes will be restricted to the release of the dispute panels' final reports along with whatever written opinions that the parties, in their discretion, wish to have released (1807.7). Provincial governments and Canadian corporations with an interest in the continental market will want to have some assured access to this crucial institution. As it stands, there is no provision for direct provincial participation in CUSTER.

Finally, if CUSTER is to make all decisions by consensus, one must wonder how many decisions will ever be made. If conflict levels between the governments of Canada and the U.S. are low, it is conceivable that their representatives on CUSTER could happily operate by unanimity. But if conflict levels are high, consensus will be hard to sustain because of the escalation from arbitration to retaliation anticipated in the agreement whenever one party resists the findings of arbitration and dispute-settlement procedures. Articles 1806.3 and 1807.9 mandate an unsatisfied complaining party to shift from moral suasion to active retaliation by suspending "the application of equivalent benefits of this agreement to the non-complying Party." Strong pressure on Canada to meet American demands could well provoke resistance within Canada that could quickly paralyze CUSTER's decision-making.

CUSTER, as we have seen, is the product of two incompatible agendas. For Canada, it was to provide a final solution to an insoluble problem — the politics of unequal power in the Canadian-American relationship. For the United States, CUSTER is the instrument to monitor and enforce a breakthrough in its global trade policy strategy. CUSTER does not jeopardize the Mulroney-Reagan deal's immediate chances, but once the agreement becomes reality, CUSTER promises to turn into a millstone for its Canadian signatories. If it serves as the focus for extended U.S. intervention in Canadian policies, it could well become the locus for increased levels of bilateral political conflict, ultimately leading a Canadian public, aroused by the inadequacy of the agreement's benefits, to demand abrogation.

The attempt to create a rational manager for the Canada-U.S. free-trade agreement has been conceived in confusion. It does not have the autonomy with which to do a neutral professional's job. Nor does it have the accountability, transparency or accessibility with which to reassure its constituencies that it can be held responsible for its actions. It hasn't the organizational coherence or administrative substance to take on the tasks it has been assigned. What is now an institutional mystery on paper is bound to become a bureaucratic monstrosity in practice.

Managing the Agreement Outside CUSTER

The establishment of CUSTER represents a radical departure from both governments' historic approach to the Canadian-American relationship. Both the dominant and the smaller partner have traditionally shied away from institutionalizing their relations in order to deal with issues on an ad hoc, case-by-case basis. That the two signatories have hedged their own bets about CUSTER is suggested by the extent to which they have left important functions outside CUSTER's grasp.

Notification

Apart from the notification provided through CUSTER, the agreement also specifies the following:

- Each Party shall publish in time for comment "any law, regulation, procedure or administrative ruling" it proposes to adopt respecting the agreement. (2102.2)
- Each side must publish its regulations concerning temporary entry for business persons. (1502.2)
- Prior to establishing a monopoly, such as a province-wide automobile insurance scheme, notification must be given. (2010.2)

Consultation

Outside CUSTER's direct mandate, the agreement specifies that consultations are to take place between "the Parties" on a number of other issues:

- Through their customs administrations they are to consult on the uniform application of the rules-of-origin principles defined in Chapter 3. (Annex 406.C.6)
- On the vast array of agricultural issues laid out in Chapter 7 of the agreement, the two governments are to consult semi-annually. (709)
- The two governments can initiate direct consultations when either finds the energy regulatory actions of the other, such as the actions of the U.S. Federal Energy Regulatory Commission or Canada's National Energy Board, to be discriminatory or inconsistent with the agreement. (905)
- They are to consult once a year to eliminate impediments to trade in tourism. (Annex 1404.B.4)
- Annual consultations are also to take place between immigration officials to facilitate further temporary entry of business persons. (1503)
- On financial services, either side may request consultations, though the Canadian Department of Finance and the U.S. Department of the Treasury maintain their own control over these discussions. (1704)

Decision-making

Beyond the purview of the formal trade commission, the agreement specifies further institutional mechanisms which will have missions of their own.

- "Equitable, timely, transparent and effective bid challenge procedures for potential suppliers of eligible goods" have to be established in Canada (1305.3) and a reviewing authority has to be created in each country to receive *and decide* challenges to its government's procurement decisions. (Annex 1305.3)

- A working group is annually to review levels of government support for wheat, oats and barley. (Annex 705.4)
- Eight working groups with equal representation from each party have to meet at least annually to further the implementation of the harmonization provisions for technical standards in agriculture. (708.4)
- The Canadian Grain Commission is charged with monitoring compliance with the elimination of import permits for wheat, oats and barley. (705.2)
- A select panel of informed persons is to assess the North American automobile industry and propose policy measures and private initiatives to improve its competitiveness. (1004)
- Canada is to amend the Investment Canada Act to comply with the new limitations prescribed in Chapter 16. (Annex 1607.3.3)
- A working group is to develop a substitute system of rules for government subsidies and unfair pricing within five to seven years. (1907.1)
- A joint public-private sector advisory committee is to review television retransmission rights and make recommendations within twelve months following Canada's changes to its Copyright Act. (2006.4)

Keeping these responsibilities outside CUSTER's domain suggests that even the signatories may have had some fears that they should not entrust the entire management of the agreement to the new joint body. Clearly the U.S. Treasury was not willing to let decisions in its area of competence pass out of its hands. The Departments of State and External Affairs do not seem to have been so jealous of their prerogatives, possibly assuming that their own officials would naturally capture the new agency.

Conclusion

Given the complexity and imprecision of the text, CUSTER's impact on the management of the overall Canadian-American relationship is impossible to predict. Much will depend on the extent to which the United States puts institutional flesh on the agreement's bones. It is quite possible that the U.S. government will treat CUSTER as casually as it did the trade negotiations themselves, devoting to it minimal resources compared to the massive effort mobilized in the Canadian Trade Negotiator's Office. This would make it difficult for Canada to exert the same leverage over American policy-making as the United States clearly expects to achieve in Canada. It stretches credulity to suppose that the Canadian government could get very far in demanding consultations and then arbitration to have the anti-union "right to work" legislation in certain southern states abolished on the grounds that it gives U.S. industry an unfair trade advantage by lowering its costs.

More will depend on how strongly the United States feels inclined to press on with its level-playing-field strategy by exploiting all the levers of influence that CUSTER offers it. Far from being an obvious step towards the more strategic management of Canada's relationship, CUSTER's Canadian half could become a Trojan horse giving the United States institutional access for its management of Canadian politics.

The Canadian government claims that the "essential features" of CUSTER's proposed institutions are "economy" and "joint decision-making." Thus the agreement will "promote fairness, predictability and security by giving each Partner an equal voice in resolving problems through...authoritative interpretations of the Agreement." It is hard to imagine how CUSTER will be economical when its proportions will likely be gargantuan. How the lion is to lie down with the lamb to engage in joint decision-making on competitive problems is equally problematic. Equal voices the two parties may well have, but how these voices will promote fairness is not clear when one voice can out-threaten the other. What is predictable is that no part of Canada's governmental operations will be secure from American requests for notification and consultation. What is not predictable is what role the provinces will be able to develop either in responding to requests for notification, consultation and dispute settlement or in putting their own grievances against American practices on CUSTER's agenda.

Prime Minister Mulroney's deal promises to actualize what would have been considered a nightmare by former generations of political leaders. Far from extracting politics from Canadian-American economic issues, this deal will introduce an American presence into many aspects of Canada's internal political life. In creating so many new kinds of bilateral quasi-diplomatic activities that will affect activity in the private sector and in the provinces, it cannot help but politicize vast areas of the continental relationship that had until now been advantageously managed outside the glare and conflict of politics.

It is no accident that the features giving CUSTER powers of notification, consultation, arbitration, negotiation and decision are most relevant for the items the United States won in the deal in the areas of services, technical standards, banking, investment, resources and energy. CUSTER gives the U.S. a legitimate institution with which to ensure that the dramatic breakthroughs it achieved with the Mulroney-Reagan deal are translated into an economic union harmonized along the patterns established by American society. In short, CUSTER promises to be the institution which will push Canada's political integration in a U.S.-controlled North America to levels barely thought possible before the Mulroney era dawned in 1984.

4

Market Access

Duncan Cameron, Stephen Clarkson and Mel Watkins

In the period leading up to the free-trade negotiations it was argued that Canada-U.S. trade relations were so important to Canada that other international issues should not stand in the way of a bilateral deal with the United States. This was particularly thought to be the case because of the overwhelming dependence of Canadian exporters on the U.S. market. Securing improved access to the U.S. market, it was argued, justified a major departure from Canada's internationalist approach to trade.

Others looked at the same situation and argued differently. Canada had become overly reliant on the U.S. market, too reliant for its own good. As a result, Canada needed to diversify its trade, and strengthen its domestic economy, before it became so vulnerable to American pressure that it gave up significant margin for international manoeuvring simply to preserve the status quo of reliance on exports to the United States.

Now that the deal has been negotiated it is necessary to reach some judgment as to which of these conflicting views better reflects the Canadian situation. Has Canada satisfactorily resolved its trade problems with the U.S., potential or otherwise? Or did the disparate power relationship work to Canada's disadvantage in the negotiations? Whatever differing interpretations may be offered of specific points in the agreement, the key question in many people's minds is, did Canada get out of this deal what it wanted: secure market access? Or did Canada get the short end of the stick?

As a result of tariff reductions through seven major GATT negotiations over forty years, trade between the U.S. and Canada was mostly tariff-free, even before the Canada-U.S. free-trade agreement was signed. In this largely open North American market, firms have been specializing and rationalizing their production so as to compete successfully on each side of the border. But, for Canada, there has been a catch. In the absence of agreed rules about what is an acceptable trade practice, successful Canadian exporters can be pushed around, threatened and eventually denied access to the American market when, as is sometimes the case, U.S. law treats as unfair trade what are normal Canadian practices stemming from regional, economic and social policy. For instance, in the case of Atlantic groundfish exports, the U.S. authorities found some fifty-one Canadian programmes to constitute practices unacceptable under U.S. trade law concerning subsidies to exporters. In such cases, the U.S. levies a countervailing duty equal to the amount of the so-called export subsidy to offset what are considered unfair trade practices by foreign competitors. In short, trade has been imperfectly liberalized. Tariffs have been reduced, but trade penalties are becoming more important in dealing with increased import penetration and balance of trade deficits (one being a consequence, the other a perceived consequence, of trade liberalization). Continued U.S. trade deficits raise the spectre of increased U.S. protectionism.

Under the competitive conditions of the North American market, a successful Canadian firm could be shipping as much as 70 or 80 per cent of its production to the United States. If that producer is hit by a countervailing duty action, it could well go under: such Canadian plants are so dependent on shipments to the U.S. that without market access they have to close. Because a successful American industry would be unlikely to ship even 10 per cent of its North American production to Canada, Canada cannot hurt the U.S. industry to nearly the same extent through the introduction of a similar countervailing duty. This assessment of the unequal impact of protectionist laws leads to the obvious conclusion that in North America, the trading rules are rigged in favour of the larger country, even when each nation has similar protectionist laws in place.

It was this basic inequality under existing laws, including those sanctioned by the General Agreement on Tariffs and Trade (GATT), and the resulting injustice for successful Canadian firms, that worried Canadian trade experts and exporters and led some of them to press for bilateral negotiations with the U.S., in part simply to establish new trade rules. For Canada, the issue of the application of American trade laws was central to the whole bilateral negotiations. As the government explained to the provinces in November of 1985: "a better, clearer set of rules to govern the largest trading relationship in the world would provide the predictability Canadian exporters need." But, as will be shown, the free-trade agreement offers Canada little protection against the protectionist impact of U.S. trade law. Since Canada sends 80 per cent of its exports to the U.S., this in itself is cause for concern. In addition, in the absence of agreed rules, more liberalized trade creates greater uncertainty about national policy initiatives. Canada's social and economic programmes are subject to American protectionist pressures already. Since the agreement does not include new trade rules, they will be subject to even greater pressure in the future.

The provisions of the agreement that deal with so-called trade-remedy law, and disputes that arise from the application of those laws, are covered in three chapters of the agreement. The treatment of the two basic trade-remedy laws — countervailing duty and anti-dumping laws — is the subject of Chapter 19. Chapter 11 deals with the emergency actions, allowed for by GATT and enshrined in national laws as safeguard measures, which come into play when a nation is faced with a sudden surge in imports. Finally, the disputes-resolution mechanism for trade law is subject to some of the general institutional provisions that fall under the Canada-United States Trade Commission (CUSTER) and that are covered in Chapter 18 of the agreement.

American Trade-Remedy Legislation

The U.S. has seven instruments of trade law that it applies to imports. As a result of the trade deal, six remain unchanged. Of the five laws of specific concern to Canada, four (the anti-dumping law, the countervailing duty law, Section 301 of the Trade Act of 1974 and Section 337 of the Tariff Act of 1930) can still be invoked as before, despite so-called free trade. Only Section 201 of the Trade Act of 1974 has been modified in Canada's favour. And in this instance, the modification is less significant than Canada had every right to expect under GATT Article XXIV.

With respect to U.S. trade action under Section 201, the emergency action against an import surge permitted under GATT rules, Canada got less favourable treatment than provided for under GATT when two nations join in a free-trade area. Free-trade areas allow participants the right to give each other special treatment, to discriminate in each others favour, so to speak. While GATT Article XIX (the article corresponding to Section 201) requires that nations which act to protect themselves against an import surge not discriminate in favour of any one country (that is, equal action must be taken against all importers), Article XXIV (8 b.) allows an exception for free-trade areas. But under the free-trade deal Canada is not entitled to exemption from Section 201 action.

The Washington D.C. law firm, Hogan and Hartson, assessed what Canada did get in the trade deal. Their brief shows the extent to which U.S. protectionism remains significant. On Section 201 they conclude: "The agreement will not affect cases in which Canadian imports are a major factor in the U.S. market." This means, for instance, that the major U.S. action against cedar shakes and shingles would have stood despite the agreement. This is the case because under Article 1102 (1) of the deal, Canada is not exempted from Section 201 actions if its imports are "substantial" (5 to 10 per cent is not substantial) and if they "contribute importantly to the serious injury or threat thereof caused by imports." Hogan and Hartson conclude that "the exemption from Section 201 restrictions where Canadian trade is not a major factor in the U.S. market could be a significant benefit" since it would prevent Canada from being "sideswiped" when the U.S. acts against others. They go on to point out, however, that Canada may have to litigate to protect its rights and that in Section 201 cases its exports will still be monitored and therefore subject to the 10 per cent ceiling. This is another way of saying that Canada would still be subject to a form of voluntary restraint, as happened in the case of carbon steel exports.

With respect to the matters of principal concern to Canada, Hogan and Hartson point out that "Canada has not been exempted from U.S. anti-dumping or countervailing duty law" and that "the substantive

U.S. law defining countervailable subsidies, sales at less than fair value [dumping] and material injury has not been changed." Thus, Canada was denied the relief from these laws it sought in negotiations. What was achieved in the deal was a new binational review process that replaces judicial review in countervailing duty and anti-dumping cases. Hogan and Hartson point out that "the binational review process will probably reach decisions very similar to those that would have been reached by U.S. courts." In favour of this process they say is that it "should operate more quickly and efficiently than U.S. courts if outstanding legal issues are satisfactorily resolved."

The proposed binational review panels are supposed to protect Canadian exporters, unjustly accused under U.S. law with benefiting from subsidies or of selling in the U.S. at prices below those prevailing in Canada, by introducing a new set of trade umpires to review U.S. decisions made under U.S. law. Article 1904 stipulates the conditions under which a chairman, drawn from one of the two countries, and two nominees from each country will sit down to sift the evidence presented in the United States. The very existence of this new review process is expected to influence the application of American law by the American authorities, or so the government says. While Canadians guilty of dumping in the U.S., or of receiving subsidies and thus open to the application of countervailing duties will still be prosecuted, the innocent will now, supposedly, be better protected. Moreover, it is further claimed that, because Canada has its own trade-remedy laws, its own countervailing duties for subsidized exports and its own anti-dumping measures, it can always act against guilty American exporters. While no doubt accurate, this argument fails to address the issue of the unequal impact of such laws on Canada.

It should be clear from the foregoing that the free-trade deal does not exempt, protect or free Canada in any meaningful way from the application of U.S. statutory protection afforded by countervailing duty and anti-dumping laws designed to deal with the unfair trading practices of other nations. On the contrary, Article 1904 (2) enshrines the relevant U.S. legal statutes in the agreement. This means that the new binational panels will merely consider whether *American* trade law has been fairly applied in the cases under review. Disputes arising from the application of these laws are covered by Article 1904, and under subsection 1 Canada exchanges the current right to appeal to

American tribunals for the new right to appeal the same laws to a binational review panel. Canada continues to consider these laws to be unsatisfactory and Article 1907 establishes a working party to develop a "substitute system of rules" in the first five to seven years of the life of the agreement.

Prospects for Canadian Exports

Of significant presumed benefit to Canada is the understanding that future modifications to U.S. anti-dumping and countervailing duty laws will be subject to binational review. Furthermore, the U.S. undertakes not only to notify Canada of changes it intends to make, but to make those changes consistent with the GATT codes on anti-dumping and countervailing duties. Finally, by agreeing that any changes to existing law would apply to Canada only if the legislation so states, the U.S. has shown that it intends to single out its free-trade partner for special treatment. But, if this provision does provide some protection from future changes, it does not alter the status quo. And it was because the status quo was unsatisfactory that Canada negotiated the agreement in the first place.

Though the new dispute provisions have been heralded by the government as a major achievement, the Canada-U.S. free-trade agreement still fails to address, in any adequate way, Canada's main concern in the talks: guarantees about access to the U.S. market. In presenting the new binational review panels as a major step towards providing the guaranteed access sought by the government, the substantive reasons that led Canada to negotiate with the U.S. in the first place — the reasons invoked by the Business Council on National Issues, the Macdonald Commission, and the government itself to sell Canadians on free-trade talks — seem to have been forgotten. While for the Americans, Canadian trade law is nothing more than an irritant, for Canada, the continued existence of American trade protection means that new investment in Canada will still not be encouraged, or existing investment any more protected under the deal than before the talks began. Indeed, since the deal provides for national treatment in the U.S. for Canadian investors, companies will have an incentive to invest in the U.S. rather than in Canada, and service the American market from a U.S. location, rather than through countervailable exports from Canada. Yet it was to encourage new investment at home that Canada went into negotiations with the U.S. in the first place. There will be no benefits to Canada from free trade if, as a result of the deal, new investment is undertaken in the U.S., not Canada, and existing investment is "rationalized" to U.S. locations.

To make matters worse, the most objectionable features of U.S. trade law are untouched by the trade deal. American companies have more scope to initiate the protectionist process in the U.S. than do Canadian companies in Canada. While no Canadian firm can proceed on its own against what it considers to be unfair competition from abroad, American companies have such rights under U.S. trade law. These rights are called "process protectionism" by critics of American trade law. This term is used because U.S.-based corporations have a legal right to take their competitors — successful Canadian exporters — through a process that amounts to trade harassment. The failure to negotiate new trade rules means that this harassment process continues.

The existence of the new binational procedure does not alter the fact that it is trade harassment that hurts exporters or scares them away. If you win, if you are competitive, if you succeed under liberalized trade, then you can be punished in the U.S. by trade-remedy law. It is this *uncertainty* that led Canada to negotiate guarantees about market access, and it was liberalized trade that led to the increased use of trade-remedy law by the United States. The trade agreement liberalizes trade yet again without changing the rules that hurt Canada and left the U.S. untouched. On this issue, Canadians are being seriously misled by the government when it claims that binational review addresses the question of secure market access.

The issue that led negotiator Simon Reisman to break off talks, before the subsequent political intervention, was precisely the issue of so-called Canadian subsidies and the American countervailing duties that deal with them: the issue of U.S. trade laws. The Americans simply refused to recognize that Canadian regional policies, industrial development grants and social policy measures were normal practices for a nation with a small population inhabiting a huge territory, with all that implies for an open economy. In interviews following the suspension of the talks, Mr. Reisman seemed appalled by the American lack of sensitivity to Canadian practices and needs. Thus Canada tried, and failed, to secure American agreement as to what constitutes fair and unfair trade laws. Obviously, since Canada failed to win agreement on a new set of trade laws, the negotiations themselves have to be considered a failure with respect to securing market access.

However, the issue of American protectionist laws and Canada's presumed subsidies is still on the table. The two countries will spend five years trying to come up with a new set of trade rules. If they fail, the agreement provides for a further two years of negotiation on trade-remedy legislation. Since the U.S. believes that its $150 billion (U.S.) trade deficit is due to unfair competition by subsidized exports from the rest of the world, it was quite simply unwilling to cut a deal on trade law concerning subsidies before the timetable for GATT negotiations had run its course. Though major concessions were made to the U.S. on investment, energy, autos, banking, services and agriculture, on the market access issue Canada signed what is really only an interim deal — nothing more than an agreement to keep on negotiating. Surely this was unwise in the extreme. Canada has the option of negotiating the same issues within the context of the current GATT round which is slated to end by 1991, fully two years earlier than the proposed new bilateral talks.

What, then, is the effect of the agreement on American protectionist laws? Simply put, it legitimizes practices that are dangerous for Canada. By agreeing, under the terms of the free-trade deal, to allow U.S. countervailing duty and anti-dumping law to continued to be applied in trade actions against Canadian exports, Canada has accepted the very practices that free trade was supposed to end. Surely the failure of the accord to address these laws is serious enough to lead anyone concerned about Canada's trading future to reconsider support for the deal.

Even Canadian measures to move workers from low- to high-productivity industry, the very rationale behind trade liberalization, are still subject to the countervailing duty power in the United States. The failure to have these measures included in the agreement either speaks very poorly of the prospects for increased productivity and efficiency under the agreement, or it flies in the face of everything we have been led to believe by free-trade boosters. Thus, for instance, the agreement fails the Macdonald Commission's test of providing "for agreed measures of transitional adjustment assistance and safeguards."

Though the provision for binational panels falls far short of what Canada was seeking in talks with the U.S., it still may fairly be asked if the situation is not improved nonetheless. In other words, though Canada did not get an independent tribunal as the court of *first* resort for trade disputes, and though Canada did not get a *new* set of trade laws that recognizes and legitimizes Canadian practices in the areas of regional assistance, social policy and industrial development, is what Canada got not preferable to the status quo?

In answering this question it should be remembered that uncertainty about the future was at the heart of Canada's complaints about U.S. trade-remedy law. But, in the deal, reference is made to the possibility of either side terminating the agreement upon sixty days notice in the case of unresolved countervail or anti-dumping actions, and upon six months in the case of failure to work out a joint subsidies code for countervail cases. Canada, as the smaller, more dependent partner in the deal, needs more protection from abrogation than the United States. Without a significant shield, even the possibility of abrogation undermines the business confidence needed for investment to take place in Canada rather than in the United States. Should intractable political differences arise with the U.S., Canada would need more than six months to extricate itself from the increasingly integrated North American economy. Yet the agreement allows for abrogation on short notice by either party. This gives the U.S. tremendous leverage when it comes to resolving trade disputes. For this reason many observers, including Ambassador Reisman, called for a long abrogation period as a condition of the agreement. Since Canada did not get this, the formalized procedures of the disputes mechanism means that Canada becomes more vulnerable to American political pressure than it would be without the treaty.

The new panels and CUSTER must be seen, in any reading of the agreement, as a substitute, and *not* as an alternative, to existing GATT panels. But Canada has much more to gain through improving the GATT panel process than from the proposed binational review process. It can hardly be envisaged that Canada would be obliged to give up anything like what was conceded in these bilateral talks in order to get improvements in trade disputes from GATT. So rather than seeing binational review as preferable to the status quo, it must be seen to be worse: first, because it effectively closes down recourse to the existing GATT procedure; and second, because it weakens Canada's commitment to GATT in the future.

When seen in this light, it should be cause for grave concern that, despite so-called free trade, what Canada got falls far short of secure access for Canadian exporters to the American market. While many observers have argued that U.S. trade laws and administrative precedents are unfair to exporters, no one ever argued that the existing judicial review process was biased or politically motivated. When the review process was mentioned as a trade impediment it was only to point out that judicial review could take much too long and be very costly. This flaw was addressed by the agreement. But, by no stretch of the imagination can shortening the review period for bad decisions be thought of as securing access to the American market. Secure access would require agreement on new trade laws; it would also depend upon the panels, and not (as is still the case) U.S. administrative bodies, making the initial decisions on the basis of the new rules.

Worse yet, under the treaty, Canada remains vulnerable to protectionist measures that could be invoked for balance of payment reasons by the United States. These measures, permitted by GATT, are enshrined in the free-trade deal. They provide that a country experiencing severe deficits in its dealings with other nations may for a time discriminate against imports from other countries. Despite so-called free trade, Canada did not win an exemption from the application of these measures, though the GATT agreement itself would allow for such an exemption in the case of a free-trade area. There is no mention that, should the U.S. find it necessary to apply exchange controls or take trade actions (such as a surcharge or quota) to counteract a serious deterioration in its balance of payments, it must do so in a manner consistent with the bilateral agreement. Article 2002 (the balance of payments clause) refers only to the need to act in a manner consistent with GATT and other agreements. This means that should the U.S. have to defend its dollar — as the Nixon administration did in 1971 — Canada will, once again, not be exempt. Under this deal, Canada is in the position of someone who buys an insurance policy that fails to cover the biggest and worst risk!

In evaluating the effects of the deal on market access it must be kept in mind that the U.S. has a serious trade deficit that must shrink at some point. The opposite side of the coin is that the rest of the world has a trade surplus with the U.S. that must likewise shrink; Canada, as it happens, has the second largest surplus and is therefore vulnerable. It is hard to see how Canada can *increase* net exports to the U.S. while the U.S. tries to *decrease* its net imports from the world. It is more likely that Canada will end up importing more from the U.S., though the government never mentions this possibility in all its literature about the deal. Indeed, the rise in the value of the Canadian dollar that occurred in early 1988 means that Canadian industries will find it harder to export to the U.S. while they become more vulnerable to U.S. competition. While the government implies that the trade deal will increase exports, spur economic growth and create more jobs, it neglects to mention that the U.S. gets improved access to the Canadian market at a time when it needs to improve its trade balance.

The GATT Alternative

The largely symbolic concessions on market access obtained bilaterally contrast sharply with what Canada has managed to gain in concessions from the U.S. under seven GATT round negotiations. There is no reason to believe that this situation has changed. If anything, the current prospects under GATT are better than at any other time in recent years. GATT was ignored by the U.S. in the early Reagan years, when the U.S. dollar was strong. And after the 1982 GATT ministerial meeting ended in failure, many Canadians despaired of another GATT round getting off the mark, and the idea of bilateral talks with the U.S. gained favour among trade officials as a result. But recent circumstances have changed the need for bilateral concessions dramatically. The stock market crash of October 19, 1987, brought home to many Americans the dangers of trade protectionism in a fragile international economy. There is now more interest in the U.S. in the new GATT round than in protectionist law. If there is one historical lesson that is well know in the U.S. Congress, it is that the protectionist Smoot-Hawley tariff bill, passed in 1930, contributed significantly to the world depression of the 1930s.

With a significant trade deficit looming large over American politics, it is highly unlikely that the U.S. will give up on efforts to open new markets through GATT. In this event, they will have to give in order to get. As its largest trading partner, Canada is likely to benefit more than any other country from American concessions under GATT. There is no reason to believe that Canada will have to give up anything like what was conceded under the free-trade deal in order to get those benefits, as past practice shows. For example, in the Tokyo round negotiations, the Americans agreed to adopt an "injury test" before laying countervailing duties against so-called subsidized exports from other countries. This test requires that domestic producers show that they have suffered material injury before protectionist measures can be invoked by the U.S. authorities. This concession was granted by the U.S. at the insistence of the European Community. The EC in a sense "paid" for the concession by granting the U.S. improved access for citrus fruit exports. But Canada is a major beneficiary. The potential value of an injury test in countervail cases is of greater importance to Canada than any concession obtained on trade law under the free-trade deal, including the binational panels.

As a general rule, under GATT, Canada gains access to the U.S. market when the U.S. makes concessions to others. Since the U.S. objective is to gain expanded access to the 80 per cent of the U.S. export market that is outside North America, the greater part of the "cost" of those concessions are paid for by others outside North America. And yet Canada wins big as a result, because nearly 80 per cent of its exports go the United States. In the bilateral talks, the U.S. granted concessions to Canada that were fully paid for by Canada in the form of equal concessions to the U.S.; multilaterally, however, concessions gained by Canada are paid for by others as well. In other words, Canada gets what others pay for in GATT, while Canada pays full value for concessions won in bilateral negotiations. On this basis, can it seriously be argued that GATT is not a superior alternative to the free-trade deal?

Under the deal, Canada received only a commitment from the U.S. to review in further talks its trade-remedy laws as they apply to cross-border trade. Meanwhile, the U.S. is already committed to reviewing trade-remedy law within the current GATT negotiations. On the secure market access issue, the conclusion is inescapable: the U.S. was unwilling to make commitments to Canada that would show its hand before the GATT talks had reached the hard bargaining stage. Thus, on trade law, Canada-U.S. talks are on the same time track as GATT. This raises doubts about the wisdom of pursuing the bilateral option. Did Canada not pay too much in bilateral talks for meagre concessions? Could Canada not have achieved more, at less cost, through GATT? The answer to both these questions is yes.

5

Assessing Economic Benefits

Riel Miller

In presenting the case for the free-trade deal, tariff reductions bear an unreasonable burden. In fact, Article 401 (2), which sets out the timetable for the elimination of duties, shoulders responsibility for most of the benefits which will accrue from the deal. In supermarkets across the country, in documents produced by various government departments, and in the technical studies leading up to the agreement, the benefits arising from Mulroney's trade deal depend on the familiar and supposedly quantifiable impact of reduced tariffs on the economy. Employment gains, productivity growth, lower prices and greater consumer choices: these are viewed as the principal sources of the benefits arising from the trade deal. Such positive expectations are justified in two ways. First, by an appeal for faith in the virtues of "liberalized" market forces, and, second, by the evidence provided by econometric models.

The Department of Finance produced "An Economic Assessment" of the deal which mixes faith and econometric results in roughly equal measures. Their case begins with the assertion that trade liberalization was the single most important factor in the unprecedented boom following World War II. Quoting from the report of the Macdonald Commission, they state that "it is through the gradually increasing exposure of Canadian producers to competitive world market forces that the Canadian economy, as a whole, has become more productive" (Volume

1, p. 234). Then, after a brief review of existing trade barriers and the provisions of the accord, the study reports on the long and medium-run econometric forecasts which attempt to predict the impact of the trade deal on the Canadian economy.

The strength of the department's approach is that it combines political assumptions with a "scientific" method for predicting future economic trends. This combination of faith and science has always packed a powerful punch. But, without delving into the technical intricacies of the models (which predict a wide range of outcomes), it is worthwhile to examine briefly the assumptions which are the real determinants of the mysterious, yet supposedly irrefutable, econometric calculations.

Free Market Faith

The Department of Finance argument in favour of the trade deal rests on seven premises: comparative advantage specialization; lower prices for consumers; third country effects; economies of scale; increased flexibility and dynamism; reduced uncertainty; and real income effects. The common thread running through all of these premises is the assumption that free markets, and the corollary of free trade, are per se beneficial, regardless of market structure, geography, social infrastructure, or history. The positive economic impact of tariff reductions relies on these premises. To the extent they are inaccurate or misleading, the case for the deal is undermined and ultimately fails.

Faith in the abstract virtues of the free market actually reflects what's currently "in vogue" for economic policy, rather than analytic rigor. Not so long ago economists were arguing that government intervention was really the main factor behind the unprecedented economic growth of the post-war period. During this era economists were fervent advocates of "fine tuning" and "pump priming." At other times, economists have pointed to the forces of war which fostered massive industrialization in the United States and set the stage for Europe to rebuild with new technology. To isolate liberalized trade, and by implication free markets in general, as the preponderant factor accounting for post-war growth is a limited approach, to say the least. For example, it neglects the role of the state in sustaining buying power for the elderly, the poor, and the unemployed. It denies the reality of how trade unions forced up real wages and stimulated growth.

Underlying the virtues of market liberalization (or "flexibility" as the Organisation for Economic Co-operation and Development calls it) is the notion, handed down from Adam Smith, that unfettered markets will allocate resources more efficiently. By freeing up the invisible hand it should be possible to overcome low productivity growth rates and labour market rigidities. In this theoretical framework the concern shifts away from purchasing power — or the demand side — to production, the supply side of the economy. But the shift by economists from demand side to supply side concerns — with factor costs, productivity and allocation as the central focus — also requires consideration of the forces shaping decision-making by firms, or "industrial structure."

Once industrial structure enters the picture, along with other specific determinants of economic behaviour such as taxes and climate, there is a change in the various premises upon which the benefits of market liberalization depend. The Department of Finance, however, excludes the facts of Canadian geography, foreign ownership, resource dependence, and corporate concentration when constructing its econometric models. This elimination of the reality of the Canadian economy calls into question the evidence produced by econometric models showing that tariff reductions will generate economic gains. If these models exclude most of the major structural influences on the behaviour of prices and investment in the Canadian economy, how much value do they really have?

Brief consideration of the seven premises used by the Department of Finance should clarify this point.

Comparative Advantage Specialization

"Trade barriers *distort* production decisions. Trade liberalization, in contrast, *ensures* that countries specialize in producing goods in which they have a comparative advantage."

If this statement is taken literally, there can be little doubt that the Canadian economy itself is the product of "distortion." After all, the National Policy championed by Sir John A. Macdonald shaped market forces in order to foster industrial development. In this sense, "distortion" is in the eye of the beholder. Moreover, without entering into an extended discussion of the two-hundred-year-old debate around comparative advantage and specialization, it is worth noting that the Canadian economy and, even more so, Canadian exports, are already highly specialized. Often, Canadian historians have described our "specialization" as resource dependency.

For many nations, Canada included, the opportunities presented by comparative advantage do not lead to an optimal outcome. If unfettered markets leave nations underdeveloped and poor, yet specialized in resource extraction, is that acceptable? If the vagaries of historical development leave a nation in the hands of foreign owners and hence less capable of generating high value-added production, is that something market liberalization will overcome? Obviously, the answer to these questions is no. The market is not an impartial arbitrator. It does not provide optimal solutions irrespective of the historical conditions or the policy objectives of a nation. In fact, trade liberalization and specialization have meant that Canada foregoes jobs in manufacturing.

In a country where research and development expenditures lag far behind what is invested in the other advanced capitalist nations, it is hard to believe that upgrading production techniques to take advantage of new technologies and emerging industries will happen by simply allowing the market to make the decisions.

Lower Prices for Consumers

"Trade barriers *distort* prices and hence consumption decisions. Trade liberalization means lower prices for both imported and domestically produced goods that compete with them. Trade liberalization also means lower costs for imported intermediate products which in turn will lead to further reductions in consumer prices."

When the Organization of Petroleum Exporting Countries raised the price of oil they argued that they were simply correcting the distorted prices which had been set for so long by the big oil companies. When Hydro Quebec signs a deal with American utilities at three times the price being charged users in Quebec, is this price distortion or effective national use of a resource?

Once again, "distortion" is in the eye of the beholder. In Canada, as in a number of other countries, governments aim both to conserve energy and to extract higher economic rent by increasing the price of fuel. Market players, with short-term horizons and profit maximization as priorities, don't consider the social costs and benefits that are by-products of their behaviour. International prices are not necessarily optimal prices, nor are they by definition set by the forces of competition.

Here is where market structure and pricing behaviour in the real world play havoc with the simple scenarios of competition and price flexibility. Global multinational corporations are not simply price takers forced to accept conditions in the marketplace as they find them. On the contrary, they seek to control prices through planning. Nor are prices particularly responsive in the short-run to changes in demand or costs. Neither Canadian consumers nor producers can expect a sudden departure in pricing behaviour due to the relatively marginal tariff reductions planned under Mulroney's trade deal. Firms will not abruptly change the pricing practices built up through experience and targeted according to production costs, global dispersion of production, and profit requirements. Perhaps, at the margin, some firms will go out of business and others will adopt new strategies, but price flexibility will not be the end result. Only in a world where fixed capital is perfectly malleable and prices are only set once supply and demand are in balance will we find price flexibility of the sort envisaged by the Department of Finance.

In the real world there is a clear link between price behaviour and market structure. Canada's market structure exhibits four main traits: a very high level of foreign ownership; dominance of multinational firms at a sectoral level; two-thirds control of Canada's imports by multinationals (intra-firm trade is an important factor here); and foreign-controlled firms in Canada are bigger and more diversified than Canadian-controlled firms. Research for Canada confirms the link between market structure and firm behaviour. Indeed, evidence suggests that there is a strong association between price rigidity and industries dominated by multinational firms.

In fact, in the Canadian case, so called market liberalization may lead to greater market concentration, less price responsiveness and lower rates of investment and job creation. Although the overall level of foreign ownership in Canada has fallen somewhat over the last decade, the role of multinational corporations has not diminished but increased. Recent Statistics Canada figures show that gradual decline in the percentage share of assets controlled by foreign corporations has not been reflected in their share of profits. Indeed, the share of total assets, sales and profits accounted for by the leading twenty-five enterprises in the Canadian economy as a whole has climbed steadily over the past decade. In other words, the riches promised by those in favour of trade liberalization and the accompanying openness to foreign investment are likely to turn into liabilities given the peculiar structure of the Canadian economy and industry.

Third Country Effects

"The elimination of trade barriers between Canada and the United States will ensure that goods produced in one country are cheaper in the other country's market. Canada's domestic producers will have a competitive advantage in the U.S. market compared to suppliers from other countries, and vice versa."

The Department of Finance hopes that Canada will become an export platform to the United States for both domestic and foreign producers. But these expectations ignore certain realities. Domestic producers in the U.S. are having a hard time competing in their own market, and not because they've been coddled by tariff protection or because they lack access to a "large consumer market." The root causes are more systemic in nature and reflect the changing international division of labour in conjunction with a significant technological transformation.

Many provisions in the trade deal work against turning Canada into a manufacturing export centre serving the American market. First of all, unless Canada harmonizes its overall tariff rates to those of the United States, producers in Canada will face, on average, higher import tariff charges than they would face in the United States. Simply put, the historically higher Canadian tariff levels mean that firms located in Canada using parts imported from third countries will face higher costs than their American competitiors. Compounding this disincentive are the all too familiar facts of Canadian climate, taxation, regulation and unionization. These details of Canada's history and geography are disturbing wrinkles in what would otherwise be a seamless flow of benefits from liberalized trade.

Further problems arise out of the specific elements of the deal. In particular, the provisions dealing with rules of origin are inadequate. The 50 per cent Canadian content rule outlined in Article 304 actually allows a firm to "Canadianize" the cost of foreign produced "energy, fuel, dies, molds, tooling, and...of machinery and equipment." As a result, firms which do take advantage of the ability to send goods to the United States because of lower duties will have no incentive to buy Canadian machinery, capital equipment or energy. Companies that want to meet the 50 per cent Canadian content requirement can buy all their capital equipment in Germany or Japan, or even the U.S., and then have the cost of that equipment count as part of the Canadian content. Without domestic sourcing for capital goods as part of rules of origin criteria, Canada may never develop any new industrial strength. Instead, Canada retreats into the "free market" of a sort of fortress North America while abandoning the policies it needs to compete in that market.

Economies of Scale

"Both foreign and domestic trade barriers impose costs. This is particularly the case for smaller economies....The capacity to specialize and to exploit the economies of large-scale production are the main potential sources of gain from free trade for a small country such as Canada which, unlike other industrialized countries, does not have *secure* access to a large consumer market."

The critical question not addressed by proponents of market liberalization is why producers operating in Canada have not already taken advantage of the apparently vast potential for realizing economies of scale? After all, the issue is not access to the American market per se, since Canada and the U.S. currently have the largest trading relationship. Realistically, neither security of access nor tariffs can be seen as having posed major obstacles to firms wishing to take advantage of the economies of scale offered by cross-border trade.

Even without questioning the supposition that there are vast untapped economies of scale to be exploited (in a world that is in fact moving towards smaller specialized production runs), it remains doubtful that the trade deal will alter the behaviour of producers deciding to invest in Canada. Pricing and investment behaviour do not change drastically because tariffs decline by a few points. At a minimum, free marketers must admit that exchange rate changes and uncertainty easily overwhelm the influence of tariff reductions. Unfortunately, the volatility of exchange rates means that they are not amenable to econometric modelling. Yet exchange rate problems become more acute as the United States looks at the puny tariff walls surrounding fortress North America and moves to a lower dollar to solve its trade deficit.

In the end, "security" of access is also in the eye of the beholder. Canadians supply the United States with a vast range of raw materials, from electricity and paper to water and natural gas. Our best security lies in the fact that Americans need what we have. If the concern is with product specialization and fitting Canadian plants into corporate strategies so that production is undertaken in Canada for the world market through the use of world product mandates, (which are the current ways of achieving economies of scale), the free-marketers need to reconsider their premises. Canada is not any better placed to gain world product mandates with or without the agreement. But, with the deal in place, Canada is certainly weaker in its ability to direct investment and control capital flows in a way which promotes the development of product specialization by domestic industry. One of Canada's proudest examples of a "world class" producer is Northern Telecom, a company that was nurtured, not by open markets but by a closed customer-supplier relationship.

Increased Flexibility and Dynamism

"Free trade implies greater exposure of Canadian business to international opportunities and competition, both at home and in foreign markets. This exposure can be expected to create incentives for greater price flexibility and faster responses to changes in market conditions."

The premise here is that greater exposure to the world market will generate greater economic flexibility in domestic markets. But does the trade deal bring about such exposure? In fact, the Department of Finance neglects the actual provisions of the accord. The move to fortress North America is designed to reduce competition from the trade tigers, like Taiwan, Korea, or even Brazil. Furthermore, as was pointed out above, market liberalization may engender even greater price and labour market rigidities.

Economies such as Sweden show greater labour market and price flexibility because public intervention facilitates it more effectively than the so-called free markets. Does it need to be pointed out that Japan's economic success has occurred because the government plays a critical role in co-ordinating private sector activities? If the Department of Finance wants to encourage flexibility and dynamism they might do well to assess the atavistic and defensive behaviour that characterizes Canadian markets.

Reduced Uncertainty

"Firms must have reasonably secure access to a market before they will undertake large investment projects dedicated to that market. The Canada-U.S. Free Trade Agreement, with its new rules and procedures for the application of trade remedy laws and the resolution of disputes, will reduce uncertainty with respect to market access and will thereby encourage investment and risk taking."

Tariffs, and even non-tariff barriers, are not the main source of economic uncertainty. Overall economic growth prospects and the cyclical volatility of the economy are much more important. An unfettered market, as Keynes pointed out, is the greatest uncertainty an entrepreneur can face.

In fact, the deal does little to reduce uncertainty. Indeed, the additional appeal procedures add another layer to the legal labyrinth. Investment decisions will not turn on the slim hope that moral suasion might prevail because Canadians are on a disputes-settlement panel. It is more likely that investors will worry that the ongoing negotiations concerning the definition of subsidies will result in major changes to Canadian economic policies that favour their operations. With the prospect of significant shifts in the patterns of public financing, regulation, and taxation because of the new set of negotiations, the degree of uncertainty in the Canadian economy has increased rather than decreased.

In order to create a climate that encourages investment and risk-taking, Canadians should look to reducing the speculative frenzy which is increasing cyclical volatility. The path towards investments which will build an economy for the 21st century is not that of liberalization, but collective decision-making on terms which put social goals ahead of multinational mobility.

Real Income Effects

"For an open economy like Canada's, the impacts of freer trade on real income depend mainly on two effects: the increase in production made possible by better and more efficient utilization of resources, and change in the relative price at which imports can be purchased and exports sold abroad, that is, the economy's 'terms of trade'."

In the abstract there is little to dispute about the virtues of higher productivity and more efficient utilization of resources. More for less is better. The problem is whether liberalized trade and free markets are likely to deliver the productivity dividend. According to the new orthodoxy, liberalized markets generate economic flexibility, which means that both workers and investors adapt more quickly to changing economic circumstances. For Reagan and his ilk, economic flexibility is a by-product of greater inequality or, in more polite terminology, sufficient incentives for capitalists to invest and for workers to change jobs and accept lower wages and poorer working conditions. For many this is not flexibility, but waste. Higher productivity is much more easily realized when the gains are not only shared but determined in a democratic fashion.

The logical chain leading from freer markets to greater flexibility, to enhanced productivity, to real income gains is broken at the very first link, in part because freer markets also break the last link which ties efficiency to equity and democracy. As for the gains or losses due to changes in Canada's terms of trade, they are simply impossible to predict. Since the tariff changes are marginal compared to likely exchange rate changes, speculation about the trade deal and Canada's terms of trade is just that, speculation.

The Politics of Greed

In making the case for the trade deal, the government works from the simple assumption that free markets and trade liberalization are superior in all circumstances. Starting from this premise, the econometric models, not surprisingly, project positive economic benefits resulting from tariff reductions. But these econometric predictions ignore two central facts. First, that the agreement is only in small part concerned with tariff reduction, and so the benefits accruing from the conventional liberalization of trade must be seen in conjunction with the other provisions of the agreement. Higher energy prices, for instance, overshadow any predicted price effects of lower tariffs. Second, the expected gains accruing from market liberalization fail to take into account the structure and history of Canada's economy.

In Canada, trade liberalization and the extension of free market conditions cannot be assumed to be positive. Market structures, how firms actually perform, must be considered as well. It is only by starting from simplified assumptions that government economists predict a rosy future resulting from the deal.

Glowing predictions about income, jobs and economic growth help politicians to sell their product to the public. For example, in a small pamphlet issued by External Affairs, Canadians are told that the "new Free Trade Agreement with the U.S. is a good deal for consumers. For *every* Canadian it will mean: lower prices, more choice, and higher disposable incomes." It seems that the Mulroney government has borrowed from Ronald Reagan and opted for the politics of greed: though the virtues of free trade are justified on the basis of abstractions like market liberalization, the federal advertising campaign appeals directly to people's pocketbooks. Unhappily, this approach is often effective. Reagan used it to sell his regressive tax reforms and Margaret Thatcher has convinced the British public to sign-up for the privatization of everything from council flats to the phone company. In a similar fashion, the Mulroney government is using the prospects of cheap goods and higher income to sell the trade accord.

The glossy, full colour pamphlets produced by External Affairs and the Department of Finance drive home the extent to which formerly neutral, professional government departments have gone into advertising. Their pitch is even tuned to take into account the results of opinion polls. For instance, survey results show that women are less likely to support the trade deal than men. Consequently, much of the advertising available on supermarket stands across the country targets women with stories about lower prices and the sanctity of social programmes. Seeing External Affairs trying to close the "gender gap" on free trade hardly adds to the respect the department once enjoyed in Canada and the world.

The Mulroney government has been unable to convince the Canadian people of the virtues of the nco-conservative agenda that underlies the trade deal. So now the agreement is being marketed as a way to make a quick buck. Voters are treated no differently than consumers. Marketing takes precedence over democratic debate; advertising becomes a substitute for democracy.

PART II

A New Economic Constitution for North America

6

North American Integration

Daniel Drache

Far from putting Canadian-American affairs on a new, more equal footing, the Canada-U.S. trade deal reaffirms the fundamental asymmetrical power relationship of the two countries. Canada's trade is already concentrated with its principal trading partner more than any other industrial nation (see Table), and this dependency on the United States is bound to grow for a specific reason — the agreement restricts Canada's ability to modify its industrial structure. It does this by laying the foundation for the integration of the two economies, the two markets, and, ultimately, the two countries on terms and conditions lar-

Five OECD Countries' GNP Ratio of Trade* with the World and with the United States

	Canada	France	Japan	U.K.	West Germany
		(Per cent of GNP)			
Total trade	43.0	37.8	23.6	42.0	48.9
Trade with laragest partner	31.2	6.2	5.9	5.3	6.0
Trade with the U.S.	31.2	2.7	5.9	5.3	3.6

* exports plus imports
Source: OECD Monthly Review of Statistics of Foreign Trade (May 1985); and OECD National Accounts, 1960-1983 (Paris, 1984)

gely favourable to the United States. As a result of granting the U.S. the right of national treatment, Canadian governments will be unable to manage the economy in Canada's national interest. For all intents and purposes, Canada, in opening its economy, has in fact given the U.S. a large role in the Canadian policy-making process.

Both governments claim to be working to harmonize their different economic and social systems for their mutual benefit. The truth is that, while Ottawa has to change and amend major pieces of federal legislation in banking, energy, agriculture, services, the Auto Pact, investment, financial services and immigration,[1] Americans have few fixed obligations to change, repeal or modify American federal laws to make them conform to the objectives of the trade deal. While the U.S. is only committed to making minor changes to three statutes, none of which are significant,[2] Canada's major regulatory agencies will be altered by the trade pact. The Wheat Board, the Canadian Transport Commission, the Canadian Radio-television and Telecommunications Commission, and the National Energy Board will find their powers substantially reduced to conform to the overall design of the trade deal. Since all provinces have important regulatory authority over resources, transportation and regional development, provincial governments will have to bring their policies in line with the terms of the agreement. When implemented, the free-trade agreement becomes, by virtue of its scope and regulatory importance, the new national policy for Canada. All other federal and provincial policies will have to conform to its framework and goals.

Disparity of Power

The bilateral negotiations could not reduce the disparity of power that permeates Canadian-American relations. In this circumstance, further policy harmonization between the two countries is particularly dangerous for Canada. When the decentralized nature of Canada's political system is coupled with the pressures leading to North American integration, the distinctly different ways Canada has of coping with economic, political and cultural issues seem fated to disappear. The vast differences in market power in the private sectors, and political power in the public sectors, between the two countries simply has not been taken into account in calculating the effects of trade liberalization. Canada will be the country with the most to lose. Henceforth, the power of American political and economic forces will be brought to bear more directly on Canadian institutions.

An example of the difference in Canadian and American rights and obligations imposed by free trade can be seen in a key provision in the agreement: rules of origin. Such rules are a crucial issue in creating a free-trade area, since they determine which of the articles partially assembled outside Canada or the U.S. can enter duty-free for customs' purposes. According to the terms of the deal, both Canadian and American manufacturers will be able to import partially manufactured goods from low-wage countries such as Mexico, Brazil and Korea. This has important implications for job creation and the future of many small and medium-sized firms, especially in Canada.

Goods assembled abroad have become a key factor for many American industries. According to a recent study by J. Grunwald and Kenneth Flamm, *The Global Factory*, "more than one-half of U.S. sales of certain products in textiles and electronics are assembled abroad."[3] In recent years, imports of these products have reached almost one-sixth of total American imports of manufactured goods and about one-quarter of imports of manufactured goods from developing countries. Thousands of American firms have relocated in low-wage countries. By comparison, far fewer Canadian firms have moved out of Canada and set up new operations in these low-wage havens.

While all industrial countries rely on foreign assembly operations to increase profits and market share, the United States has gone further than any other industrial country. As the authors of the above study stress, over the years the definition of assembly has been expanded by a series of decisions of the U.S. customs courts to such a degree that, in 1983, imports under this provision amounted to more than $21 billion.[4] Rules of origin in the deal permit low-cost goods, largely manufactured outside North America, to enter the Canada-U.S. free-trade area duty-free. This will inevitably result in plant closures in those sectors of the Canadian economy that are import-sensitive. According to a confidential study carried out by the Bank of Nova Scotia, the sectors likely to be most hurt include clothing, automotive small parts producers, truck assemblers, shipbuilding and ship repair, organic and specialty chemicals, footwear and major appliances. These industries are high risk and "the losers will be hit up front." Small manufacturers will bear the greatest brunt in the short-term while larger manufacturers will face a "neutral or slightly positive outlook" down the road.

Tying Down Government

Article 103 unilaterally extends the rights and obligations of the final agreement to spheres of provincial jurisdiction. For instance, provinces will not be permitted to discriminate in favour of local suppliers over American companies.

Article 2010, dealing with the establishment of public monopolies, also affects provincial powers. Its terms would limit a government's authority to create a public monopoly in the areas of resource management, auto insurance, public housing, non-profit services such as daycare and cultural policy. The article restricts Canadian use of public powers for purposes that could be interpreted as creating or leading to "anticompetitive practices that would adversely affect a person of the other party." Grounds include alleged discrimination against an American multinational by a Crown corporation, or predatory practices on the part of state enterprises!

Articles 903 and 1407 are particularly onerous because they restrict Canadian legislative authority to impose new taxes on American multinationals and American businesses. Article 903 prevents any Canadian government from imposing export taxes, duties or charges on energy destined for the United States unless the same tax is applied to energy consumed domestically. Effectively, under its terms, no Canadian legislature will be able to develop national energy policies in Canada's self-interest. Article 1407 is equally far-reaching for the service sector. In the future, no Canadian government will be allowed to introduce "any new taxation measure that constitutes a means of arbitrary or unjustifiable discrimination."

Article 1603 prevents Canadian governments from demanding performance requirements and job or production guarantees from American capital. Under the agreement, provincial and federal governments, for instance, are prohibited from mounting an industrial strategy which requires industrial targeting or other measures restricting or interfering with American investment rights. In the past, the federal government supported large-scale aid to the textile and clothing industries which were being undermined by imports from low-wage competitors. A similar rationale was adopted to keep Massey-Ferguson and Chrysler solvent in order to protect the jobs and the companies themselves. Similarly, the government purchase of Canadair and de Havilland is an example of government intervention to maintain a highly competitive position in a strategic industry. In the future, Canadian governments will not be able to mount an industrial strategy that threatens foreign ownership rights. In fact, the overall effect of the agreement dramatically reduces the role of government in planning and managing the economy. Any control that Canada introduces must not be "a disguised restriction on trade." This reduces the action that a government may take to correct a market failure, alleviate regional disparity or regulate foreign ownership.

Article 1402 creates a new regulatory norm to regulate health and safety and consumer protection in service sectors covered by the Mulroney-Reagan trade deal. The aim of this provision is to reduce significant differences in existing regulatory standards. Where Canadian programmes and standards are different from the American ones, Ottawa has agreed that the difference be "no greater than is necessary for health and safety and consumer protection." The wording suggests that a minimal standard is not only permissible but preferable. In other words, tougher criteria to protect the consumer or the workplace could be considered a violation of the agreement.

Article 1605 creates far-reaching legal and political norms with respect to nationalization (misleadingly entitled "expropriation" — a word that ignores the national purposes served by such state action). Any Canadian legislature wanting to repatriate sections of the economy now in foreign hands will find that this has been made very difficult by the free-trade agreement. Article 1605 specifies four reasons for expropriation: "for a public purpose; in accordance with due process of law; on a non-discriminatory basis; and upon full payment of prompt and adequate and effective compensation." As the text reads, nationalization must meet all four criteria. Specifically, a violation of *any one* of these criteria would be grounds for dispute under the deal. Further, the criteria of "a non-discriminatory basis" will create difficulties for any Canadian government that wants to Canadianize foreign-owned sectors such as resources. In fact, had the agreement

been in force, it is doubtful whether the government of René Lévesque
would have had the authority to nationalize Quebec's American-owned
asbestos industry. Certainly, under the terms of the free-trade agreement, the creation of Petro-Canada, a national oil company, could not
have happened.

U.S. Business Rights

The principle of removing barriers to the flow of goods and services
in order to ensure "open and competitive trade" between Canada and
the U.S. does not interfere with the right of American-owned companies to receive support from the Canadian state. On the contrary, the
Mulroney-Reagan deal protects the rights of American businesses to
receive subsidies for private gain; it encourages support for the private
sector, in particular, for American resource companies and investors.
Article 906 protects existing and future subsidies for exploration,
development and related activities in the oil and gas industries in order
to maintain the "reserve base for energy resources." Article 1609
protects rights of American corporations to receive investment subsidies. All that is required is that the subsidy not "become a means for
unjustifiable discrimination between investors or a disguised restriction on the benefits accorded the parties to the agreement." Rights to
public support are guaranteed by Article 2011 dealing with nullification and impairment. This clause gives the U.S. the right to use the disputes-settlement mechanism if American firms are denied reasonable
benefits due to them under the free-trade agreement. It may be invoked
even though the agreement has not been breached. Given its broad
scope and flexibility, it gives American firms a powerful legal and
political device to circumvent a broad range of Canadian policies. Essentially, it could be used to restrict the enlargement of the public sector at the expense of the private sector.

In extending the right of business-persons to move back and forth
between the two countries with minimal restriction, the trade deal
grants multinational business one of its long-time goals. It lays the
foundation for a common market in management personnel. The first
step towards this common market is the elimination of the labour standards test which stipulates that among two qualified candidates a com-

pany is required to hire the Canadian one. Abolishing these procedures will limit the ability of the Canadian government to protect jobs for its citizens. Specifically, not only does it facilitate intra-company transfers between branch-plants and head-office but it allows American corporations to bring technical support staff or other business-people (broadly defined) into Canada on a temporary basis to work for them. The implications are far-reaching. American corporations may hire advertising, business consulting or other specialized personnel from the U.S. to work in Canada without having to justify their reasons to Canadian authorities. As well, in radically expanding the definition of a business-person, over forty different kinds of professionals will have the right to work in Canada in the areas of research and design, marketing, sales and distribution; these professionals will include insurers, bankers and investment brokers, computer specialists, scientists, teachers and management consultants. They will be able to work in Canada on a "temporary" basis for up to five years. As a consequence, Canadian governments will be left with less control over immigration and the contracting out of services.

Free Trade and Canadian Democracy

Given the extent and number of these restrictions on Canadian legislative authority, as well as the asymmetrical nature of the rights and obligations imposed on Canada compared with the U.S., it is conceivable that, when and if the trade pact is signed, Canadian governments will not be able to initiate major changes to legislative programmes without prior consultation and, in the end, *American approval*. The risk of proceeding unilaterally would be too great. As well, the deal opens the door to lengthy and bitter constitutional challenges in which the courts will shape the course of Canadian public policy. In short, the trade deal creates a legal and political nightmare for all levels of Canadian government.

The legalization of the public policy process will make Canada more dependent on American judicial processes and practices and, ultimately, on the whim and mood of Congress. Major policy questions will be viewed in light of their legal merits rather than their intrinsic policy worth. Not only does American business stand to profit from its enhanced access to all sectors of the Canadian market but, in fact, the trade deal gives the U.S. a powerful influence over the Canadian policy-making process. Canada, in return, receives nothing of equivalent value. Canada has not been granted any rights to participate in the American political process.

The End of Free-Trade Orthodoxy

In a world of stiff competition, the U.S. has all but abandoned free-trade orthodoxy. It now accepts the need to protect its markets and its welfare from further global economic shocks. The instability of the international economy, combined with its own industrial decline, has forced the U.S. to reassess its commitment to defend the principle of open trade irrespective of what other countries may do and irrespective of the costs of adjustment on its industries, its regions and employment. In its place, American policy-makers are concerned first and foremost about their economic security. This reversal of American commercial policy is evidenced not only by a change of rhetoric, but also by the fact that in the new legislation known as the Omnibus Trade Bill, old-fashioned trade liberalization has ceded ground to a blunt realism based on an older concept of reciprocity — that a country reserves the right to limit the damage unrestricted free trade now poses.

Faced with these new circumstances, the U.S. has used American trade-remedy legislation along with specific policies to exclude foreign products and protect American industry. As well, despite all the talk about other countries not playing by the rules, in 1985, U.S. government spent over 13 per cent of the Gross National Product, more than $60 billion, in direct and indirect support to its industries.[5] A 1983 International Monetary Fund study confirms that the U.S., more than any other industrial nation including Japan, protects and assists its industries with an extensive net of subsidies, tax credits and other programmes aimed at imports.

Then there is Canada. After three decades of tariff reduction, Canada continues to depend on a few high-performing industries, mostly resource- and energy-related, such as chemicals, agriculture and mining, and forestry products.

In the 1980s, two-fifths (by value) of Canadian exports consist of primary and crudely processed goods; two-fifths consist of other manufactured goods and one-fifth of automobiles and trucks. Compared to other industrial countries, Canada's export structure had barely evolved:[6] through the 1970s it continues to have an extremely high concentration of exports to one country, namely the U.S., as well as a heavy orientation towards primary and crudely processed goods, and motor vehicles still account for a high proportion of its manufactured exports. Despite some positive developments, the most disturbing fact is that Canada's deficit in manufactured goods continues to be one of the highest in the world. Clearly, then, trade liberalization has not transformed Canada's export-led economy into a world-class competitor.

The slowdown in the world economy has inevitably changed the rules of global trade and Canada's relations with the United States. Between 1950 and 1979 the international system worked because industrial countries had similar cost and production structures. Manufactured goods were sold between industrial countries and to the newly industrializing states of Africa, Asia and Latin America. Western countries bought mineral, agricultural and lumber resources, used in the manufacture of capital and consumer goods, in the Third World. But, in less than a decade, the high-wage industrial economies have been thrown into competition with new, highly efficient industries located in low-wage nations. Today, shifts in trade patterns seem to benefit one nation at the expense of another. "Adversarial trade," according to the leading authority on management practices, Peter Drucker, "is conducted not for purposes of exchange on a comparative basis but to destroy an opponent. New markets can only be obtained by destroying rival industries. The target is the declining smokestack industries where hundreds of thousands of blue collar workers are employed."[7] Therefore, given this shift in trade strategy, Canada has to rethink its economic strategy on the continent and globally.

Key to a strong international performance is the ability to arrive at a "negotiated understanding" between the principal social groups which link their welfare to a successful national economic effort; in this way, nations like Canada can expect to enhance their competitiveness. By contrast, free trade is essentially a confrontational strategy. In its pure expression, it ignores the economic dislocation that a policy of open markets causes. Free traders want competition between workers and industries to determine the pattern of economic adjustment. Accordingly, the aim of the agreement is not to control the conditions of industrial adjustment and competition but to accelerate the process of economic restructuring.[8]

For Canadian public policy, this kind of adjustment process has always been highly problematic. Being active in the international marketplace has meant that Canada has had to favour certain industries and let others stagnate. While productivity and incomes have risen in the internationally competitive sectors of the economy, the costs have been high. Trade liberalization has reinforced the existing structural weaknesses between the economically prosperous and the economically deficient regions of the country, between the internationally competitive sectors and those that produce mainly for the home market, and between workers in well-paid, stable jobs and those in low-paid marginal occupations.

The essential problem is no longer access to the American market. With more than $160 billion in cross-border trade, Canada has more access to the American market than any other industrial country. With the grooves of economic geography solidly established, the real issue is that, with capital increasingly mobile and technology largely portable, Canada's industries are able to prosper even though the have-not regions of the national economy grow progressively poorer.

Competition forces firms to reduce their workforces. In the past, business accepted the idea of tying increases in productivity to increases in wages. In the aggregate, the upward pressure on wages was thought of as positive so long as the economy was strong and productivity was increasing. In the new global economy, business sees less need for maintaining even the appearance of a social contract between itself and labour. It aims largely to reduce wages and the size of the workforce in order to make itself price competitive. It sees no need to balance welfare of key producer groups against competitive efficiency.[9] The drive to be competitive has already resulted in the loss of over 400,000 industrial jobs in Canada since 1981. It is predicted that by the year 2000, one-third of the industrial work force will be forced to look for jobs elsewhere.[10]

As North American business has reorganized itself to exploit world economic changes, the successful firms will be the multinational giants that have the resources, technology and marketing strategy to sell goods in the major markets of the world. Canada's branch-plant economy remains highly vulnerable to shifts in trade and investment flows. In a world of mobile capital, multinational corporations are no longer dependent on their Canadian operations for traditional kinds of "engineered commodities" that were critical to profitability in the past. Canada is a net importer of high technology in such industries as data processing, telecommunications, fine chemicals and the like. As corporations search for low-cost, high quality locations for these capital-intensive industries, they will be investing less in Canada and more elsewhere. In these circumstances, Canada's reliance on free trade is only going to worsen its economic problems.

In the new global economy, the free-trade model is not a viable growth strategy for the future. It cannot guarantee Canada the high standard of living it has had in the past. Nor can it strengthen Canada's international performance. With its weak industrial sector, sharp regional divisions and stark social equalities, the Mulroney-Reagan trade agreement commits Canada to the crude logic of market-based liberalism, a liberalism that lets the market determine competitive advantage while requiring that governments give up the right and ability to intervene in the economy.

A better solution for the uncertain times that lie ahead is to plan and manage the strategic goals of the economy. In the words of *New Republic* economics editor Robert Kuttner, "in the real world there are so many affronts to the pure theory of free trade, the practical policy question has long since changed. It is no longer *whether* to manage trade, but to manage it according to *which* criteria and to *what* degree."[12] The Mulroney-Reagan free-trade arrangement, far from doing this, cedes power to market economics. In accepting a North American vision of the world, Canada's negotiators may have sacrificed Canada's ability to determine its fate.

7

Investment

Mel Watkins

It is called a free *trade* agreement. Yet Chapter 16 is entitled "Investment." It is evident that we face a problem of misleading labelling. This agreement is much more than a trade agreement; indeed, much of what the critics object to in the agreement are the features that go far beyond "free trade" in the sense in which that is usually understood, namely, as removing barriers to trade in goods.

This agreement removes barriers to trade in services (Chapter 14), meaning that companies in either country are given complete freedom to operate in the other. There can only be free trade in "management services," for instance, if American management firms are free to set up operations in Canada — which is called the right of establishment — and are not discriminated against in any way by Canadian governments (federal, provincial or municipal). This is dealt with by a blanket provision in the agreement (Article 105) which reads: "Each Party shall, to the extent provided in this Agreement, accord national treatment with respect to investment and to trade in goods and services."

In order for there to be truly national treatment with respect to investment, there is a further necessity: the parties must agree, by and large, to eliminate restrictions on foreign investment. Foreign companies must be given rights of entry with minimal exclusions. Furthermore, they must not be discriminated against by performance requirements (such as domestic content requirements) imposed at the time of entry or subsequently.

These sweeping changes go well beyond the existing provisions of the General Agreement on Tariffs and Trade (GATT), which mostly bear on *trade*, and in *goods* only. The American government is pressing for such changes multilaterally in the present Uruguay round of GATT and elsewhere, and Article 1610 informs us that Canada shall now support that American agenda: "The Parties shall endeavour, in the Uruguay round and in other international forums, to improve multilateral arrangements and agreements with respect to investment."

Investment rules of the type found in this agreement are not usually thought to be part of a free-trade area — which is what Canada and the U.S. supposedly become under this deal. Rather, they are normally associated with common market arrangements, where both capital and labour are granted mobility rights. Under the Canada-U.S. agreement, capital has virtually complete mobility; labour has virtually none (though there are temporary entry provisions for business-persons to facilitate trade in services — Chapter 15). In that important sense, this agreement is so comprehensive that it is already half-way toward a common market arrangement.

The Corporate Agenda

Free trade, so understood, fits the contemporary corporate agenda. Companies trade, and prefer to do so with as little interference as possible from governments. They also invest abroad as well as at home, and they likewise prefer that governments not impede that process. The Canada-U.S. free-trade deal meets that corporate agenda so far as North America is concerned. It gives both American and Canadian companies *North American* citizenship. It is *their* Charter of Rights. Since it does not apply to companies outside North America, it means that Canadian policy henceforth discriminates in favour of American investment relative to overseas investment.

From the corporate perspective, this speaks to certain realities. Not only do Canada and the United States engage in a level of bilateral trade that is the largest in the world, there is also a level of cross-border investment that is unique. Canada has the highest level of foreign, mostly American, ownership of any country in the world, while (in per capita terms) there is an even higher level of Canadian investment in the United States.

But because Canada is the much smaller country, American control of the Canadian economy is a fact of life, while Canadian control of the American economy is self-evident nonsense, suggesting tongue-in-cheek articles in trendy American magazines. And because foreign economic control is widely perceived as compromising political sovereignty, it is not surprising that Canadian governments have, over the years, laid down some rules and regulations about foreign, including American, ownership. While the United States has not felt it necessary to respond in the same way to the "threat" of Canadian ownership, it nevertheless prohibits foreign investment in such industries as shipping, domestic air transport, dredging, nuclear-power generation, telecommunications and broadcasting. Yet Article 1607, which deals with "Existing Legislation" has a detailed Annex (1607.3) on *Canadian* legislation, but not on American. U.S. restrictions remain in force.

Though Canada has had some legislation with respect to the entry and performance of foreign-owned firms (notably the Foreign Investment Review Act), careful students have usually evaluated the effect to be minimal. The present Conservative government has, nevertheless, further emasculated such policies, turning the Foreign Investment Review Agency that screened foreign investment, and may occasionally have discouraged some of no apparent benefit to Canada, into Investment Canada with a mandate to encourage more of it. This agreement yet further reduces any restrictions on the operations of American companies in Canada, and then enshrines what little remains in such a way as to make it impossible for any future Canadian government to pursue a more interventionist policy.

The Mulroney government and other supporters of the free-trade deal have had a further obsession: a conviction that in recent years Canadian firms have been putting new investments in the U.S. as a hedge against American protectionism. There is little hard evidence of this, but insofar as the present agreement offers no effective protection from American protection (see chapter four), it does not deal with the problem.

New Rules for Investment

Annex 1607.3 spells out the new, and lesser, set of Canadian rules that will apply to American takeovers of Canadian companies. Investment Canada presently reviews foreign takeovers of Canadian firms with a worth in excess of $5 million (CDN) for the purpose of determining "net benefit" to Canada. This will rise in stages over a three-year period to $150 million, and will then remain at that level as measured in constant-dollars (corrected for inflation). Only a few hundred companies, rather than the present thousands, will then be eligible for review. (True, under the present government, no takeover had been turned down anyway, but this now locks any future government into a laissez-faire policy.)

Investment Canada is also currently empowered to review indirect acquisitions, where the ownership of a Canadian subsidiary changes from one American parent to another as the result of a takeover in the United States — a frequent occurrence in this age of mergers. Three years into the agreement, Canada ceases any such screening.

A policy that the late Walter Gordon was fond of was that American subsidiaries, which are typically wholly-owned by their American parents, would be required to divest some of their shares, say 25 per cent, to Canadian shareholders; this might mitigate the fullness of foreign control and permit Canadians some access to big profits being reaped solely by foreign shareholders. Such a requirement is forbidden under the free-trade agreement (1602.2).

Meanwhile, the financial press is reporting that American-controlled companies in Canada with minority shareholders are, in fact, buying them out in anticipation of the free-trade agreement coming into effect. The rationale given is the desire for tighter managerial control at the American head office, the better to rationalize continental production.

Either country, (read Canada), is precluded from imposing on a company in the other country any requirements with respect to exporting some specified portion of its production, or to buying domestically rather than importing. Domestic content requirements — such as those in the Auto Pact which have been so helpful to Canada — are similarly proscribed (1602.1). These concessions would seem virtually to preclude, amongst other things, the use of government policy to encourage secondary industry and build a more diversified economy around Canadian resources.

The Government of Canada's preamble to Chapter 16 insists that "the negotiation of product mandate, research and development, and technology transfer requirements with investors" is "not precluded," but the government would appear to have disarmed itself in conducting such negotiations.

This agreement, though between the governments of the United States and Canada, further insists that "national treatment" means "provincial treatment" (or "state treatment") as well. Hence, no province in Canada could apply any rule to an American company with terms less favourable than those which it applies to one of its own provincial companies. As well as being a significant intrusion on provincial rights, this article has the bizarre effect of permitting a provincial government to discriminate against companies from other Canadian provinces, but not companies from the United States! (Of course, it is also true that, under this agreement, we get free trade between Canada and the United States but not within Canada.)

In some cases, past Canadian policies will be allowed to remain. The $5 million threshold for review by Investment Canada is retained for takeovers in the oil and gas and uranium sectors. The cultural industries are exempted (Article 2005). This grandparenting provision, by its nature, makes no allowance for any extension of such Canadianizing policies into any new sectors in the future (see chapter twenty).

In the past, public enterprises at both the national and provincial levels have sometimes been created as alternatives to private American ownership; cases in point would be the CBC, Petro-Can, and provincial hydro-electric companies. Article 2012 of this agreement calls that phenomenon "designating a monopoly," (this is American phrasing; Canadians would call it "creating a Crown corporation"), and will require us in the future to operate the "public monopoly" in such a way as to "minimize or eliminate any nullification or impairment of benefits" — the benefits in question being those presently accruing to private American firms.

Had this agreement been in place in the past, would we have had to compensate American insurance companies when we set up medicare? Would we, in fact, have been able to create CBC, Petro-Can, Ontario Hydro and so on? How about denticare or publicly-run auto insurance in the future? Yet scholars tell us that a fundamental difference between Canadian and American society is our greater reliance on public enterprise.

The briefing notes on the agreement prepared by American officials for Treasury Secretary James Baker and Trade Representative Clayton Yeutter tell us what this all adds up to: "We could not end the life of Investment Canada, but we greatly circumscribed the scope of its activities....We have achieved a major liberalization of the investment climate in Canada and embedded it permanently so that in the future Canada's investment policies cannot retrogress to the old policies of the NEP and FIRA."

Once-upon-a-time, tariffs (the so-called National Policy) required American companies to set up branch-plants in Canada and produce here for the Canadian market rather than simply export from the U.S. to Canada. Over time, Canadian policy shifted to trying to make the branch-plants perform better, and in some cases, trying to exclude them. A struggle going back to the mid-1950s to impose some constraints on the rights of American capital in Canada ends in this agreement with a resounding defeat. American companies will largely be free in the future to do in Canada as they wish, and no future Canadian government will be able to do anything about that, short of tearing up the whole agreement — which would be hard to do after it had been in place for an extended period and companies had become accustomed to roaming freely throughout the continent.

Economic Consequences

Does it matter? The Mulroney government believes that letting capital have its freedom is a benefit rather than a cost, not only for the companies — which is true — but for the rest of us as well. However, there are reasons that suggest the contrary. Everyone agrees that one reason that American branch-plants came to Canada in the past was because of the Canadian tariff. But as the tariff completely disappears, how do we know the plants will not disappear too, as the American head office decides to service the Canadian market from the United States?

Unfortunately, there are some quite specific reasons for being pessimistic about what may happen to Canadian production and jobs under a free-trade agreement when so much of the Canadian economy is under foreign control. The first is that Statistics Canada data show that Canadian companies have been creating jobs while foreign-owned companies have been eliminating them.

Secondly, a number of Canadian subsidiaries of American firms are restricted by their parents from exporting to the United States (in order to preserve the American market for the parent). This is a well-documented problem that has been around for a century; the free-trade deal does not touch this issue and it will not go away just because governments decree free trade.

A third reason for concern is that the process of restructuring comparative advantage will now very likely be taking place during an economic downturn. All companies will experience higher levels of unused capacity. In the case of Canadian subsidiaries, their American parents may be sorely tempted, and pressured by domestic political considerations, to cut back production in Canada rather than in the United States. The rationalization on a North American basis that is compelled by free trade could provide the excuse for phasing out, or down-sizing, Canadian plants and jobs.

It may be claimed that this is too pessimistic, particularly given the experience with rationalization in the auto industry, where we have seen plant specialization for the continental market, a much increased level of cross-border trade, and a satisfactory level of production in Canada. But this best-possible outcome is the result of managed trade rather than of free trade proper. Further, even in the case of the auto industry, rationalization has been accompanied by increasing centralization of decision-making in the United States and by greater Canadian technological and design dependence. The branch-plant has been rendered more efficient but the branch-plant status does not change; rather it is deepened and entrenched.

Will Canadian firms not expand their production in Canada the better to service the American market, tending to offset any flight of U.S. firms out of Canada? This view is excessively sanguine, for it ignores the brute fact — reported by the Science Council of Canada some years ago — that the American market, being more than ten times larger than the Canadian, acts like a magnet to pull unto itself those very external-ly-based firms which are most successful in selling there. Consider, for instance, the case of the Maritime provinces within the free-trade area called Canada in the post-Confederation period. The Maritimes had its winners, like Max Aitken and the Bank of Nova Scotia, but they ended up moving their operations to central Canada (see chapter seventeen). Aitken himself kept on moving until, as Lord Beaverbrook, he was wheeling and dealing in the yet larger imperial world.

The fundamental issue underlying all of this is the extraordinary mobility of capital and of corporations in the pursuit of profit, in contrast to the much more limited mobility of workers and their families with their commitments to community and to country.

The stakes for workers are high. They may lose their jobs with no certainty of finding another. If they do keep a job, they may find that their wages shrink and their working conditions deteriorate as they are whipsawed by companies that are free to flit across the border. At the same time, unions will be less able to protect them as companies lobby legislatures for the kind of anti-union legislation that is rife in the United States, such as right-to-work laws, threatening otherwise to pull up stakes and service the Canadian market from, say, the southern United States or perhaps from across the border in a free-trade zone in Mexico.

Investment is vital to economic growth. In an economy such as Canada's, the bulk of that investment takes place within the corporate sector. That sector is dominated by a small number of large corporations that are typically multinational. In the nature of North America, most of the corporate head offices are in the United States.

With the best will in the world, it would be no easy task for the Canadian government effectively to influence the behaviour of these companies and make them operate in a way more beneficial, or less costly, to its citizenry. But not to try, while tying the hands of future governments so they cannot try, is necessarily to erode Canadian sovereignty and compromise Canadian control of the Canadian economy; indeed, it will make it increasingly difficult even to define a Canadian economy — and perhaps ultimately a Canadian society and a Canadian polity.

8

The Trade Deal and the Resource Sector

Andrew Jackson

Notwithstanding its declining share of total employment and national income, the natural resource sector remains of absolutely fundamental importance to the health of the Canadian economy. Certainly agriculture, forestry, mining, the energy sector, the fishery and their associated processing sectors continue to dominate industrial employment in the regions outside southern Ontario and Quebec, and Canada as a whole would have a massive trade deficit if our huge ($20.8 billion in 1986) deficit in the trade of manufactured products were not offset by an even greater ($26.7 billion) surplus in the trade of crude and fabricated materials. National reliance upon resource production is further underscored when our large, continuing deficits in services and financial payments are taken into account.

To a very large degree, Canada's competitive edge in the world economy and our continuing comparative advantage in world trade is the result of access to a rich endowment of renewable and non-renewable natural resources in a world of scarcity. This fundamental fact has receded from view in recent years as central Canada has boomed, despite the prolonged post-1981 downturn in the price of raw materials. What has been overlooked is that the contraction and uneven recovery of the resource sector underlies continuing high unemployment in the West, the North and the Atlantic regions, and has contributed to the alarming accentuation of regional disparities. It can be confidently predicted that international demand and prices for resources will revive, and expansion in this sector may again contribute to national economic expansion, as in the 1970s. More contentiously, it can be argued that any future set of Canadian industrial policies designed to expand secondary manufacturing will be most soundly based if it is built upon our underlying national strengths in the resource sector.

Managing the Resource Economy

The strongest argument of the proponents of the Canada-U.S. trade deal is that Canada needs "secure and enhanced access" to the American market; but market access is scarcely the greatest problem of the resource sector. To be sure, lumber, potash and other exports have been subject to a degree of protectionist harassment by uncompetitive American industries in recent years, but the fundamental reality is that the American economy as a whole needs, and will continue to need, access to Canadian resources. If Canadian supply were to be significantly constrained, the U.S. would have to endure massive price increases and outright shortages of construction lumber, newsprint, natural gas, electricity and a host of other goods essential to an advanced industrial economy. Indeed, one finds that American countervail actions tend to be fought vigorously by affected American industrial customers of Canadian resources, and that measures taken against our exports tend to be quickly modified or withdrawn in response to domestic American pressures. (The American farm lobby against protection of their U.S. potash industry is a recent case in point.)

Numerous reports and studies could be cited to document American awareness of looming supply deficits for natural gas, lumber and electricity. Evidence of the American desire for secure and stable access to Canadian resources can readily be found in the virtual non-existence of tariff barriers against all but the most highly manufactured resource goods for the past fifty years; in the significant presence of American multinationals in the Canadian forest, energy and mining industries; and in strong American opposition to past Canadian attempts to implement nationalist policies in the resource sector. To justify the trade deal as a solution to the problem of access to the American market is, then, misleading. In addition, the creation of a U.S.-Canada trading bloc may itself jeopardise access to the Pacific Rim and European Economic Community markets which are of vital importance to the mining, forest, and fishing industries.

The real problem of the resource economy is not long-term market access but cyclical instability compounded by over-dependence upon crude extraction and processing as opposed to higher value-added fabrication and manufacturing activities. Canadians may no longer be "hewers of wood and drawers of water," but we certainly tend to be producers of pulp and newsprint rather than fine papers, of lumber rather than finished building materials, of raw rather than processed fish products, and of mineral concentrates rather than smelted metals and finished metal goods. We have, in short, failed to exploit fully a wide range of opportunities for further processing and addition of value to resource commodities (so called "forward linkages"), and we have failed to develop a wide range of industries serving the need of the resource sector for advanced machinery and equipment of all kinds.

While report after report has lamented our national failure to fully capitalise on our resource base, the gap between potential and reality is most keenly felt in the resource dependent regions where the boom-bust cycle of demand for primary products has not been adequately alleviated by relatively more stable employment in further processing of raw materials and manufacturing activities. Indeed, the dangers of over-reliance upon crude resource processing are growing as these activities become increasingly capital-intensive, and as the physical limits of resource extraction are encountered. In British Columbia, for example, young workers must seek employment in regional economies dependent upon forestry in the context of massive restructuring of the forest industry and depletion of the forest resource. As the proponents of the trade deal say, the status quo is indeed not an acceptable option.

Policies to diversify resource-based economies and to stimulate higher value-added resource manufacturing activities have been pursued by both levels of government, but the provinces have played a particularly important role by virtue of their resource ownership rights. Unlike the U.S., most natural resources in Canada (mineral rights, forest land, etc.) remain the property of the community as a whole through the Crown. They are made available to the private sector in return for royalties, stumpage fees and so on, and in return for the fulfillment of certain obligations such as reforestation or adding value to the resource through further processing. The provinces have used these powers of ownership and control — enshrined in Section 92A of the Constitution — to regulate the rate of exploitation of resources, to raise money to finance social services and economic development activities and, on occasion, to encourage, or force, the private sector to upgrade resource products rather than simply ship them in raw form. These powers were fully defined in 1982, but only after protracted federal-provincial conflict, and serious ambiguities remain as to the status of provincial resource ownership rights relative to the exclusive federal power to regulate international trade. It is nonetheless clear that an important part of provincial jurisdiction is affected by the terms of the trade deal.

Canadian governments have used a wide range of policy instruments to encourage higher value-added resource processing and to diversify the resource economy. Restrictions on the export of unprocessed resources have been imposed by both levels of government in an attempt to force processors to locate close to the resource base. For example, current federal regulations prohibit the export of certain species of unprocessed salmon caught on the West Coast, while Newfoundland and the other Atlantic provinces maintain similar restrictions. Controls on the export of unprocessed logs date back to before the First World War, and an export restriction on nickel led to the establishment of a smelting industry in the Sudbury Basin in the same period.

Another policy tool has been the use of a two-price system for resources to "discriminate" in favour of domestic industries. Alberta in the 1970s, for example, sold natural gas at incentive rates to its infant petrochemical industry, and Canada as a whole maintained a two-price system for oil and gas throughout much of the same decade, in part to give a competitive advantage to Canadian industry. (A two-price system may, of course, also be used to protect a basic resource industry against depressed world prices.) Interestingly, while the federal government and the resource producing provinces fought heated battles over resource ownership rights and revenues in this period, neither contested the view that ownership could and should be used as a tool for stimulating economic development through the establishment of non-market prices for basic resources. Former premier of Alberta Peter Lougheed was at least candid enough to concede the point when he defended the trade deal before the House of Commons Committee on International Trade.

Virtually all Canadian provinces maintain a *de facto* two-price system for electricity through the pricing policies of their hydro Crown corporations. Generally speaking, when power is exported it is sold for what the market can bear, while power sold in the provincial market is made available to industry at favourable rates (at or near average cost) so as to bolster the competitive position of industry. Low power rates have been particularly important for resource processing industries such as pulp and paper and smelting and, on occasion, individual companies have been given special incentive rates in order to encourage them to locate in a particular province.

When resources were at a premium, in the 1970s, the producing provinces consciously attempted to maximise resource "rents" in order to accumulate capital for economic diversification purposes. The key example is, of course, the Alberta Heritage Fund, while in B.C., the Barrett government established the BC Petroleum Corporation to collect massive windfall profits from the sale of natural gas to the U.S. at premium prices. In principle at least, these windfall gains were to be recycled to other areas of the economy in order to promote the cause of diversification and enhanced stability. At the same time, both B.C. and Alberta enjoyed domestic energy prices which were well below the level of export prices.

The central argument to be developed in the balance of this paper is that the trade deal — and more specifically Articles 407 to 409 and the parallel provisions dealing with energy — significantly curtails the ability of Canada or a province to use these policy instruments and thus circumscribes effective Canadian sovereignty over Canadian natural resources. Seen from this perspective, the trade deal solves the American problem of securing access to Canadian resources and limits the exercise of policy options to address some of the enduring problems of the Canadian resource economy.

A Continental Market for Resources

Articles 407 to 409 of the trade deal limit the capacity of Canada or a province to prohibit or restrict resource exports to the United States, and constrain Canadian governments from taking measures which would result in the export price of a resource being higher than the price paid by Canadians. These clauses place significantly greater limits on Canadian policies than is currently the case under the General Agreement on Tariffs and Trade (GATT), and grant the U.S. certain defined rights of access to Canadian resources in the future.

Articles XI and XX of GATT call for the elimination of restrictions or prohibitions on exports through export licences and other measures. These articles are, however, subject to a wide range of exceptions, such as measures to promote the conservation of natural resources or to relieve critical domestic shortages of essential goods. The trade deal generally eliminates these allowable exceptions under GATT and further prohibits Canada (or a province) from levying export taxes, a measure which is permissible under GATT.

Article 407 of the deal affirms Canadian and American rights and obligations under GATT with respect to trade prohibitions and restrictions, and notes that "the Parties understand" that these rights and obligations prohibit minimum export and minimum import price requirements "in any circumstances in which any other form of quantitative restriction is prohibited." Despite the misleading wording, Canada's GATT obligations have not precluded the maintenance of minimum export prices for a wide range of energy commodities in the past and, indeed, up to the present. (For example, the National Energy Board has in place a requirement that electrical power exported to the U.S. not be sold below the price of the least cost alternative available to the purchasing utility (see chapter nine). This and other requirements eliminated by the trade deal have never been challenged before GATT.)

As noted above, in the 1970s, Canadian natural gas was sold at a very substantial price premium in the American market, and the National Energy Board maintained a minimum export price in order to help maintain this differential. A minimum price proved difficult (and, arguably, counterproductive) to maintain as natural gas supplies in the U.S. expanded and Canadian export volumes were substantially cut in the 1980s. As a policy decision, minimum export prices and other export restrictions — such as the requirement to prove to the NEB that surplus supplies were available for export — were relaxed, and then eliminated by the Conservative government. The key point, however, is that the trade deal would eliminate the *possibility* of returning to past policies, even if circumstances change.

Article 408 on Export Taxes further provides that Canada shall not "maintain or introduce any tax, duty or charge on the export of any good" to the U.S., unless this is also levied on domestic consumers. As noted above, such export taxes *are* permissible under GATT, though they have been used only infrequently by Canada. In conjunction with Article 407, this provision severely limits the right of Canada or a province to charge export customers more for a good or, conversely, to give preferential treatment to domestic consumers or industries. (Ironically, the only recent Canadian export tax — that imposed on softwood lumber — was exempted from the deal because it resulted from American pressure to increase prices.)

At the national level Articles 407 and 408 will make a return to a two-price system for energy or any other good impossible, even if the price of such a good was skyrocketing because of international shortages. Similarly, an energy producing province could not use its resource ownership rights to charge export customers more (or provincial residents less) for an energy resource. In effect, the competitive advantage of owning renewable and non-renewable resources has been undercut by this deal because Canadians will no longer be able to grant themselves preferential access to their own resources.

The purpose of the deal is, in essence, to establish a single Canada-U.S. market for all goods, in which the price in both countries will be set by the market, and not by government taxation or regulation. Neither Canada nor a province will be able to "discriminate" against American customers by charging them an artificially high price by government regulation. Concretely, these clauses would preclude any return to a regulatory regime in energy like the National Energy Policy of the early 1980s or its predecessors.

What has been less well noted is that provincial regulation of resource export prices (for example, through the establishment of a provincial border price) is also precluded. This, in turn, significantly undercuts the ability of the provinces to pursue economic development initiatives which rely upon facilitating domestic processing through the maintenance of favourable pricing and supply conditions for provincial industries. It also undercuts the ability of the provinces to maximise revenues from resource exports while cushioning provincial industries through the establishment of a border price.

The government and the Trade Negotiator's Office insist that nothing in the deal stops us from charging Americans a higher price for Canadian resources. All that is prohibited, we are told, is discriminatory action by governments. There is, however, a critical grey area which remains to be clarified — namely the pricing policies of Crown corporations.

While Exxon or Texaco will understandably sell for what the market can bear in both Canada and the U.S., provincial hydro-electric utilities generally seek to maximise revenues and profits only in export markets. As a rule, provincial consumers and industries are charged power rates which are only intended to cover costs and provide funds for system expansion, and these rates can be set by provincial government policy or by provincial regulation. Provincial consumers generally pay less than export customers. For example, in 1984, export profits reduced Ontario Hydro's rate increase requirement by 4.5 per cent.

The deal clearly prohibits the establishment of a minimum export price by regulation, but some government officials maintain that Crown corporations can continue to "discriminate" through their pricing policies. It would, however, seem possible — and indeed likely — that a major American utility buying power from, for example, Quebec Hydro, at significantly higher rates than Quebec consumers, could argue that the provincial policy producing the price differential amounts to a prohibited export "charge" under Article 408. Certainly there are no clear grounds for excluding such a challenge on the basis of the language of the deal, and it seems unlikely that the U.S. would allow us to do through public ownership what we are unable to do through regulation.

U.S. Access to Canadian Resources

Article 409 further limits Canadian powers to restrict exports for reasons which are now permissible under GATT. Specifically limited are our rights under articles of GATT which allow us to introduce restrictions "to prevent or relieve critical shortages of foodstuffs or other products essential to the exporting contracting party" (GATT Article XI(2)a); to take measures "relating to the conservation of exhaustible natural resources" (XX(g)); to restrict exports as part of a plan to stabilise a processing industry through holding the price of raw materials below the world price (XX(i)); or to restrict exports when a commodity is in short supply (XX(j)). As can be seen, most of these GATT exceptions deal with export restrictions involving resources or raw materials.

Under the terms of the trade deal, Canada may apply such a restriction only if it does not reduce the proportion of American exports "relative to the total supply" of the good. In other words, we must continue shipments at a defined level. In effect, this means that Canada or an energy-producing province could not suspend exports of, for example, conventional light oil even if oil was in short supply or if we simply wished to conserve a non-renewable natural resource for future use. Under certain circumstances we are, then, obliged to sell or to make goods available to American buyers (contrary to government statements that there is no obligation to sell). It is specified that American customers must continue to be supplied with the same proportion of total supply as they received over the previous three years, even if an otherwise permissible restriction is introduced.

In effect, this means that the U.S. has gained the right of permanent access to whatever share of a Canadian resource they are now purchasing. Assume, for example, that 25 per cent of total oil production is now exported. We would still have to ship the U.S. their share of total supply if a production and export restriction was introduced, and the proportionate U.S. share would continue to be defined at the same level so long as they continued to buy as before and thus maintained their share of total supply. (Note that the obligation to make supplies available for sale to American customers exists even if no long-term contracts are in place.)

In the deal, "total supply" is defined as domestic production and inventory *plus* imports "as appropriate." Assume that Canada produces 9 billion barrels (bbl) of oil per year, of which 6 are consumed domestically and 3 are exported to the United States. Assume further that we import 3 bbl per year from foreign countries. (This is a valid example since Canadian oil imports and exports are, indeed, in rough balance.) The U.S. share is thus 3 bbl of a total supply of 12 bbl, or 25 per cent.

Assume further that the Canadian or Albertan government decides to restrict production and export to conserve a depleting resource for future use, and to minimise uncertainties relating to future supply. If production is cut from 9 bbl to 6 bbl we could, at present, simply eliminate exports to the U.S., and domestic supply would be unchanged. In effect we would have conserved a depleting resource for future generations by stopping exports.

Such actions will clearly no longer be permissible, and a cutback in Canadian production would have to be shared between domestic consumers and the export market. In other words, as production was cut from 9 bbl to 6 bbl, production for domestic consumption would fall from 6 bbl to 4 bbl and exports would fall from 3 bbl to 2 bbl. To meet domestic needs, imports would have to increase from 3 bbl to 5 bbl. In other words, to conserve resources for our future use we should have to increase imports rather than just suspend exports.

As if this were not bad enough, there is an interesting problem raised by the wording of the deal. In the above example, "total supply" after a cutback would be reduced from 12 bbl to 11 bbl (production of 6 bbl plus 5 bbl of imports). The U.S. share would, then, be 2 bbl out of 11 bbl, or 18 per cent rather than the 25 per cent level existing before the cutback. Since we are not allowed to cut the U.S. share, it would have to be increased. Thus the mathematics of the deal implies, astonishingly, that Canadians would have to bear the proportionate burden of a production restriction *to a greater extent than the U.S.*!

The Trade Negotiator's Office maintain that, under these circumstances, the wording of the definition of total supply to include imports "as appropriate" is crucial. The argument is that imports would not be included in the calculation if we were restricting production for conservation reasons, but only if we wished to restrict exports because of an interruption to our foreign imports. This is, however, to assume what is hardly obvious — that the definition which serves Canadian interests will be the operative one if a dispute should arise.

The terms of Article 409 also raise a potential problem with respect to the renewal of long-term export contracts for hydro-electricity. A provincial government in B.C. or Quebec in the year 2010 might well decide that power which had been exported under an expiring contract should in the future be reserved for provincial use because of a shortage of power to meet industrial needs. They could then instruct their hydro export utility not to sell but instead to sell or seek new customers in the domestic market (even if the American customer was willing to pay more). However, under the terms of Article 409, export of a good can be restricted by a government (even for reasons of short supply) only if American customers continue to be served on a proportionate basis. In other words, American utilities could argue that non-renewal of a contract by a Crown corporation amounted to a restrictive government policy, and thus insist that export contracts be renewed (and that the export price be no greater than the provincial price). This, in turn, means that the U.S. may have gained permanent access to power (and other resources) which are now sold on the premise that they are surplus to provincial or national requirements. As a result, prospects for future industrial expansion could be severely curtailed. Such a scenario is hardly unlikely, for it seems eminently plausible that a government directive to a Crown corporation not to export indeed amounts to a government "restriction" on exports.

Protection of Existing Resource Export Restrictions

A problem with the terms of the deal also arises with respect to existing Canadian restrictions on exports which are ostensibly "grandfathered," that is, allowed to continue in place. Any new restriction can, under the terms of Article 407, be introduced only if the U.S. is given proportional access, so effective protection for existing restraints on the export of raw logs and unprocessed fish was sought by the affected Canadian interests.

Article 1203 grandfathers both American and Canadian controls on the export of raw logs. It seems likely that such controls are indeed effectively safeguarded since they are applied in both nations. The U.S. does, however, retain the right to appeal Canadian restrictions to GATT.

Article 1203 also purports to allow for the maintenance of provincial legislation in the Atlantic provinces governing the export of unprocessed fish. Newfoundland, for example, attaches processing conditions to a fish buyer's licence, meaning that all fish landed in the province must be processed to a specified degree. Premier Peckford was very insistent that these conditions be protected as part of any trade deal with the U.S., observing that, in their absence, market forces could lead to the trucking of unprocessed fish to American markets and a consequent loss of provincial jobs.

It is questionable whether these requirements have indeed been protected. Provincial restrictions on interprovincial and international trade are of dubious constitutional validity in the first place and, most importantly, under Article 1205 the U.S. retains the right to challenge fish processing requirements before GATT.

While its decision has neither been published nor made final, the November 16, 1987, GATT panel interim decision against federal fish processing requirements on the West Coast suggests that such restrictions are, to say the least, hardly immune from effective challenges before GATT. Further, the fact that the West Coast fish processing requirements challenged before GATT by the U.S. have not been grandfathered under the deal suggests that the U.S. intends to continue their attack on these restrictions. The fact of the matter is that East Coast processing requirements are no safer from American challenge than before the deal was signed.

The effect of the trade deal as a whole is to undermine the Atlantic restrictions which are ostensibly grandfathered. It is clear that these requirements, at best, stand on an "as is" basis and cannot be improved. Most important, if they are successfully challenged before GATT, neither the provinces nor the federal government will be able to implement effectively an alternative policy instrument.

As noted in the earlier analysis of export restrictions, GATT allows for the imposition of export taxes. Thus, if processing requirements were struck down, Canada could implement the policy alternative of an export tax on unprocessed fish, a measure which would have the equivalent effect of prohibiting unprocessed fish exports if the tax were set at a sufficiently high level. Under the terms of Article 408 of the deal, however, an export tax could not be imposed, and the same holds true of related policy alternatives.

Conclusion

Articles 407 to 409 of the trade deal severely curtail the ability of
Canada or a resource-producing province to regulate the level of
resource exports and export prices. The creation of a single continental market for resources, combined with the restriction of national
powers and provincial resource ownership rights, will constrain
governments from pursuing policies which would maximise revenues
from resource exports while protecting domestic industries. It will also
place severe limits on the ability of governments to force and encourage greater domestic processing of raw materials. Canadians will
no longer be able to pursue policies which give us favourable access
to *our* resources and the resource-dependent regions will, as a result,
be even more confined to their traditionally subordinate role of
producers of raw materials rather than finished goods. For its part, the
United States has ensured that American consumers and industries will
have access to Canadian resources at a price no greater than that paid
by Canadians, and they have forced Canada to recognise an obligation
to export resources even in circumstances where Canadian restrictions
would be clearly permissible under existing international trade law.
These clauses, then, amount to a major concession on the part of
Canada and to a major restriction on national sovereignty and provincial rights.

9

Continental Energy Policy

John Dillon

When the bilateral trade deal was first announced on Oct. 4, 1987, Ronald Reagan himself emphasized that the agreement would "improve our security through additional access to Canadian energy supplies." Few Canadians even knew that energy was on the bargaining table.

If ratified, the deal will make permanent policies already initiated by the Mulroney government for deregulation and continental integration of Canada's energy sector. These policies reflect the view that this sector is managed best if it is controlled by the major energy corporations, with little or no interference by Canadian governments, federal or provincial. More important still, any effort in future to pursue alternative energy policies will require that Canada abrogate the entire accord.

Shortly after his election, Prime Minister Mulroney told an audience of 1,500 powerful corporate executives in New York that the Liberals' experiment with government intervention under the National Energy Program (NEP) was next on his government's "hit list," after it dismantled the Foreign Investment Review Agency. His finance and energy ministers asked the corporate sector what specific energy policies they wanted to replace the NEP and what kind of incentives they required before resuming investments in energy projects. The result was a policy embodied in the "Western Accord," signed in March of 1985 by the governments of Canada, British Columbia, Alberta and Saskatchewan. The editor of *The Investor's Digest* dubbed the new policy "A Private Enterprise Energy Program." The essential elements of the new deal included world market prices for oil, phasing out of the Petroleum and Gas Revenue Tax, replacement of the Petroleum Incentive Program grants with tax incentives, and elimination of volume and price restrictions on oil exports.

The executive director of the Canadian Petroleum Association (CPA), which represents the largest energy companies operating in Canada, declared that the Mulroney energy policy was "virtually identical" to that demanded by his association's members. The trade deal would now make these pro-corporate policies permanent. The vice-chairman of the CPA has welcomed the deal as an "insurance policy that we will be able to enjoy our present arrangement," without fear of any future government price or export regulation.

The energy chapter of the agreement extends far beyond the boundaries of a trade deal. It effectively concedes to trans-national corporations control over the allocation of Canada's non-renewable energy resources. In periods of shortages, Canada is obliged to make available to American importers the same proportion of our total supply of non-renewable hydrocarbons as was sold to the U.S. over a recent three-year period. The export price cannot be any higher than the price charged domestically.

During the most recent three-year period for which data are available, 1984-1986, three out of every ten barrels of oil produced in Canada were exported to the United States. In the event of a global oil shortage, Canada would be obliged to make the same ratio of domestic production available for export to the U.S., unless domestic prices rose so high that Canadian oil was priced out of the American market. Under prevailing conditions of global oil surplus, and with export restraints forbidden by the agreement, energy corporations will no doubt strive to increase the volume of oil exports from Canada to compensate for low world prices.

Canada's conventional oil reserves are now estimated at about 4.5 billion barrels, down from a peak of 10.5 billion barrels in 1969. Even if all oil exports were eliminated, these reserves would be sufficient only for about eleven years. Sharing these reserves with the U.S. at the same ratio as prevailed during 1984-1986 would reduce their viability to only about eight years. Canadians will end up paying dearly to replace these low-cost conventional reserves with more expensive resources from frontier areas.

In an effort to sell the free-trade deal in western Canada, Prime Minister Mulroney is appealing to traditional western resentment of Ontario's relative prosperity. In a November 1987 speech to the Calgary Chamber of Commerce, Mr. Mulroney proclaimed that the deal could "do for the West what the Auto Pact has done for Ontario." The Prime Minister promised that both western Canada and the Atlantic provinces would benefit from energy "mega-projects" because there would be larger markets and no possibility of export restrictions. An examination of the recent historical record, however, shows that, despite the freedom to export enshrined in the Western Accord, there has been a recession in the Canadian petroleum industry. Low world petroleum prices, not lack of access to markets, brought on the most recent downturn.

While the taxation and revenue-sharing provisions of the Liberals' National Energy Program did discriminate against western petroleum-producing provinces and favour the federal government, the tactic of playing on western alienation to sell the free-trade agreement is dangerous. It obscures the fact that the Western Accord failed to yield its promised prosperity because it was committed to the rule of world oil prices. Also hidden is the common interest that everyone in Canada, east and west, shares in a diversified economy and a broadly based energy industry which responds to Canadian needs independently of world market forces. Further, the Mulroney tactic seeks to veil the sacrifices made under the deal. Contrary to government propaganda, provincial control over natural resource pricing and allocation has been turned over to corporate head offices located in New York or Chicago.

Lessons of the Past

The need for strong provincial and federal regulatory powers is evident from a brief review of recent corporate exploitation of Canada's petroleum resources. During the 1960s and early 1970s the giant petroleum corporations promoted Canadian oil exports to the United States. More oil was exported than was consumed in Canada every year from 1969 through 1973, when exports amounted to 66 per cent of Canadian production. In its 1972 annual report, Exxon's Canadian subsidiary, Imperial Oil, was still praising hydrocarbon exports: "In the current debate, the export of Canada's energy resources is being questioned...Canada is not in any way deficient in energy resources. Our present energy reserves, using present technology, are sufficient for our requirements for several hundred years."

One year later, after the "energy crisis" had begun, Imperial's annual report told a different story: "Within the next ten years, production rates from existing reserves in Western Canada will be inadequate to supply markets now being served." Canada then began to curtail crude oil exports. From 1975 through 1982 Canada was a net importer of crude. In 1983 Canada again exported marginally more than it imported. By 1984, exports of crude petroleum had grown to about one-fifth of Canadian oil production. During 1985 the volume of crude exports rose to 30 per cent of production and in 1986 reached 37 per cent, as energy corporations sought to compensate for falling oil prices by increased export sales.

These larger exports did not bring prosperity to the oil-producing provinces. The Mulroney government had predicted that the Western Accord would induce the energy corporations to create between 100,000 and 300,000 new jobs by 1990. Instead the policy of moving to world petroleum prices backfired. World oil prices fell from $32 (U.S.) a barrel in November of 1985 to around $13 (U.S.) a barrel in March 1986, the first anniversary of the Mulroney energy policy. Exploration declined and there were massive layoffs in the western Canadian oil industry. It was the smaller, Canadian-owned energy companies that experienced the most serious financial difficulties. Their larger cousins began to pick up oil and gas properties at fire-sale prices. Companies that hired acquisitions experts instead of geologists did well. *The Financial Post* wrote about the "Americanization" of the Canadian oil industry as "U.S.-owned multinationals...cash in hand [were] on the prowl for oil reserves, the value of which has fallen dramatically."

Rather than investing in new exploration, foreign-controlled petroleum corporations took $1.8 billion in interest, dividends and service fees out of Canada during 1986 alone. With relatively depressed world oil prices now likely for several years to come, private corporations will be reluctant to invest in expensive frontier energy projects. This haemorrhage of capital could continue well into the 1990s. Ratifying the free-trade deal will render Canada powerless to stop the capital drain. Article 1606 explicitly denies Canada the right to control corporate transfers of "profits...royalties, fees, interest [or] other earnings."

During the first half of 1987, the Canadian petroleum industry experienced a partial recovery. Profits for the first six months of 1987 rose to $1.8 billion, an increase of 148 per cent over the comparable period in 1986. The Canadian Petroleum Monitoring Agency attributed the profit gains to a partial recovery of world oil prices (a recovery which now appears to have been short-lived), the elimination of the Petroleum and Gas Revenue Tax, reduced provincial royalty rates and royalty holidays, and lower interest rates. Nevertheless, even these higher profits did not lead to substantial new investment activity. Only 59 per cent of total industry cash flow was reinvested during the first half of 1987, compared to 98 per cent a year earlier.

Another decline in world oil prices began in August, 1987. Even as Canadian and American negotiators were finalizing the trade deal, corporations were contemplating renewed cutbacks in their exploration programmes. It is estimated that some $20 billion in energy projects — including the heavy oil upgrader at Lloydminster and the development of oil reserves offshore in the Atlantic — could be delayed by falling oil prices.

Adhering to world oil prices and giving full rein to trans-national corporate investment decisions — including the trans-national corporate decision to largely ignore diversification — are the crux of the problem for Canada's petroleum-producing provinces. The free-trade agreement will make permanent the very policies that have brought economic decline to these regions. While the deal would protect foreign corporations' ability to drain capital out of Canada, it would explicitly exclude policies that favour Canadian producers willing to explore and develop energy supplies that Canadians will need in the future.

Free Trade and Energy Security

The Mulroney government's interpretation of the accord claims that "Canada has no obligations to supply energy to the U.S." In fact, what the deal obliges us to do is to concede to energy corporations the right to sell in American markets as much or as little of our non-renewable energy resources as they choose. Canadian governments, federal and provincial, will have little or no control over the process. Depletion of Canada's more accessible reserves of non-renewable hydrocarbons is inevitable as trans-nationals attempt to satisfy the American appetite for petroleum imports. Moreover, this appetite is likely to increase. At the end of 1985, remaining crude oil reserves in the United States were equivalent to only five years of consumption, natural gas reserves to only eleven years. Canada's remaining conventional oil reserves are equivalent to only a nine-month supply for the U.S.

As already noted, with the deal in place, Canada could not reassert control over its domestic energy supplies even during periods of shortages. Corporations would retain the right to export to the U.S. the same proportion of our energy supplies as had been the practice over a recent three year period, and the prices could not be higher than those paid by Canadians (Article 904). Furthermore, Canada could not alter the mix of products sold, for example by substituting more plentiful heavy oil for scarcer lighter grades. Even if the U.S. precipitates global shortages through military intervention in the Persian Gulf, they would still be entitled to supplies from Canada.

Damage to Canada's energy security would not only occur after another "energy crisis" blooms and the proportional sharing clause is invoked. Much of the damage could have already been done as our cheaper, more accessible supplies of non-renewable hydrocarbons are depleted. Canadians could end up subsidizing American consumers by exporting comparatively low-cost western Canadian hydrocarbons at depressed world market prices, and later being forced to replace them domestically with more expensive resources from Canada's frontiers. During 1986, oil was selling for around $14 (U.S.) a barrel in American markets, while the cost of replacing each barrel with more expensive frontier resources was estimated at $24-$28 (U.S.).

With regard to natural gas, a recent ruling by the Federal Energy Regulatory Commission (FERC) prevents Canadian natural gas producers from passing on to American buyers the cost of transporting gas through Canadian pipelines. The Canadian natural gas industry has complained that this ruling will cost it as much as $400 million a year in lost revenue. In May 1987, Energy Minister Marcel Masse called the FERC ruling an "unacceptable...[extension of] U.S. regulation into Canada... [and] a serious setback in our joint efforts to move towards market-oriented energy trade." Nevertheless, Canada's free-trade negotiators failed to win any changes in current FERC regulations.

This failure explains the lukewarm reception that the Canadian natural gas industry has given to the free-trade agreement. The *Natural Gas Market Report* sums up the industry's attitude this way: "What has the natural gas industry gained? The popular answer is unrestricted access to the U.S. market; however, the real answer is nothing....Access to the U.S. market was already more or less assured because of market conditions...Canadians, in effect, could be subsidizing the export of gas to the U.S. in the long-term."

The newsletter uses National Energy Board (NEB) projections for supply, domestic demand and exports to show that the proportional sharing requirement could cause a shortfall of natural gas within Canada. The report examines a hypothetical case in which the proportional sharing clause for natural gas is invoked in 1995, and 1990 levels are used to determine the amount of gas which would have to be made available for export to the United States. Under the NEB's high-price scenario the result would be a 1995 supply shortfall, relative to Canadian needs, of 165 billion cubic feet (Bcf). Calculations based on the NEB's low-price scenario result in an even larger shortfall of 500 Bcf, equivalent to about one-fifth of the projected Canadian demand for 1995.

The Mulroney government has already substantially weakened the ability of the NEB to assure that adequate energy supplies are conserved for Canadians. For instance, Canada has had restrictions on the export of natural gas since 1907. Between 1959 and 1986 natural gas producers could not export to the U.S. unless they had a twenty-five-year supply available for sale in Canada. This "surplus test" was first reduced to fifteen years and then eliminated altogether by the Mulroney government. It is the weakened NEB which would become enshrined in the deal. If the agreement becomes law, the National Energy Board will be reduced to the role of a monitoring agency. Annex 905.2 of the accord specifies that "the administration of any 'surplus test' on the export of any energy good...[would be] consistent with articles 902, 903 and 904." These articles prohibit minimum export prices and export taxes and require the proportional sharing of supplies in times of scarcity.

Furthermore, Article 905 gives the U.S. the right to initiate direct consultations concerning any future regulatory action by the NEB or by any provincial agency which it deems to be inconsistent with the principles of the accord. The U.S. can appeal any regulatory action that might result in "discrimination against its energy goods or its persons inconsistent with the principles of this Agreement." Article 201 defines "persons" as including corporate enterprises.

Surrendering Control Over Canadian Resources

Article 906 recognizes that energy corporations rely on a variety of government programmes to provide them with incentives for engaging in hydrocarbon exploration and development. Since the Mulroney government designed its current subsidies in close collaboration with the giant energy corporations, it is not surprising that the Reagan administration did not object to existing subsidies. But under the foreign investment rules contained in Chapter 16 of the agreement, no future incentive programme could discriminate in favour of Canadian companies because the agreement guarantees "national treatment" for foreign corporations. However, there is no corresponding guarantee that countervailing duty actions will not be initiated against future Canadian incentive policies.

Existing laws governing the ownership of oil, gas and uranium companies are exempted from the investment code contained in Chapter 16. Thus the 50 per cent Canadian ownership requirement for production from the federally-owned "Canada Lands" in the Arctic and off the Atlantic Coast is allowed to continue. The law allowing Canada to review foreign takeovers of energy corporations with assets above $5 million remains intact. But this provision has little meaning under the current Conservative government, given its willingness to allow foreign takeovers of any energy company in financial difficulty. The purchase of Dome Petroleum by Chicago-based Amoco Corporation is the most notable example.

Export or import restrictions are permitted under Article 907 when necessary to ensure energy supplies for the military in peacetime and in response to "a situation of armed conflict." Both parties may also restrict trade in uranium in order to "implement national policies or international agreements relating to the non-proliferation of nuclear weapons" to other countries. However, the United States retains the right to "respond to direct threats of disruption in the supply of nuclear materials for defense purposes." Otherwise, trade in uranium is deregulated so that Canada can no longer require that uranium be upgraded to the maximum extent possible prior to export. The U.S. exempts Canada from a law prohibiting the importing of enriched uranium (Annex 902.5.1&2).

In the event that there is a conflict between the bilateral accord and the Agreement on an International Energy Program (IEP), Article 908 states that the provisions of the IEP are to take precedence. The IEP was established as a "consumers' cartel" in 1974 at the initiative of U.S. Secretary of State Henry Kissinger, ostensibly to counter the power of the Organisation of Petroleum Exporting Countries (OPEC). Both Canada and the U.S. are signatories. The IEP has a plan for sharing oil among member nations in the event of a reduction in the daily rate of a member country's energy supplies amounting to 7 per cent or more of its average daily consumption.

Any global emergency affecting petroleum supplies could trigger the International Energy Agency, which administers the IEP, to assign to a group of trans-national oil companies headed by Exxon the role of allocating scarce oil supplies among member nations "in accordance with historical supply patterns." Canada would be expected to share its oil with its traditional customer, the United States. This commitment is to be cemented if the deal is ratified.

Annex 902.5.3 gives Canada access to 50,000 barrels a day of Alaskan crude oil, provided that the oil is shipped to Canada from a suitable location within the lower forty-eight states. This latter provision is another concession to the U.S. shipping industry, which won changes in the preliminary transcript of the Elements of the Agreement to protect its monopoly over coastal shipping.

The apparent concession of access to Alaskan oil may prove meaningless. No Canadian refinery has yet shown interest in importing Alaskan oil. "We've asked every refiner. No one wants it," an official of Canada's Department of Energy, Mines and Resources told the *Globe and Mail* (speaking on condition of anonymity). "The Vancouver refineries are not geared to run heavy crude," the official added, "why should they buy and run heavy crude when they can get light crude from Western Canada?"

Currently, the NEB applies three price tests to the export of energy. The first price test requires that sales of energy from Canada be priced high enough to recover an appropriate share of the cost of production. This test is for practical purposes incorporated into the deal, because charging less would be considered a subsidy and, at least from the American point of view, an unfair trading practice.

The second price test requires that the selling price should be not less than that which is charged to Canadians for an equivalent energy service. It is also embodied in the agreement without being specifically mentioned. As the result of anti-dumping provisions in American trade law — provisions incorporated into the deal — any American competitor objecting to such sales could launch an anti-dumping action against the Canadian seller. Assuming that the objection was properly applied under U.S. law, it would be successful under the agreement. For example, Manitoba Hydro is concerned that coal-fired electrical utilities in the U.S. might lodge successful dumping complaints against low-priced hydro exports from Manitoba. The Mulroney government has allowed occasional exceptions to this rule. For instance, early in 1985 gas exports through the "pre-built" sections of the ill-fated Alaska Highway Natural Gas Pipeline were sanctioned at prices five to six cents per thousand cubic feet below the Toronto City Gate price.

The only NEB price test ruled out by the trade deal, and this is done explicitly (Article 905.2), is the "least cost alternative test." This test requires that energy exports be sold at a price no lower than that which the foreign customer would pay if he had to buy from the lowest price *alternative* supplier. This third price test was originally adopted in 1967 when the Westcoast Transmission Company was applying to sell gas to an American importer. Aware that the Canadian company had few alternate markets, this importer was using its position to bargain for an unusually low price. In 1970 the NEB extended the test to cover electricity exports. Then in October 1985, the test was eliminated for natural gas exports.

At NEB hearings in 1986 every major provincial hydro utility, except for the New Brunswick Electric Power Commission, pressed for the elimination of the least cost alternative test. They argued that it is difficult to obtain information on the prices of alternatives available to potential customers. More to the point, the provincial utilities and their privately-owned corporate cousins want the third price guideline dropped because it limits their ability to compete aggressively for American markets. Interests south of the border have come to view the test as an unfair trading practice. While its application cannot be construed as either dumping or a subsidy, it might produce higher American import prices. Removal of this third price test not only permits lower energy prices to American consumers; it also permits Canadian utilities to undercut each other in order to gain larger shares of American markets.

Power From the North

In the forefront of the utilities' campaign to undermine the regulatory powers of the NEB has been the present Quebec provincial government, and specifically Hydro Quebec. Premier Bourassa campaigned for election on a promise, elaborated in his book *Power From The North*, to build a second James Bay mega-project. Urged on by Bourassa, Hydro Quebec has staked its multi-billion dollar corporate future on winning large-scale American markets. It sees the least cost alternative test and other NEB regulations as obstacles in its path.

Hydro Quebec recently suffered a setback when the NEB rejected its application to sell $3 billion worth of electricity to the New England Power Pool. The utility had failed, the NEB ruled, to prove that the electricity was surplus to foreseeable Canadian needs. The NEB found that Hydro Quebec had not offered the electricity first to other provinces before selling it to the New England Power Pool. Giving preference to domestic energy markets would be prohibited under the agreement.

Removal of the third price test and preferential options for domestic users is entirely consistent with the Mulroney energy policy. When Energy Minister Marcel Masse promised that he would announce "during the winter" of 1987-88 a new government policy for deregulating electricity sales, he declared: "We believe as a Government that the market is the best protector for the consumer." Unfortunately, if a new wave of energy mega-projects including another James Bay hydro development results from the trade accord, it is the people of Canada — and Quebec in particular — who will end up paying the highest price. Such capital-intensive investments create relatively few jobs and divert money from other economic and social programmes. They are also a threat to our environment and to the aboriginal rights of native nations. Finally, they effectively impede progress towards a "soft" energy future, that is, one based on conservation and the development of renewable sources of energy.

Another part of the energy mega-project package is massive new foreign borrowing. This would increase the already major burden of Canada's international debt. In order to earn foreign exchange to pay these debts even more energy exports become necessary. Another round of energy mega-projects would also discourage the diversification of resource-dependent regions like western Canada by reducing the investment capital available for other projects.

An Alternative Energy Policy

Fortunately, we do have an alternative to the continental energy policy of the trade deal. A self-reliant energy policy, directed to meet community and individual needs, could stabilize energy prices at levels that would ensure a prosperous domestic energy industry even in times of low world prices. It would certainly sustain Canadian companies, especially the large oil service and supply sector that is in danger of disappearing under free trade. A self-reliant policy would require controlling energy exports so as to conserve our non-renewable supplies of light oil and natural gas and reduce our dependence on imports. Community control over the surpluses generated by the sale of non-renewable energy resources would ensure that investments are directed into conservation programmes, the development of renewable energy sources and regional diversification.

A community-oriented, self-reliant energy policy is also needed so that Canadian consumers and industries can be protected in times of global shortages. Ratifying the trade deal means accepting that energy prices and supplies will be determined by the continental, and ultimately the global, market. Faced with global shortages, Canadian industries would then find it even harder to survive the roughly 20 per cent cost disadvantage imposed by our climate and long haulage distances relative to American competitors. Only made-in-Canada prices will enable us to achieve energy security, responsible energy stewardship, and diversified economic development in every part of Canada.

10

Manufacturing

Duncan Cameron and Hugh Mackenzie

Proponents of free trade say that it is the best, most efficient way to develop a strong domestic manufacturing sector. At the heart of their case is the belief that the unhampered operation of the competitive price system provides all the signals that entrepreneurial firms need to make the best investment decisions. Free traders argue that access to a wider market guarantees the economies of scale necessary for productivity gains: the ability to produce more with less. The removal of remaining North American tariffs and some non-tariff barriers to trade, they say, should allow Canadian firms to close the 20 per cent gap in manufacturing productivity with the U.S.

For critics of free trade, this perspective is far removed from the way that the manufacturing industry has developed in Canada and, most important, is an inadequate guide for the future as well. Canada already has significant access to the American market, but this access has not produced the sort of domestic manufacturing sector envisaged by free traders. Similarly, the U.S. obviously has full access to its own market, yet its ability to export manufactured goods or even compete against foreign imports has been repeatedly questioned and is a matter of great concern in that country. This fact in itself should lead to considerable scepticism as to the benefits of more open borders for domestic manufacturing. Finally, the various econometric studies of the deal fail to identify any particular manufacturing growth in Canada as a result of it.

Winners and Losers

It is usually argued that exports are the basis of Canada's economic prosperity. While this view is not incorrect, it does require clarification. First, if one wants to argue that exports increase national production, and create jobs in the process, then one must also admit that imports decrease national production and eliminate jobs. In this line of argument, what creates extra wealth for Canada from trade is net exports, the surplus of exports over imports. The trade deal, by opening the Canadian and American markets, is designed to increase two-way trade. In this case, both countries would benefit. So long as the increase in exports offsets the increase in imports, Canada would maintain its net export benefits. But the overall impact of the deal economically depends largely on which sectors forge ahead and which sectors suffer under expanded trade. While it is difficult to assess how Canada's labour-intensive sectors in manufacturing will fare under free trade, it does seem likely that Canada's competitive advantage in capital-intensive resource production will lead to more activity in that sector rather than in services or manufacturing where jobs are more easily created.

Since Canada had a higher average tariff on dutiable goods to begin with, 9.6 per cent as opposed to 4.2 per cent, it gave up more than the U.S. — nearly twice as much tariff protection for weak industries, in fact. But Canada also gained. The American market is roughly ten times larger than the Canadian market, and so reduced tariffs in the U.S. mean that competitive Canadian firms have much more to gain from the American market than competitive U.S. firms from the Canadian market. At this point, however, the economic advantages from tariff reduction are unclear. Losers on the Canadian side can be pin-pointed. Winners are more difficult to predict. No one really knows how many Canadian firms are poised to take advantage of lower tariffs.

This becomes clear when the schedule for tariff reduction is examined. Different timetables are established for three categories of goods: in the first category, tariffs are removed immediately on the deal taking effect; in the second, they are eliminated over five years; and in the third over ten years. The first category is relatively limited, covering some non-agricultural raw materials (fur, unwrought aluminum, leather) and products where the trade is already largely one-way (computers and equipment, airbrakes for rail cars) and where tariff removal will have little direct impact on the importing country. The second category includes products made from duty-free raw material and machinery used in manufacturing and processing. Thus, accelerated tariff elimination is concentrated in raw materials and processed raw materials — Canada's greatest strength — and in higher technology products — Canada's greatest industrial weakness. In other words, the deal looks to reinforce Canada's strengths *and* weaknesses.

Most of the secondary manufacturing sector is subject to the phased-in elimination of tariffs over ten years. This is where the winners and losers will be determined. The losers are easily identified: food processing, furniture, textiles, clothing, leather goods, footwear, plastics, paper products and household appliances. Though American firms are not necessarily world leaders in these sectors, the preferential treatment afforded them under the deal should allow U.S.-based firms to take market share from Canadian firms and undercut third country competition as well. No list of winners has yet to be produced, but it is clear that some potential winners are not helped by the deal. Canadian steel producers, for instance, will not be allowed to win under the agreement, since they will continue to be subject to American protectionist laws.

The case for tariff reduction is a general one. In all the documentation released by the government to support its trade deal, there is no mention of specific costs to Canada from reduced tariffs — the firms that are going to go under, the jobs that will be lost. The lack of concrete information from the government has allowed adversaries of the deal to have the field to themselves. Estimates of job losses furnished by the Ontario government and obtained from the Quebec government are so high as to put all presumed job benefits from the deal into doubt. According to these estimates, so many jobs will be lost as a result of tariff reductions that it would require the creation of some 500, 000 to 800, 000 new jobs just to offset those that will be lost.

Closing the Door on Industrial Strategy

In the past, Canada's industrial strategy in manufacturing has consisted mainly of tariff protection and tax concessions. While tariffs increase domestic competitiveness only negatively — they make it more difficult for foreign firms to compete in the national market — tax policy is a positive measure designed to encourage domestic investment. Unfortunately, taken alone, tax measures, such as accelerated depreciation for investment expenditures, have not produced the expected results in Canada. And the reason is simple. Investment in manufacturing is subject to much wider considerations than just tax incentives. In Canada, public sector programmes that promote exports, fund research and development, educate workers and use government purchasing power to assist new industry have been significant as well, but less important than in other rich industrial countries with small populations, such as Austria, Sweden, or the Netherlands. Indeed, an almost complete reliance on market forces, combined with an open door to foreign investment capital, has characterized Canadian industrial thinking in the post-war period. The free-trade deal enshrines these same approaches despite evidence that changing conditions in the world economy have modified the investment decision-making process in manufacturing.

The need for strategic thinking about industrial development increases as international competition grows. The problem with the way the deal treats manufacturing is that strategic intervention to enhance the prospects for individual firms is constrained by specific provisions of the agreement. For instance, Article 405 eliminates customs duty-waiver programmes where these are tied to industrial performance requirements. These measures have been used extensively by Canada (but not the U.S.). They allow firms to import duty-free where the intention is to further process, or export, a given product. The elimination of such a trade policy tool for industrial development leads to a question. What is the point of having increased access to the American market if, under the deal, Canada limits its ability to adopt the measures necessary to benefit from market access?

In Canada, the all-important economic infrastructure of transportation and communications is publicly regulated by bodies like the

Canadian Transport Commission and the Canadian Radio-television and Telecommunications Commission, but large chunks, like Air Canada (until recently) and the CBC, have been publicly owned and controlled. Under the deal, the creation of new public monopolies would be subject to severe new restrictions as set out in Article 2010. If Canada decided to create a new public corporation to develop products based on publicly funded biotechnology research, for instance, it would now have to consult with the U.S. before doing so. If it were deemed that such a corporation affected existing American markets in Canada, Articles 2010 and 2011 of the deal would require Canada to compensate the American producers. This means that the cost of creating a new efficient Crown corporation increases under the deal. Under the free-trade agreement, it is fair to ask if Canada could ever again create a cost efficient Crown corporation.

General public services and social expenditures on education, health services and welfare programmes account for an important share of Canada's domestic market. Yet the role of the public sector in economic development is characterized only negatively by the deal. Reference is made to "trade distortions" caused by government policy; no reference is made to trade enhancement by government policy. Though, obviously, industry, including manufacturing, has been a major beneficiary of government spending and American industry in particular has thrived thanks to defence spending, the links between such spending and industrial development go unrecognized. Worse, such links are thought best to occur under conditions approaching that of a wider North American market. This puts Canadian governments in the awkward position of having to compete to attract industry, not only with each other, but with American governments as well.

In a changing world economy, the structural deficiencies of domestic manufacturing have become increasingly evident. Tariff reductions through the General Agreement on Tariffs and Trade (GATT) mean that trade liberalization replaces tariff protection as "national policy." But the dominant role played by multinational corporations in the restructuring of industry on a world-wide basis makes the presumed benefits of trade liberalization more difficult to capture for individual national economies. Thus, one of the major paradoxes of public policy is that governments have been subsidizing rich corporations through the tax system to assure that manufacturing capacity remains a strong presence in the national economy. In the context of North America, the "level playing field" imposed by the deal means that the smaller economy must adjust its industrial incentives to those available in the United States.

Problems arise because corporations play an ambiguous role in economic development. As employers, they struggle with their own workers over shares of output as either profit or wages and often work to restrict or block the social benefits which are so important to individual workers. In doing so, of course, corporations hamper the ability of Canadians to maintain a high standard of living. Their strategy in this regard is damaging to the economy as a whole because, while higher wages may mean higher costs for one company, they also represent more purchasing power and an expanded market. In light of all this, it is clear that, given the wider labour market created by the free-trade deal, the tendency will be to force wages, working conditions and social benefits down to the lowest level prevailing in North America. Such a tendency must be considered as offsetting presumed benefits from the workings of a larger market.

The key, then, to understanding the nature of the manufacturing sector is to recognize that the wealth created must be translated into improved working conditions, wages, and social benefits, if Canadians are to recoup the public costs of supporting industry indirectly through government services and directly through industrial policy. The problem with the trade deal is that, rather than representing an industrial policy option that recognizes the importance of creating a high standard of living for all Canadians, it in fact closes off industrial policy options open to Canada other than the North American market option — and that option, for reasons just outlined, probably will result in a *lower* standard of living. Instead of constituting an alternative to the status quo, it represents a continuation of past practices, practices that may be even less relevant in today's world economy.

The major firms that dominate world manufacturing have been pursuing new strategies. To reduce costs, they have been moving production facilities "offshore" to low-wage locations and "hollowing out" the economies of the industrial nations in the process. As well, firms have been looking abroad for lower-cost sources of material inputs into the production process. Such strategies often bring multinational firms into conflict with national goals of employment and wealth creation. This agreement, while it imposes requirements for domestic content that must be met by producers in order to qualify for duty-free treatment for traded goods, also basically accepts and encourages off-shore sourcing for manufacturing. Rather than seeing the advantages inherent in encouraging domestic production for the national market, it encourages multinational manufacturing. As a result, it is hard to accept the view that relatively minor tariff reductions in North America will have any positive influence on investment in domestic manufacturing by major international firms.

All manufacturing is subject to market forces and international competition — of that there is little doubt. But industrial competition is not purely market driven. The price system works in an imperfectly competitive way. Large firms control resources, seize access to markets and determine labour costs (and working conditions) under circumstances at least partly of their own making. Within Canada the five hundred largest firms account for 85 per cent of all private production — goods and services alike. They compete all right, amongst themselves and with foreign companies, but the competition cannot be reduced to the question of who is the lowest-cost producer. Industrial, economic and social policy measures are important as well. Firms compete for tax breaks, industrial subsidies, and government defence and civilian contracts. The impact of the trade deal on Canada's manufacturing industry must be judged in the context of world industrial restructuring where the role of public policy is important.

Successful manufacturing performance requires more than "a leap of faith"; it requires planning, a long term commitment to development, finance, and technical expertise. Markets are no substitute for industrial policy, as even prominent free-trade economists such as Richard Harris of Queen's University acknowledge. Capitalizing on our "comparative advantage" — specializing in those activities we do best — entails taking advantage of differences. In the manufacturing sector, such differences have to be consciously created. The process of creating and bringing new products to the competitive marketplace is more complicated than simply letting the market decide. For instance, even mainstream economic theory has always suggested that in the case of infant industries, special assistance and protection my be in order for them to eventually compete successfully with established firms. However, this agreement does not recognize the special needs of fledgling industry.

Who Pays?

The cost of economic adjustment from free trade will be paid by workers that lose jobs as a result of the deal. It is worth noting that workers likely to lose their jobs are concentrated in industries that are often small-scale, and labour-intensive, where working conditions and salaries are below average standards. Such workers are often immigrants who experience language difficulties. Many of them are women who have little job mobility because of family responsibilities. As a rule, workers in vulnerable industries are poorly educated and unlikely to find work that requires retraining in tasks more sophisticated than manual labour. The logic of free trade is to move workers from low productivity industries to high productivity industries. That is how Canadian manufacturing would become stronger as a result of free trade. Curiously, the government has argued that, for workers, little economic dislocation will take place. Since this is another way of saying that few benefits will result from free trade with the U.S., one is entitled to ask if, for manufacturing, there is much point to this agreement.

11

Free Trade and the Auto Industry

Hugh Mackenzie

Chapter 10 of the Canada-U.S. free-trade agreement is essentially an elaboration of the general tariff rules governing trade in goods set out in Chapters 3 and 4 that takes into account the special characteristics of the auto industry. In particular, this section of the agreement addresses the Auto Pact, Canadian duty-waiver programmes applied to the auto industry, and used automobiles. Because automobiles and spare parts are also covered by Chapters 3 and 4, however, the impact of the agreement in the auto sector can be determined only by reading Chapters 3, 4 and 10 of the agreement together.

When these three chapters are seen as a whole, it is clear that, despite repeated assurances from the government that the Auto Pact would not be affected in any way, the agreement in fact includes important provisions which will:

- undermine the effectiveness of the Auto Pact in maintaining Canada's share of North American automobile production by companies that now meet the Auto Pact's content requirements;
- make the Auto Pact essentially a dead letter by preventing any additional producers from qualifying;
- prevent Canada from negotiating an agreement similar to the Auto Pact with any other country; and

- outlaw Canada's use of performance-based duty waivers as an incentive for companies that do not qualify as Auto Pact producers.

The Auto Pact: What it Does

Negotiated in 1965, the Canada-U.S. Automotive Trade Agreement, known as the Auto Pact, has provided the basis for the development of an auto industry in Canada. Essentially an agreement to manage cross-border trade in motor vehicles and parts, the Auto Pact guarantees that as many cars will be produced in Canada as are sold in Canada. This is accomplished through a "carrot and stick" approach. The carrot is that auto makers that meet specified requirements, known as safeguards, are allowed to import vehicles and parts duty-free. The stick is that if they fail to meet the rules of the pact, they must pay the 9.2 per cent Canadian tariff on all imports of vehicles and parts. In order to preserve their duty-free privileges, auto companies operating in Canada must ensure that 60 per cent of the value of their production is of Canadian origin (purchased or made in Canada) and they must undertake to assemble one car in Canada for every car they sell in Canada.

The safeguards in the Auto Pact were acceptable to American-owned companies because they gave those producers duty-free access to the seventh-largest market for automotive products in the world. In return, Canada got the investment and job benefits associated with industrial production. In the first ten years of the pact, auto parts production rose by 200 per cent, vehicle production by 100 per cent and employment in the industry increased by 30 per cent. Centred in Ontario, automotive trade now accounts for 60 per cent of Ontario's exports to the U.S. and 50 per cent of imports. Despite not having a domestically-owned auto industry, Canada has been able — thanks to the Auto Pact — to capture fully 14 per cent of North American auto production.

The Impact of Free Trade

Article 1001 of the free-trade agreement commits both countries to continue the Auto Pact as originally negotiated. When the provisions of Chapters 3 and 4 are taken into account, however, it becomes clear that the agreement maintains only the form of the Auto Pact. The substantive provisions of the Auto Pact are made irrelevant by other sections of the agreement.

Companies that qualify under the Auto Pact are still entitled to ship duty-free between Canada and the United States and to import parts from third countries into Canada duty-free. But the agreement limits the role of the Auto Pact for Canada in two important ways. First, Article 1002 (together with Annex 1002.1) limits participation in the Auto Pact to those companies that currently qualify or those that can qualify by no later than ninety days after the end of the 1989 model year. This means that, with the possible exception of the new General Motors-Suzuki joint venture, none of the new Japanese or Korean plants now in operation, or planned for the future, will be able to qualify for Auto Pact status.

Second, duties on all motor vehicles and motor vehicle parts that meet the test set out in the Rules of Origin established in Chapter 3 of the agreement will be eliminated in accordance with the tariff elimination schedule in Chapter 4. Tariffs are to be eliminated by January 1, 1993, on vehicles and original equipment parts, and by January 1, 1994, on after-market (replacement) parts. This, of course, means that companies can get duty-free status through the agreement by 1993 even if they do not meet the Canadian content requirements under the Auto Pact. If manufacturers can get the principal benefit of Auto Pact qualification without meeting the production targets in the safeguards, then the safeguards, and the Auto Pact itself, become meaningless.

Under free-trade rules, the Canadian government no longer has available the stick of withdrawing duty-free status in order to force compliance with the safeguard provisions. Indeed, under Section XVII of the Rules of Origin, vehicles, aircraft, vessels and associated transport equipment will qualify for duty-free entry into Canada or the U.S. provided that they meet a new 50 per cent North American content requirement. This North American content rule replaces the

Canadian content rule. It means that duty-free status will be accorded to Auto Pact companies even if they decide to produce nothing in Canada.

The only remaining benefit from Auto Pact qualification is the right to import duty-free from third countries; however, the companies that would be most attracted by this benefit — the Asian manufacturers — are frozen out of the Auto Pact anyway. This aspect of the deal may, in fact, be in violation of the General Agreement on Tariffs and Trade (GATT). When the Auto Pact was first negotiated, Canada did not have to obtain a GATT exemption because participation was open to any manufacturer that met the content requirements. With the free-trade agreement, Auto Pact participation is no longer open; Canada is also prohibited from entering into an agreement similar to the Auto Pact with any other country. Indeed, as limited by the agreement, the Auto Pact would be open to a challenge under Article II of GATT.

Article 405 of the agreement requires Canada to phase-out all of its performance-based duty-waiver programmes by January 1, 1998. Duty-waiver programmes were introduced by Canada as part of a strategy to attract investment in the Canadian auto industry from new sources. Companies that had won a share of the Canadian market by exporting from Europe, Japan or Korea were offered incentives to locate and produce in Canada in the form of rebates and import duties if they met certain requirements, such as exporting production (export-based duty waiver) or purchasing from Canadian sources (value-added duty waiver).

Under the free-trade agreement, Canada's export-based duty waivers are limited to current recipients; on January 1, 1989, they will cease to operate for exports to the U.S., and on January 1, 1998, they will be terminated entirely. Duty waivers based on value added in Canadian production are also limited to current recipients and must terminate by January 1, 1996. Value-added duty-waiver requirements that expire prior to January 1, 1996, cannot be renewed.

Article 1003 (Import Restrictions) phases out Canada's restrictions on the import of used cars. Because this measure will increase significantly the supply of corrosion-free used vehicles available to the Canadian market, it is likely to depress the resale value of Canadian used cars.

The Future

These changes are a long way from the Mulroney government's oft-repeated promise that the Auto Pact would remain untouched. Perhaps because of that fact, the government has tried very hard to convince Canadians that the deal is good for the auto industry. It argues that the new 50 per cent North American content rule is actually better than the Auto Pact's 60 per cent Canadian content rule. Whereas the Auto Pact's 60 per cent Canadian content rule can be met with non-production costs, only production costs count towards the trade agreement's 50 per cent criterion. In actual fact, the argument goes, the new 50 per cent rule is equivalent to a much tougher rule (the government says 70 per cent but industry experts say that is a gross exaggeration) in the Auto Pact terms.

It is an interesting argument, but it misses two crucial points. First, as we pointed out above, it requires Canadian *or* American content, not Canadian content. The requirement can be met without any Canadian production. Second, the argument conveniently ignores the fact that the "big three" manufacturers already far exceed the 50 per cent criterion. The 50 per cent rule in fact gives the "big three" considerable scope for reducing its Canadian-U.S. content.

The most significant part of the agreement, however, has nothing to do with its impact on the "big three" auto makers. It is generally agreed by auto industry experts that when currently planned offshore investments in North America are included, production capacity exceeds demand in North America by about 3 million cars a year. Clearly, the auto industry is heading for a big shakedown. The share of the "big three" will shrink, while the share of offshore producers will increase. Attracting offshore — principally Japanese — investment to Canada will be critical to maintaining our share of the North American automobile market.

But how are we going to attract that investment? We cannot use the Auto Pact. No more firms can qualify. And in any case, offshore investors will not need to meet Canadian content rules to get duty-free access to our market. They can gain access to Canada by producing in the United States. We are also precluded by the agreement from using performance-based duty remission agreements — the kinds of agreements that encouraged Honda, Hyundai and Toyota to locate in Canada.

The location of new offshore investment in Canada will be determined entirely by the market. Consider, for example, the choice faced by a Japanese corporation considering a North American location. If it locates in Canada, it will have to pay duty on its shipments into the American market until it meets the North American content rule. It will also have to pay (higher) Canadian duties on the parts it imports. If it locates in the United States, it will have to pay duty to ship to the Canadian market (one-tenth the size of the American market) and will have to pay (lower) U.S. parts duties. The market factors facing offshore investors clearly do not favour Canada.

If the auto industry in North America were stable, the argument that the trade deal will not adversely affect Canada's share of the market might hold up. But the North American auto industry is anything but stable. It is in the middle of its most massive adjustment since Ford and GM refined assembly-line technology. The agreement makes it impossible for Canada to influence the outcome of that adjustment.

12

Government Procurement

John Calvert

Traditionally, governments in Canada and elsewhere use their buying power to promote social and economic objectives. But under the Canada-U.S. trade deal, policies to encourage local sourcing, regional development, employment equity, Canadian investment and other domestic goals will be weakened, as private American business interests are given new legal mechanisms that will enable them to open up the Canadian public sector to competitive tendering. Under the agreement, the process of government tendering will be made more "transparent." That is, the criteria for evaluating bids will be public so that American firms will be able to submit tenders on an equal footing with Canadian firms. Most important, a new bid-review body will be established to deal with appeals by firms that feel they have suffered from discriminatory treatment. Not only will this body have the authority to investigate individual claims, it will also have the power to make recommendations on changes to the procurement practices of governments. Thus government procurement, formerly a national policy instrument, will become subject to North American rules.

The Dollars at Stake

The amount of federal government procurement open for competitive tendering to American firms will move from a threshold of $171,000

(U.S.), which is the current requirement of the General Agreement on Tariffs and Trade (GATT), down to $25,000 (U.S.). One study estimates that this will open up an additional market of $600 million to American firms operating in Canada. The amount of American government procurement opened to Canadian firms is estimated at $3.5 billion. The deal covers non-military procurement only and existing arrangements under the Defense Production Sharing Agreement remain unchanged.

A detailed list of the various federal government departments and agencies which will be required to follow the new rules is included in Chapter 13 of the agreement. This chapter is silent on any new obligations the treaty will place on provincial and municipal governments in Canada (and state and municipal governments in the U.S.). But in Chapter 1 there is an explicit commitment to extend the agreement eventually to all other levels of government. It seems clear that the intent is to apply the new procurement rules throughout the Canadian public sector.

The situation of Crown corporations — what the Americans refer to as "public monopolies" — is not mentioned explicitly in the chapter dealing with procurement either. But the logic of the deal is such that they will likely be included as part of the five to seven year period of negotiations on a new subsidies code. Moreover, the fact that we have accepted American terminology in referring to this matter (Article 2010), with its implied assumption that monopolies are undesirable, suggests that the thrust of the treaty is towards adopting the restrictive American approach to public ownership.

The significance of the procurement provisions of the treaty only becomes clear when the amounts involved are examined. In 1983, total purchases by all levels of government, including Crown corporations, amounted to $71.1 billion. By any standard, these expenditures have a significant economic impact. Canada's Gross National Expenditure in the same year was $389.9 billion. Thus, procurement expenditures represented 18.2 per cent of the total, or roughly one-fifth of all purchases in the economy. The reason the U.S. would like access to our government purchases is more readily understood in light of figures of this magnitude.

For 1983, Canadian federal government purchases amounted to approximately $8.6 billion, or only 12.1 per cent of the total. Federal

Crown corporations spent another $16.1 billion, or 22.6 per cent. The remaining two-thirds of Canadian procurement expenditure is in the hands of other levels of government or provincial Crown corporations. The table provides a further breakdown of government procurement expenditures by level of government and/or agency.

As indicated above, the procurement chapter of the agreement states that only the federal government's direct purchase of goods and goods-related services will be affected. But under other chapters of the agreement, the federal government has made the commitment that the deal will eventually apply to provincial and local levels of government as well as provincial public enterprises, hospitals and other provincially-supported agencies. This suggests that the federal government's estimate that only $600 million of Canadian government procurement will be affected by the treaty is misleading, since it is based on its 12.1 per cent share of all government purchases. The real amount with respect to "goods and goods-related services" could be eight times as much and even more if the category of services to which the treaty applies is interpreted liberally.

Even if we take the suggested amounts at face value, the share of the American and Canadian federal governments' procurement opened up by the agreement is not proportional. Since the U.S. economy is approximately twelve-times the size of the Canadian economy, the

Table 1
Government Procurement Expenditures in Canada (1983)

CATEGORY	BILLIONS $	PER CENT OF TOTAL
Federal Government	8.6	12.1
Provincial/Territorial Governments	14.5	20.4
Local Governments	9.1	12.8
Hospitals	3.8	5.3
Universities	1.3	1.9
Fed. Govt. Enterprises	16.1	22.6
Prov. Govt. Enterprises	13.9	19.6
Local Govt. Enterprises	3.8	5.3
TOTAL	71.1	100.0

Source: Department of Supply and Services

amount of purchasing which should be subject to the deal in the U.S. federal sector is $7.2 billion. In fact, as we have seen, it is only $3.5 billion, less than half the amount that Canada has provided. Proportionately, we are giving up twice as much access to the Canadian market as the U.S. is conceding to its market.

Procurement and the Larger Picture

The procurement chapter of the agreement must also be read in the overall context of the deal. For instance, the inclusion in the deal of the services sector has significant implications for the future role of government procurement in the economy.

A closer look at procurement expenditures provides some surprising information concerning the relative share allocated to the purchase of services. Approximately $34.6 billion, or 48.7 per cent of all government purchases, went to services. The relevant data are shown in the following table.

Of even greater interest is the overwhelming proportion of services currently being provided by domestic suppliers. While services amounted to almost one-half of all government procurement in 1983, only $1.5 billion or 4.3 per cent of this total was imported. In contrast, approximately $8.8 billion or 33.4 per cent of manufactured goods was imported. While manufactured goods represented only 37.0 per cent of total government purchases, they accounted for 77.2 per cent of imports arising from government procurement spending.

Table 2
Government Procurement Expenditures by Economic Sector
1983

Industrial Sector	Amount Billions $	Per Cent of Total
Service Industry	34.6	48.7
Manufacturing Industry	26.3	37.0
Primary Industry	10.2	14.3
TOTAL	71.1	100.0

Source: Department of Supply and Services

If the same share of services were imported as manufactured goods, the impact on the balance of payments would be dramatic. A rough calculation indicates that an additional $10.1 billion of imports would result. Of course, it is not simply the balance of payments which would suffer. To the extent that American firms succeed in utilizing their new opportunities under the deal, they will transfer large numbers of jobs out of Canada.

There is another aspect of the free-trade deal that deserves close attention. Following the logic of the "right of establishment" and the "right to national treatment" provisions, the agreement provides for prospective bidders on government contracts to be supplied with adequate information and forbids practices which would give domestic firms any "unfair" advantage over American firms in this regard. One of the key concepts embodied in this section of the agreement is that of "transparency." The procedures used to draw up tender specifications, the specifications themselves and the process of evaluating bids must be public and accessible to prospective bidders. In other words, the rules must be made fully known to American firms so that they will be able to enjoy the same advantages as Canadian firms. There will also be a new appeal system to enable firms which feel their bids have been unfairly treated to launch a bid challenge. A bid-review authority will have the power to examine the evidence and make recommendations regarding whether the award of a contract was fair or unfair, that is, whether the procurement rules were followed properly.

The scope of the review body, however, is not limited simply to assessing the application of existing procedures. It will be able to make recommendations concerning how procedures should be changed to bring them into conformity with the intent of the treaty. To put this another way, the agency will have the power to make policy as well as implement it. In the words of the text:

> The reviewing authority should be authorized to make recommendations in writing to contracting authorities respecting all facets of the procurement process, including recommendations for changes in procedures in order to bring them into conformity with the obligations of this Chapter. The procurement body or covered entities shall normally follow such recommendations.

In agreeing to such a provision, the Canadian government has signed away to a North American common market its decision-making authority over a Canadian tool of economic policy. In the process, it restricts future governments from using their large volume purchases to promote a wide range of domestic goals, including regional development, local sourcing, special support of particular industries, research and development, and affirmative action.

Affirmative Action Threatened

On the subject of affirmative action, one of the side effects of the deal is that it will undermine the work that has already been done in this area. Under the current federal government Employment Equity Program, suppliers of goods and goods-related services must demonstrate that they are complying with existing employment standards for federal contractors. In the January 1988 issue of the Department of Supply and Services publication *The Supplier*, the point is made that American firms bidding on Canadian government contracts will not be required to meet Canadian standards:

> *Question*: Would U.S. suppliers be requested to comply with the Employment Equity Program for Federal Contractors?
>
> *Answer*: The Employment Equity provisions will continue to apply only to Canadian suppliers as will be the case for the American Affirmative action programs which now apply exclusively to American contractors. These contractual requirements fall outside the purview of the Trade Agreement on procurement as they are not meant to and do not inadvertently confer an advantage to domestic suppliers.

The problem is not that American suppliers will be at a disadvantage. It is that Canadian suppliers will claim to be. They will argue that compliance with the Employment Equity Program for Federal Contractors will make them uncompetitive. This will generate pressure to abandon our standards so that Canadian firms will not be at a "disadvantage" in relation to American bidders.

It may be argued that this paints too gloomy a picture. It is true that the U.S. has extensive legislation promoting affirmative action in many sectors of its economy. Some of it is better, on paper, than ours. However, most of this legislation pre-dates the Reagan presidency. During the past eight years enforcement of affirmative action has been eroded and the federal government's active role has been undermined by Reagan's commitment to deregulation.

In contrast, Canada has been moving in quite the opposite direction. We have improved our equal-pay and affirmative action legislation in recent years. Moreover, there is every reason to believe that Canada may continue to make modest improvements in the future, as witnessed by the recent legislation on pay equity in Manitoba, P.E.I. and Ontario. What the deal will do is limit our ability to make further advances in this area by entrenching a competitive dynamic which will tend to keep standards at the lowest common denominator.

This example provides considerable insight into how the adoption of the principle of national treatment of American firms undercuts Canadian social objectives — even when enacted in law — by generating pressure to harmonize our standards with those in the U.S.

A related, much more significant point, concerns the negative impact of the deal on the promotion of equal pay and affirmative action in the public sector itself. The thrust of the deal is to entrench market forces more firmly in our economy. In practice, this means opening up the public sector to competitive tendering wherever possible. Specifically, it means adopting the American practice of providing government services through private contractors rather than with public employees. The U.S. views the Canadian practice of providing services through the public sector as an undesirable "public monopoly."

To the extent that the American practice of private contracting of public services is introduced into a wide range of areas of the Canadian public sector, efforts to implement equal pay will be undermined. This is because the employment conditions and pay of employees of private contractors in the service sector tend to be substantially inferior to those in the public. Wages are frequently less than half, benefits are minimal, job security is virtually non-existent, and the level of unionization is low because employers tend to be hostile to unions.

Where women workers in the public sector succeed in achieving progress towards pay equity by raising wages and improving other conditions of employment, they will inadvertently make the service they supply less competitive than that supplied by private contractors. This is not a problem when the service is provided "in house" and the question of tendering does not arise. However, where competitive tendering becomes a requirement — and this is where the American commitment to limiting "public monopolies" becomes a key factor — private contractors who do not adhere to similar affirmative action policies will have a significant cost advantage. They will be more "competitive" precisely because they have not implemented equal pay. Ironically, the more successful the drive towards equal pay in the public sector, the more likely public services will be contracted out because of the resulting higher labour costs.

Regional Development

The impact of the procurement chapter of the deal on regional development will also be substantial. Although government purchasing policy has been subject to the abuses of patronage and "pork-barrelling," the fact is that governments at all levels in Canada have used their purchasing power to promote the goal of regional development. Many provinces have followed policies of giving preference to provincial suppliers unless their bids were in excess of 10 per cent above those of out-of-province firms. Similarly, the federal government has been sensitive to the view that it should source its purchases locally wherever practical as an indirect method of providing regional support. All this will gradually be abandoned under the deal.

Yet while Canadian governments will no longer be able to use purchasing power as an instrument of regional development, the U.S. will still be free to use its major regional development tool — arms spending. As with so many other components of the deal, we have given up our traditional policy instruments while allowing the U.S. to exclude its methods from the treaty. Of even greater concern is the prospect that the federal government will begin to adopt the American military contract system of regional subsidies once the door is shut on using civilian procurement.

That this is not idle speculation is confirmed by another statement in the Department of Supply and Services publication, *The Supplier*:

> *Question*: Will the federal government still be able to use procurement as a vehicle for promoting industrial and regional development?

> *Answer*: The Canadian government, and more particularly, Supply and Services Canada, will be able to continue supporting regional economic development through the procurement activities falling outside the purview of the agreement. For example, defence equipment requirements and the purchasing needs of Transport Canada, Communications and Fisheries and Oceans, which are not covered by either the GATT Code or the proposed FTA [free-trade agreement], have and will continue to be important instruments of our economic strategy.

Conclusion

While the chapter on government procurement may seem, at first glance, to be one of the less important aspects of the Mulroney-Reagan trade deal, this is an illusion. With total government purchases of goods and services amounting to over $70 billion in 1983, the loss of effective government control over the terms and conditions governing the award of public contracts is of profound significance. A key lever which governments use to manage the economy will be abandoned. Imports will increase because of the asymmetrical access provided in the deal and because many smaller Canadian firms dependent on public contracts will be pushed out of business. The use of public purchasing to promote Canadian investment will be sharply curtailed. And jobs will be exported as American firms penetrate a larger and larger share of the public sector market.

This will not happen at once, of course. It will probably take two or three decades for the full and wide-ranging effects of the deal to be felt throughout the Canadian public sector. But there is no question of the direction in which the deal points us: away from democratic control and towards an even greater reliance on market forces.

13

Services: The Vanishing Opportunity

Marjorie Griffin Cohen

The Canadian government's introduction to the chapter on services states that trade in services represents the frontier of international commercial policy, because dynamic economies are increasingly dependent on the wealth generated by service transactions. This is true. The service sector is the major source of wealth and employment in all industrial countries. Canada is no exception to this international trend: services generate about two-thirds of the national income and provide 70 per cent of the jobs.

The unusual feature about Canada's service economy is that, unlike most other industrialized nations, Canada is not a major exporter of services. For the past thirty years this country has experienced a trade deficit in services which has been growing at an alarming rate. The contrast with the U.S. is startling. American service firms are truly dominant in international trade, accounting for about one-fourth of the entire world trade in services. Since its service sector is the only one that consistently generates a trade surplus, the U.S. government has been eager to ensure that its services trade expands internationally.

Expansion requires not only increasing the export of services from the U.S., but also creating conditions so that American firms can easily invest in service industries in other countries. Some services, such as day-care, educational services, and services related to goods production, simply cannot be carried out across borders. Since this type of trade accounts for the major source of service revenue, the right to provide services within other countries is recognized in the U.S. as critical for improving balance of trade problems. Therefore, the American agenda in international trade includes improving the ability to invest in foreign countries in order to deliver services within those countries, and the creation of clear rules about how firms who deliver these services will be treated.

Investment in services is the true frontier for international investment, and can be seen as offering the same attraction that American investment in the resource and manufacturing sectors has historically provided. With the drop in world prices for resources and increased global competition in manufacturing, resource and manufacturing investment opportunities in Canada have become less lucrative for American firms. In contrast, the tremendous expansion of the Canadian service market and the opportunities for penetrating that market, have made the service sector increasingly attractive.

Over the past few decades, the ability of large multinational companies to provide services globally has expanded enormously. But the problem for them is that they are increasingly faced with trade restrictions as countries try to protect their own industries and maintain control over their economies. Many countries vehemently oppose free trade in services because it threatens control over the infrastructures of their own economies — particularly in areas as vitally important as banking, investment, insurance, transportation, telecommunications, social services, and culture.

The U.S., at the urging of giant American service firms like American Express, American Telephone and Telegraph, the American International Group and Citibank, has repeatedly tried to include free trade in services in international trade agreements, such as the General Agreement on Tariffs and Trade (GATT). Although in the past this campaign has had little success, free trade in services will be an important issue in the Uruguay Round of GATT. According to a congressional report published in July 1987, the U.S. has three objectives in GATT relating to services. These are, first, that "national treatment" should govern services trade. This means foreign firms should be treated in the same manner as are domestic firms. Second, the U.S. wants "transparency" in regulations and barriers that affect services trade. This means that all new regulations made by a country regarding services should explicitly state the impact they will have on trade. The third objective is that all trade agreements include a disputes-settlement mechanism which will relate specifically to services.[1] The report goes on to say that the U.S. has made reductions in barriers to services trade a primary goal in the Uruguay Round of GATT: "Although immediate payoffs in terms of U.S. jobs and U.S. exports will be small, the *long-run strategic importance of services makes the goal a vital one*.[emphasis in the original]"[2]

During the Canada-U.S. trade talks, Canadian negotiators paid amazingly little attention to the implications of free trade in services and the problems this would cause Canada. In the agreement the U.S. has received extraordinary concessions from Canada in the area of services — concessions which go considerably beyond those the U.S. is pushing for, and certainly beyond what it expects to achieve in the Uruguay round of GATT negotiations. This agreement is the first comprehensive agreement in services ever negotiated.

The Agreement

Chapter 14 of the agreement applies to 299 service industries (see Appendix); however, services are also covered in other sections of the agreement, most notably the chapters which cover investment, temporary entry for business-persons, financial services, and institutional provisions, and also the articles in Chapter 20 (Other Provisions) which deal with monopolies, cultural issues, and nullification and impairment.

As the government's introduction to the chapter on services indicates, the issue is "more than a matter of opening up service markets." Its point is that trade in services is an integral part of trade in goods since services are related to the production, sale, distribution, and maintenance of goods. Therefore, in order to increase trade in tangible items, their servicing needs to be included in trade agreements. But the matter of opening up service markets is also more than simply identifying services as an adjunct to the goods-producing sector. They are a big business in their own right and some services, particularly social services, are quite distinct from their relationship to trade in goods.

The government, in its introduction, maintains that "basic economic efficiency and competitiveness gains expected from the removal of barriers to trade in goods between Canada and the United States also apply to the service sectors." This is an assertion which has not been demonstrated by any studies. The effect of increased competition in services has been virtually ignored and no specific study of any industry indicates that Canada's export performance can improve once barriers to trade in the covered industries are removed. Considering the seriousness of Canada's international indebtedness, the deterioration of our service account with the U.S., and the very fragile nature of our service exports, pursuing a free-trade agreement in services without any real examination of its impact seems foolhardy.

A most serious consequence of the agreement will be the inability in the future to introduce protection of our service industries should the optimistic predictions of the government not materialize. This agreement weakens the ability to introduce any new national policies for services.

National Treatment

The chapter on services opens up enormous privileges for the services industries covered under the agreement. These privileges include the right to invest; the right to produce, distribute, sell, market and deliver a service; the right to use domestic distribution systems; and the right to establish a commercial presence.

Article 1402:8 specifies that foreign firms must receive treatment from a province or a state "no less favourable than the most favourable treatment accorded by such province or state." This means that American firms must be given the same treatment as Canadian firms with respect to taxes, laws, regulations and requirements. The provision extends beyond the "national treatment" principle in that it involves provincial treatment as well. The agreement insists that provinces must treat American firms as they do any other firm in the province.

The result of this provision will be to introduce peculiar anomolies in Canada. Provinces may continue to discriminate against Canadian service firms located in another province while being forced to treat American firms as if they were local provincial enterprises. With this agreement, U.S. firms will have increased access to provincial markets in all cases — rights which are not accorded to other Canadian firms.

The right of national treatment does not apply only to American firms which are located in Canada. The agreement (Article 1402.8) states that "neither Party shall introduce any measure, including a measure requiring the establishment or commercial presence by a person of the other Party in its territory as a condition for the provision of a covered service." This means that for the almost three hundred service industries covered in Chapter 14, American firms must be treated as are Canadian firms, *even if they are not located in this country*. This provision could result in serious job losses in industries where services can be provided from entirely outside the country.[3]

Disputes-Settlement Mechanism for Services

The agreement provides a binding mechanism for settling disagreements about trade in services. This is one area where rules are new and binding, unlike disputes over trade in goods. Yet, ironically, it is also an area where a genuine, binding disputes-settlement mechanism will definitely work against Canada.

Discussion of disputes settlement has centred on how effective the new binational panels will be in helping Canadian exporters fight anti-dumping and countervailing duty cases. Since the disputes-settlement mechanism outlined in Chapter 19 of the agreement does nothing to change the impact of U.S. trade-remedy law, that mechanism is ultimately not going to be very important (see chapter four). In contrast, the disputes-settlement mechanism for services is truly significant.

To date there has been no clear way to resolve disputes which involve services which are not traded across borders, but which are delivered domestically by a foreign-owned company. Existing trade-remedy legislation applies only when cross-border trade occurs. When American firms operating in Canada have experienced some sort of trade barrier here, there has not been any clear and strong mechanism to deal with these companies' complaints. Section 301 of the U.S. Trade Act of 1974 is technically able to remedy foreign government practices which affect the competitiveness of American service firms in foreign markets. However, the U.S. has rarely used section 301 provisions and it would find it difficult to retaliate against what it perceives to be unfair practices in services because there has been no agreement about what constitutes fair or unfair trade practices in services.

Now, with the free-trade agreement, clear rules are established. The institutional mechanism of Chapter 18, which provides for binding arbitration, ensures that these rules would be enforced. In essence, the disputes-settlement mechanism for services protects the American service sector in the same way that the manufacturing and resource sectors are protected by U.S. trade-remedy legislation. Indeed, it is a heightened form of American protectionism — one that will apply within our border! While technically the same measures will be available to Canadian service firms operating in the U.S., the balance is tipped dramatically in favour of American service firms, since the Canadian presence in the American service sector is negligible.

Social Services

There are a great many ways that social services will be affected by the agreement, contrary to the government's assertion in the introduction to the chapter on services that "doctors, dentists, lawyers, childcare and government-provided services (health, education and social services)" are excluded from the agreement. Even within that same chapter they are explicitly *included*.

The agreement lists the covered services by their Standard Industrial Classification Numbers, not by name. The kinds of services covered include post-secondary non-university education and health and social service industries (Divisions O and P of Appendix). While the chapter on services extends free trade to the management of institutions such as hospitals, homes for children, ambulance services, and health clinics, this is not the only part of the agreement which rules on these services — the chapter on investment also extends right of establishment and right of national treatment to all aspects of these industries. The effect of free trade, then, is not just increased American access to the management of social service industries, but also to the ownership of them. So, for example, while the services chapter gives a American ambulance service the right to manage this industry in Canada, the chapter on investment also permits the American firm to own the industry here.

The full implication of these provisions will undoubtedly take considerable time to understand and will probably only be resolved through legal challenges to the agreement. It could be argued, for example, that any government capital grants to establish health or social institutions would have to be also open to American firms, if they are available to non-government institutions. This is especially important in areas where government supports non-profit private services, such as nursing homes, day-care, and hospitals. Since there is no specific clause which allows a distinction between governments' treatment of profit and non-profit industries, under the deal no government will be able to favour non-profit industries in health and social services if American firms choose to operate in Canada. Thus, although health and social services are a provincial responsibility, the power of provincial governments to pursue social policies of their own design will be seriously limited by this agreement.

Provincial power regarding social services will also be affected by the section of the agreement which covers monopolies (Article 2010). This is an extremely powerful article which, in practical terms, will make it virtually impossible to extend public provision of services into any areas which are now in the private sector.

While formally recognizing the prerogative of governments to maintain or designate a monopoly, the restrictions on their ability to do so are enormous. Before Canada can designate a monopoly (such as public dental care or auto insurance) the U.S. must be notified and consulted about the way in which this will occur. Canada would also be required to "endeavour to introduce such conditions on the operation of the monopoly as will minimize or eliminate any nullification of impairments of benefits under this Agreement" (Article 2010.2b). Here is where the very powerful section on "Nullification and Impairment" (Article 2011) takes effect. This section says that if any action occurs which affects a benefit a firm would reasonably expect to receive, "whether or not such a measure conflicts with the provisions of this Agreement," the issue would be resolved through the disputes-settlement mechanism which could ultimately lead to binding arbitration. So, for example, an American insurance company which is unhappy with the idea of losing its lucrative auto insurance market in Canada could challenge any move on the part of a provincial government to introduce a public insurance plan, since this would obviously conflict with benefits the Americans expect to receive by being in Canada.

But, even if the American challenge was defeated, there would still be another problem. American firms would have to be provided with "prompt, adequate and effective compensation" (Article 1605) for whatever losses they would expect to incur. This is not a minor issue. In most cases it would involve costs so great as to make impossible the whole attempt toward increasing public involvement in the provision of public services.

In most cases, Canadian social services are superior to American social services. Canadian systems of health care, for instance, cost less and cover more people than the more privatized American system. Yet under the deal, the Canadian public would have to compensate the American private sector providers of services before introducing more efficient public services. Ultimately, the cost of compensating the private producers would price publicly delivered, universal social services out of the market. No new initiatives for services (such as public dental care) would be possible under free trade.

Although the agreement makes it impossible to bring more social services into the public sector, its provisions make it extremely easy for public services to be increasingly privatized. Clearly, the right of national treatment will make Canada very attractive for American social service investors. But equally significant are the cost pressures provincial governments face in providing these services. As federal transfer grants cover a smaller and smaller proportion of the total costs of providing social services, provincial governments attempt to solve their problems by involving the private sector. This usually results in the private provision of a service (such as nursing homes and day care) which is either partially or fully funded by taxpayers. Public funds, then, support social services operating for profit. The result is usually a deterioration in the quality of the service provided, since a considerable portion of public funding goes, not to the service itself, but toward providing profits for the private provider.

Rules of Origin

This agreement does not require that services imported into Canada be mainly produced in the U.S. in order for American service firms to receive benefits of the agreement. This is in stark contrast to the rules of origin provisions for goods which require that at least 50 per cent of the value of goods exported must be produced in the exporting country. Having rules about where items are produced prohibits firms from shifting production to low-cost places and admitting them into our free-trade area. The implications for goods-producing industries are clear — if most of the production of an item could take place off-shore, in countries where labour costs are substantially lower, and then the product could be re-shipped to Canada by American firms, the price of the item could clearly be much lower, and Canadian firms would be at a terrific disadvantage.

The same danger applies to production of services. There are no rules in the agreement about what proportion of a service can be produced in a third country in the agreement. While the agreement permits benefits to be denied if a third country is involved, there is no indication of just what constitutes third-country involvement (Article 1406). Also, benefits can only be denied "subject to prior notification and consultation," and the onus is on the country denying benefits to establish proof that an unacceptable activity is taking place.

The result of having no clear rules of origin provisions could be dramatic. Data processing, for example, could be done in the Carribean and exported by American firms to Canada. This would escalate the importation of very cheap data processing in Canada and result in dramatic job losses in the clerical sector.

Telecommunications

The United States is pursuing an aggressive approach toward free trade and policy harmonization in the telecommunications industry. The deregulation of the communications industry within the U.S. has resulted in serious trade problems for that country. While the American market has become more open to the rest of the world as a result of divestiture and deregulation, American firms face restrictions in the markets of many of their competitors.[4] Deregulation, consequently, has not been a happy experience in the U.S. The push towards international free trade in telecommunications by the U.S., and the consequent "harmonization" of policy to provide a "level playing field," is an attempt to rectify domestic problems caused by deregulation by exporting them.

Telecommunications used to mean local and long-distance telephone calls. It is now a much broader industry and includes all electronic transmission of information, including computer services. In 1979 a Canadian government commission (commonly known as the Clyne Commission) investigated the problems of international trade in telecommunications. It called for increasing protection for the industry to avoid greater dependence on American provision of these services, saying that this trend posed "the most dangerous threat to Canadian sovereignty, in both its cultural and commercial aspects."[5]

The danger areas arising from the greater use of foreign telecommunications services identified by the commission are as follows: reduced Canadian power to ensure protection for privacy, confidentiality, and crime; reduced control over disruptions resulting from breakdown; loss of control over companies operating in Canada which store and process their data in the U.S.; increased influence of American databanks emphasizing American values, goods and services; and increased ability of the U.S. to make its laws applicable outside U.S. territority.[6]

To deal with these dangers, the commission recommended a comprehensive telecommunications strategy for Canada which would include requirements that data processing related to Canadian business operations be performed in Canada, and that the exporting of client data for processing and storage abroad (as now exists with regard to banking data) in information sensitive industries (such as the insurance and loan industries) be prohibited.

The free-trade deal has ignored, rather than addressed, the dangers of trade liberalization in communications. Moreover, since it is a comprehensive agreement, it would prevent any further consideration of these dangers at any time in the future. The agreement covers all computer services and telecommunications with the exception of basic telecommunications networks (local and long-distance telephone service). The objective is to "maintain and support the further development of an open and competitive market" (Annex 1404.C1).

American telecommunications companies will have all the same rights of establishment and national treatment as other industries covered in the chapter on services. In addition, they are given access to all telecommunications networks in such a way that, for instance, private firms will be able to acquire flat-rate private-line services (which offer big volume users of telephone services a substantial advantage in costs) and resell them. At the moment, the use of private lines for the development of intercorporate networks is allowed, but the resale of the service is not. Telephone companies providing basic service have been discontented with the flat-rate provision because payments are not related to volume. This leaves them with telephone networks that are losing business to the private line firms which are getting the lucrative end of the market. Their concern has obviously been ignored in the free-trade agreement, which would allow the private sale of huge volumes of telecommunication services.

The agreement places no restrictions on the "movement of information across the borders and access to data bases or related information stored, processed or otherwise held within the territory of a Party" (Annex 1404.C3f). Currently, there are restrictions on cross-border data flows; some of them are substantial and involve tax regulations and outright prohibitions against the processing and storing of data outside the country. These have been instituted for reasons of privacy and security, but the effect has also been important for retaining a substantial number of jobs in Canada.

While there has been a significant shift toward greater amounts of Canadian data being processed in the U.S., resulting in large job losses, some important protections remain.[7] The most significant is the Bank Act, which requires that all banking data be processed and stored in Canada. American firms have long maintained that the Bank Act is an unfair barrier to trade. According to the American journal *Inside U.S. Trade*, the provision on data processing in the free-trade agreement is very important and is "a significant precedent in our efforts in the Uruguay Round to achieve a similar multilateral understanding."[8] The journal notes that the removal of data restrictions in the Bank Act was not included in the agreement, but it feels that this issue would soon be cleared up. As it points out, "the services code allows for future negotiatins to remove barriers and we have a process to deal with these isolated restrictions."

Conclusion

The services provisions in the agreement are in the process of being extended. Article 1405 explicitly states that the U.S. and Canada will work to eliminate existing measures inconsistent with the intent of the agreement, to include other industries in the sectoral annexes, and to consult periodically for the purpose of including additional services and identifying further opportunities for increasing access to each other's service markets. Whatever industries have escaped the current round of negotiations will have little protection when the spotlight is off the agreement. So services, such as postal services and transportation, which had been included in negotiations but did not make it to the final text, will undoubtedly be major targets in the future. The intention of the agreement is clear — to integrate the service sectors of the two nations.

With international trade in services expanding rapidly, rules about international competition are essential. In negotiating with the U.S., Canada has been at an extreme disadvantage. The government has little understanding of the true significance of the service sector in generating wealth and income in this country, and even less understanding of the impact of increased American penetration in our service markets. Canada would be in a much stronger position in bargaining with the U.S. if we showed solidarity with other smaller nations in negotiating through GATT. While we would undoubtedly face the might of the U.S. in this arena as well, we would be doing it with allies who recognize the dangers of unrestricted free trade in services. The bilateral agreement with the U.S. is a massive and unthinking abandonment of control over our service industries.

Appendix

Services listed in the agreement, by Standard Industrial Classification numbers

Division A — Agricultural and Related Service Industries
0122 Farm Animal Breeding Services (Except Poultry)
0121 Poultry Services
0219 Other Services Incidental to Livestock and Animal Specialties
0221 Soil Preparation, Planting and Cultivating Services
0222 Crop Dusting and Spraying Services
0223 Harvesting, Baling and Threshing Services
0229 Other Services Incidental to Agricultural Crops
Division C — Logging and Forestry Industries
0511 Forestry Services Industry
Division D — Mining (Including Milling), Quarrying and Oil Well Industries
0911 Contract Drilling Oil and Gas Industry
0919 Other Service Industries Incidental to Crude Petroleum and Natural Gas
0921 Contract Drilling Industry (Except Oil and Gas)
0929 Other Service Industries Incidental to Mining
Division F — Construction Industries
4011 Single Family Housing
4012 Apartment and Other Multiple Housing
4013 Residental Renovation
4021 Manufacturing and Light Industrial Building
4022 Commercial Building
4023 Institutional Building
4111 Power Plants (Except Hydroelectric)
4112 Gas, Oil and Other Energy Related Structures (Except Pipelines)
4113 Gas and Oil Pipelines
4119 Other Industrial Construction
4121 Highways, Streets and Bridges
4122 Waterworks and Sewage Systems
4123 Hydroelectric Power Plants and Related Structures (Except Transmission Lines)
4124 Power and Telecommunication Transmission Lines
4129 Other Heavy Construction
4211 Wrecking and Demolition
4212 Water Well Drilling
4213 Septic System Installation
4214 Excavating and Grading
4215 Equipment Rental (With Operator)
4216 Asphalt Paving
4217 Fencing Installation
4219 Other Site Work
4221 Piledriving Work
4222 Form Work
4223 Steel Reinforcing
4224 Concrete Pouring and Finishingj
4225 Precast Concrete Installation
4226 Rough and Framing Carpentry
4271 Plastering and Stucco Work
4272 Drywall Work
4273 Acoustical Work
4274 Finish Carpentry
4275 Painting and Decorating Work
4276 Terrazzo and Tile Work
4277 Hardwood Flooring Installation
4278 Resilient Flooring and Carpet Work
4279 Other Interior and Finishing Work
4291 Elevator and Escalator Installation
4292 Ornamental and Miscellaneous Fabricated Metal Installation
4293 Residential Swimming Pool Installation
4299 Other Trade Work n.e.c.
4411 Project Management, Constructin
4491 Land Developers
4499 Other Services Incidental to Construction n.e.c.
Division G — Transportation and Storage Industries
4599 Other Service Industries Incidental to Transportation n.e.c. (packing and crating only)
Division I — Wholesale Trade Industries
5111 Petroleum Products, Wholesale
5211 Confectionary, Wholesale
5212 Frozen Foods (Packaged), Wholesale
5213 Dairy Products, Wholesale
5214 Poultry and Eggs, Wholesale
5215 Fish and Seafood, Wholesale
5216 Fresh Fruit and Vegetables, Wholesale
5217 Meat and Meat Products, Wholesale
5219 Other Foods, Wholesale
5221 Beverages, Wholesale
5213 Drugs, Wholesale

5232 Toilet Soaps and Preparations, Wholesale
5239 Drug Sundries and Other Drugs and Toilet Preparations, Wholesale
5241 Tobacco Products, Wholesale
5311 Men's and Boys' Clothing and Furnishings, Wholesale
5312 Women's Misses' and Children's Outerwear, Wholesale
5313 Women's Misses' and Children's Hoisery Underwear and Apparel Accessories, Wholesale
5314 Footwear, Wholesale
5319 Other Apparel, Wholesale
5321 Piece Goods, Wholesale
5329 Notions and Other Dry Goods, Wholesale
5411 Electrical Household Appliances, Wholesale
5412 Electronic Household Appliances, Wholesale
5421 Household Furniture, Wholesale
5431 China, Glasswear, Crockery, and Pottery, Wholesale
5432 Floor Coverings, Wholesale
5433 Linens, Draperies and Other Textile Furnishings, Wholesale
5439 Other Household Furnishings, Wholesale
5511 Automobiles, Wholesale
5512 Trucks and Buses, Wholesale
5519 Other Motor Vehicles and Trailers, Wholesale
5521 Tires and Tubes, Wholesale
5529 Other Motor Vehicle Parts and Accessories, Wholesale
5611 Iron and Steel Primary Forms and Structural Shapes, Wholesale
5612 Other Iron and Steel Products, Wholesale
5613 Non-Ferrous Metal and Metal Products, Wholesale
5619 Combination Metal and Metal Products, Wholesale
5621 Hardware, Wholesale
5622 Plumbing, Heating and Air Conditioning Equipment and Supplies, Wholesale
5631 Lumber, Plywood and Millwork, Wholesale
5632 Paint, Glass and Wallpaper, Wholesale
5639 Other Building Materials, Wholesale
5711 Farm Machinery, Equipment and Supplies, Wholesale
5721 Construction and Forestry Machinery, Equipment and Supplies, Wholesale
5722 Mining Machinery, Equipment and Supplies, Wholesale
5731 Industrial Machinery, Equipment and Supplies, Wholesale
5741 Electrical Wiring Supplies and Electrical Construction Material, Wholesale
5742 Electrical Generating and Transmission Equipment and Supplies, Wholesale
5743 Electronic Machinery, Equipment and Supplies, Wholesale
5949 Other Electrical and Electronic Machinery, Equipment and Supplies, Wholesale
5791 Office and Store Machinery, Equipment and Supplies, Wholesale
5792 Service Machinery, Equipment and Supplies, Wholesale
5793 Professional Machinery, Equipment and Supplies, Wholesale
5799 Other Machinery, Equipment and Supplies n.e.c, Wholesale
5911 Automobile Wrecking
5919 Other Waste Materials, Wholesale
5921 Newsprint, Wholesale
5922 Stationery and Office Supplies, Wholesale
5929 Other Paper and Paper Products, Wholesale
  Agricultural Feeds, Wholesale
5932 Seeds and Seed Processing, Wholesale
5939 Agricultural Chemical and Other Farm Supplies, Wholesale
5941 Toys, Novelties and Fireworks, Wholesale
5942 Amusement and Sporting Goods, Wholesale
5951 Photographic Equipment and Supplies, Wholesale
5952 Musical Instruments and Accessories, Wholesale
5961 Jewellery and Watches, Wholesale
5971 Industrial and Household Chemicals, Wholesale
5981 General Merchandise, Wholesale
5991 Books, Periodicals and Newspapers, Wholesale
5992 Second-Hand Goods, Wholesale (Except Machinery and Automotive)
5993 Forest Products, Wholesale
5999 Other Products n.e.c., Wholesale
Division J — Retail Trade Industries
6011 Food (Groceries) Stores — management
6012 Food (Specialty) Stores — management
6031 Pharmacies — management
6032 Patent Medicine and Toiletries Stores — management
6111 Shoe Stores — management
6121 Men's Clothing Stores — management
6131 Women's Clothing Stores — management
6141 Clothing Stores n.e.c — management
6151 Fabric and Yarn Stores — management
6211 Household Furniture Stores (With Appliances and Furnishings) — management
6212 Household Furniture Stores (Without Appliances and Furnishings) — management
6213 Furniture Refinishing and Repair Shops — management
6221 Appliance, Television, Radio and Stereo Stores — management

6222 Television, Radio and Stereo Stores — management
6223 Appliance, Television, Radio and Stereo Repair Shops — management
6231 Floor Covering Stores — management
6232 Drapery Stores — management
6239 Other Household Furnishing Stores — management
6311 Automobile (New) Dealers — management
6312 Automobile (Used) Dealers — management
6321 Motor Home and Travel Trailer Dealers — management
6322 Boats, Outboard Motors and Boating Accessories Dealers — management
6323 Motorcycle and Snowmobile Dealers — management
6329 Other Recreational Vehicle Dealers — management
6331 Gasoline Service Stations — management
6341 Home and Auto Supply Stores — management
6342 Tire, Battery, Parts and Accessories Stores — management
6351 Garages (General Repair)
6352 Paint and Body Repair Shops
6353 Muffler Replacement Shops
6354 Motor Vehicle Glass Replacement Shops
6355 Motor Vehicle Transmission Repair and Replacement Shops
6359 Other Motor Vehicle Repair Shops
6391 Car Washes — management
6399 Other Motor Vehicle Services n.e.c. — management
6411 Department Stores — management
6412 General Stores — management
6513 Other General Merchandise Stores
6521 Florist Shops — management
6522 Lawn and Garden Centres — management
6531 Hardware Stores — management
6532 Paint, Glass and Wallpaper Stores — management
6541 Sporting Goods Stores — management
6542 Bicycle Shops — management
6551 Musical Instrument Stores — management
6552 Record and Tape Stores — management
6561 Jewellery Stores — management
6562 Watch and Jewellery Repair Shops — management
6571 Camera and Photographic Supply Stores — management
6581 Toy and Hobby Stores — management
6582 Gift, Novelty and Souvenir Stores — management
6591 Second Hand Merchandise Stores n.e.c. — management
6592 Opticians' Shops — management
6593 Art Galleries and Artists' Supply Stores

— management
6594 Luggage and Leather Goods Stores — management
6595 Monument and Tombstone Dealers — management
6596 Pet Stores — management
6597 Coin and Stamp Dealers — management
6598 Mobile Home Dealers — management
6599 Other Retail Stores n.e.c. — management
6911 Vending Machine Operators
6921 Direct Sellers
Division K — Finance and Insurance Industries
7211 Investment (Mutual Funds) — managed by insurance co.
7212 Retirement Savings Funds — managed by insurance co.
7213 Segregated Funds — managed by insurance co.
7291 Trusteed Pension Funds — managed by insurance co.
7311 Life Insurers
7331 Health Insurers
7339 Other Property and Casualty Insurers
7499 Other Financial Intermediaries n.e.c. — franchising
Division L — Real Estate Operator and Insurance Agent Industries
7511 Operators of Residental Buildings and Dwellings
7512 Operators of Non-Residental Buildings
7599 Other Real Estate Operators
7611 Insurance and Real Estate Agencies
Division M — Business Service Industries
7711 Employment Agencies
7712 Personnel Suppliers
7721 Computer Services
7722 Computer Equipment Maintenance and Repair
7731 Offices of Chartered and Certified Accountants
7739 Other Accounting and Bookkeeping Services
7741 Advertising Agencies
7742 Media Representatives
7743 Outdoor Display and Billboard Advertising
7749 Other Advertising Services
7751 Offices of Architects
7752 Offices of Engineers
7759 Other Scientific and Technical Services
7771 Management Consulting Services
7791 Security and Investigation Services
7792 Credit Bureau Services
7793 Collection Agencies
7796 Duplicating Services
7799 Other Business Services n.e.c.
Division O — Educational Service Industries
8521 Post-Secondary Non-University Education — commercial

Division P — Health and Social Service Industries
8611 General Hospitals — management
8612 Rehabilitation Hospitals — management
8613 Extended Care Hospitals — management
8614 Mental (Psychiatric) Hospitals — management
8615 Addiction Hospitals — management
8616 Nursing Stations and Outpost Hospitals — management
8617 Children's Paediatric) Hospitals — management
8619 Other Specialty Hospitals — management
8631 Ambulance Services — management
8632 Drug Addiction and Alcholism Treatment Clinics — management
8633 Health Rehabilitation Clinics — management
8634 Home Care Services (Including Home Nursing) — management
8635 Public Health Clinics/Community Health Centres — management
8654 Other Non-Institutional Health Services — management
8651 Office of Physicians, General Practice — management
8652 Offices of Physicians and Surgeons, Specialists — management
8653 Offices of Dentists, General Practice — management
8654 Offices of Dentists, Specialists — management
8661 Offices of Chiropractors and Osteopaths — management
8662 Offices of Nurses, Registered — management
8663 Offices of Nurses, Practical — management
8664 Offices of Nutritionists/Dietitians — management
8665 Offices of Physiotherapists/Occupational Therapists — management
8666 Offices of Optometrists — management
8667 Offices of Podiatrists and Chiropodists — management
8668 Offices of Denturists — management
8669 Offices of Other Health Practitioners — management

8671 Offices of Psychologists — management
8672 Offices of Social Workers — management
8679 Offices of Other Social Service Practitioners — management
8681 Medical Laboratories — commercial
8682 Radiological Laboratories — commercial
8683 Combined Medical and Radiological Laboratories — commercial
8684 Public Health Laboratories — commercial
8685 Blood Bank Laboratories — commercial
8689 Other Health Laboratories — commercial

Division Q — Accommodation, Food and Beverage Service Industries
9111 Hotels and Motor Hotels — management
9112 Motels — management
9113 Tourist Courts and Cabins — management
9114 Guest Houses and Tourist Homes — management
9211 Restaurants, Licensed
9212 Restaurants, Unlicensed (Including Drive-Ins)
9213 Take-Out Food Services
9214 Caterers

Division R — Other Service Industries
9725 Linen Supply
9911 Industrial Machinery and Equipment Rental and Leasing
9912 Audio-Visual Equipment Rental and Leasing
9913 Office Furniture and Machinery Rental and Leasing
9914 Other Machinery and Equipment Rental and Leasing
9921 Automobile and Truck Rental and Leasing Services
9941 Electric Motor Repair
9942 Welding
9949 Other Repair Services n.e.c
9951 Disinfecting and Exterminating Services
9952 9953 Janitorial Services
9959 Other Services to Buildings and Dwellings
9999 Other Services n.e.c.

14

The Trade Pact, Deregulation and Canada's Financial System

Kirk Falconer

In the area of financial services, Canada's trade pact with the U.S. relinquishes to American financial and business interests additional control over a sector that has for a long time been almost entirely Canadian-owned and controlled. Of equal importance is that the agreement gives U.S. residents acquisition and ownership opportunities in a financial environment that is now markedly more open than the one south of the border. Of all the changes that have hit the Canadian financial system of late, the most important has been government deregulation of the financial services industry. Understanding this development is essential to coming to terms with the impact of free trade on financial services.

Deregulation Canadian Style

Financial deregulation has been fashionable public policy in a number of nations in recent years. While the face of deregulation differs from jurisdiction to jurisdiction, commonly it involves the removal of prudential restrictions established in the aftermath of the Great Depression. Whatever its supposed merits for increasing short-run competition and efficiency, deregulation adds considerably to financial uncertainty. This was the view of the Bank of International Settlements (the international forum of central bankers), whose April 1986 report warned that financial re-structuring, in tandem with deregulation, would reduce the scope of domestic regulatory and monetary policies in ways that could not be precisely forecast. Canada's Superintendent of Financial Institutions, Michael Mackenzie, expressed a similar view in a September 1987 speech to an international meeting of supervisors, noting that these developments would lead to increased risks and potential insolvency among financial institutions. Both the Bank of International Settlements and Mackenzie called for more international co-operation and reform to manage the trends.

Deregulation, ironically, does not always mean increased competition. For instance, the Mulroney government's new domestic ownership rules tolerate broad commercial and financial links, especially among large financial conglomerates. Corporate giants like Trilon Financial, Genstar Financial and E.L. Financial are permitted under deregulation to remain the major shareholders in a number of closely-held, non-bank financial institutions. These conglomerates are, in turn, run by some of Canada's wealthiest entrepreneurs — the Reichmanns, Edward and Peter Bronfman, Hal Jackman and Paul Desmarais. Interestingly enough, the government has argued that the objective of its ownership policy is to provide fair competition for a heavily concentrated financial sector. Apparently, this is to be done by fighting the bank oligopoly with corporate concentration of another variety.

Accompanying deregulation have been dramatic changes within the industry. Financial structures are being reshaped, largely in response to technological change. Financial innovation has spawned a vast and complex array of consumer products and services and added to the volume of transactions conducted in Canada on a daily basis. Because all financial institutions — banks, trust companies, insurance companies, investment dealers, credit unions and *caisses populaires* — are contributing to innovation, the once clear distinctions between financial activities themselves are becoming blurred. Globalization of financial services is occurring at an accelerated pace. Sophisticated communications systems have brought financial markets closer together. Capital is becoming more mobile. New and important financial instruments play an increasingly large role in international finance. Large corporate customers have influenced an important shift in credit flows away from loans, through international banks, into securities markets.

Financial deregulation and technological innovation have tended to feed on one another. As competition in financial services intensifies, large financial institutions are scrambling to position themselves in promising global markets. To accomplish their goals, financial and commercial shareholders press the government to lift regulatory obstacles to growth. At the same time, regulatory authorities are finding it increasingly difficult to monitor financial developments — much less control them — using contemporary policy tools. As policymakers implement deregulation, it remains to be seen whether the domestic supervisory apparatus will be able to cope with change that includes broader financial powers for institutions.

Canadian financial deregulation has also been characterized by the government's commitment to increased foreign participation. Prior to 1980, Canadian policy on foreign participation in the financial industry was chiefly influenced by the 1964 Royal Commission on Banking and Finance (the Porter Commission), which concluded that "a high degree of Canadian ownership of financial institutions is in itself healthy and desirable, and that the balance of advantage is against foreign control of Canadian banks." Among the disadvantages to non-resident participation identified by the commission were a lack of compliance with the objectives of Canadian monetary policy and the already high degree of foreign ownership in the economy. The recommendations of the Porter Commission found expression in 1967 changes to the Bank Act introducing tough limits on foreign ownership for the first time.

In 1980, the government amended the Bank Act to allow U.S.-controlled institutions to be established in Canada on a subsidiary basis. The growth of American and other foreign bank subsidiaries, (called Schedule B banks to distinguish them from the Canadian chartered banks now known as Schedule A banks), was to be contained by an assets ceiling. Within six years of the 1980 Bank Act changes, foreign bank subsidiaries held 8 per cent of the total domestic assets of chartered banks or half of the allowable 16 per cent threshold. In 1986, this share rose to roughly 12 per cent following the acquisition of the ailing Continental Bank by British-controlled Lloyds Bank Canada in October, and the Hongkong Bank takeover of the equally troubled Bank of British Columbia in November. In both situations, the government appeared, at best, ambivalent about the prospect of finding a Canadian buyer for these institutions. With respect to the purchase of the Bank of British Columbia, the government even went so far as to entice a bid from the Hongkong Bank (with a $200 million recapitalization promise) over the bid of the viable and regionally-based Vancouver City Savings Credit Union.

Approximately sixty foreign banks operate in Canada with total subsidiary assets of almost $40 billion. Of this number, one-third are U.S.-controlled institutions, with the $4.5 billion Citibank, a subsidiary of New York's mighty Citicorp, ranking second only to Lloyds Bank Canada. In general, most Schedule B banks derive their profits from wholesale banking and by working the upper end of the commercial lending market. These banks have tended to shun retail banking, despite its value as a source of low-cost funds and stability. Recent statements by Schedule B banks such as Citibank suggest that this too will change, once the Canada-U.S. trade pact has been fully implemented.

The Free-Trade Agreement

Chapter 17 of the trade agreement details the terms and conditions which apply to financial services. In this chapter, financial services include any service or product offered by a financial institution, with the exception of securities and insurance, the present trade arrangements for which are simply codified elsewhere in the agreement. Even a cursory examination of Articles 1701-1706 reveals the disproportionate benefits accruing to American financial interests. This was certainly the judgment of many in Canada's financial community upon disclosure of the final text, including Robert MacIntosh, President of the Canadian Bankers' Association, who said that "the balance of advantage (in the trade deal) is very much on the side of the American banks, because the United States has made no hard commitments." These sentiments were echoed by Cedric E. Ritchie, Chairman of the Bank of Nova Scotia, in a letter to the Business Council on National Issues in November 1987: "we [Canadian bankers] know what we are giving up, but what we get in return remains to be seen and probably would eventually be available in any event."

In Chapter 17 of the agreement, the government abandoned the principle of reciprocity — the very principle which it had previously held to be a crucial factor in determining foreign participation in our financial sector. This principle was stated clearly in the government's December 1986 blueprint for financial deregulation which assured "that non-residents' access to Canadian domestic markets [would] reflect Canadian firms' access to markets abroad." It is apparent from the text of Chapter 17 that these words carried no weight in the trade negotiations. Further, it can be argued that the government's side-stepping of reciprocity may well have sacrificed a considerable amount of Canadian sovereignty over our financial system and, hence, over our ability to regulate institutions in order to maintain their solvency in the interests of a sound and healthy economy.

Canadian Gains

Article 1702 refers to the commitments of the United States to Canada. They are modest indeed. In Article 1702 (1), the U.S. agrees to permit domestic and foreign banks operating in the U.S. and who deal in U.S. bills, notes and bonds to also deal, underwrite and purchase Canadian-guaranteed securities. While the Canadian Bankers' Association welcomed this commitment as a useful business opportunity, Mr. MacIntosh also noted that "most Canadian banks regard that type of business as of rather marginal profitability." Furthermore, 1702 (1) does not represent a concession by the U.S. — the Federal Reserve Board has always had the discretionary power to allow a bank to deal in the debt obligations of a foreign government.

Article 1702 (2) says the U.S. will continue to provide Canadian banks with that access to American financial markets which they held as of October 4, 1987. This provision "grandfathers" those operating privileges accorded Canadian banks under Sections 5 and 8 of the 1978 International Banking Act — privileges that otherwise would have been up for review. In effect, the status quo for Canadian bank activity in the U.S. has been preserved — no more, no less.

In terms of asset size, Canadian banks are presently more active in the United States than are the subsidiaries of their American counterparts in Canada. It should be noted, however, that American financial markets are ten times the size of Canada's, and that half of Canadian operations are confined to New York State. Canadian bank expansion in the U.S. is obstructed by interstate banking which gives state legislatures the right to prohibit or limit non-resident entry into their jurisdictions. This is the reason why Canadian institutions had little confidence in the government's power to negotiate an American federal guarantee of nation-wide access. While a 1986 U.S. Supreme Court decision will lift state-imposed restrictions by the early 1990s, it is expected that the large American banks and other non-residents will be better placed to take advantage of the open field than Canadian banks, simply because they are bigger and thus better placed to capture new business. The rhetoric of Chapter 17 aside, there is little in the agreement that assures Canadian bank growth beyond the current level secured under Article 1702 (2).

Article 1702 (3) expresses a commitment to give Canadian-controlled financial institutions the same treatment as American financial institutions when and if the Glass-Steagall Act is amended by Congress. For some time, American politicians have deliberated over the question of amending Glass-Steagall and associated legislation to allow American banks to engage in the securities business. Opinion is sharply divided on the issue. While, for instance, the U.S. Federal Reserve Board is in favour of amendments, New York regulatory authorities are strongly opposed. The irony of 1702 (3) is that, while Canadian federal and provincial governments have already thrown open securities markets in Canada to non-residents, reciprocal treatment for Canadians in the U.S. must await the outcome of a cumbersome and unpredictable American legislative process.

Because of American equivocation over Glass-Steagall, Canadian negotiators failed to obtain an American commitment to relax the prohibition requiring a Canadian bank which owns an investment dealer to close down the American office or operations of that dealer's subsidiary. This situation will create hardships for Canadian banks that recently entered the securities business and further preclude their growth in American financial markets.

Canadian Concessions

Article 1703 expresses Canadian commitments to the United States. These are, without doubt, the most substantive elements of Chapter 17.

Most important, Canada agrees to allow all U.S. residents to be treated as nationals when investing in Canadian-controlled financial institutions; American investors are exempted from those statutory restrictions that prevent non-residents as a group from acquiring more than 25 per cent of the shares of banks or federally-regulated trust and insurance companies. All that prevents an American entity from purchasing 100 per cent of the shares of chartered banks is the retained legal requirement that these institutions be widely-held and that no one individual own more than 10 per cent of total shares. Widely-held ownership is not required for small banks on a start-up basis, however, or for non-bank financial institutions with a capital base of less than $750 million.

Approximately five hundred small and medium-sized trust, loan and insurance companies will be open to foreign acquisition. They constitute a considerable share of Canadian financial markets. For example, while three large trust companies — Canada Trust, Royal Trust and National Victoria and Grey Trust — are responsible for most fiduciary activity in Canada, and are probably not vulnerable to takeover by a group of American investors, that still leaves almost one hundred other trust companies, many with important retail networks in Canada's regions, that are. This point was made by the Trust Companies Association in their response to the trade deal.

Article 1703 (1) will also permit U.S. exemption from Bank Act requirements on institutions loosely defined as "foreign banks" to obtain federal government approval before establishing a significant interest in a Canadian financial business. This will give large American non-bank financial institutions unprecedented acquisition opportunities and a chance to enter Canadian financial markets. Article 1703 (3) denies the government use of its review powers to block entry or acquisition on the part of these U.S.-controlled institutions.

While, as mentioned, Canada limits the growth of the non-resident sector to 16 per cent of the total assets of chartered banks, Article 1703 (2) says that Canada agrees to remove restrictions on the asset size of American banks (Schedule B subsidiaries). This provision of the agreement will enable an American subsidiary to seek further capitalization from its parent and compete on an equal footing with Canadian financial institutions. Once again, this is an unreciprocated gesture that will allow American institutions to displace other foreign subsidiaries in Canada, possibly inviting recrimination from abroad, particularly from European and Japanese financial institutions and investors. 1703 (2) also frees American subsidiaries to open additional branches at will and transfer loans to its parent.

Other provisions of Chapter 17 commit both parties to further liberalization of financial services and to extend national treatment to each other in that event. This is not mere rhetorical excess. The fact that the agreement cannot "be construed as representing the mutual satisfaction of the parties concerning the treatment of their respective financial institutions" in large measure means that the American financial community has further concessions from Canada in mind. These would include eliminating restrictions requiring U.S.-controlled banks to operate in subsidiary rather than branch form, as well as shareholder's equity requirements, lending limits and other regulatory standards observed in Canada. For U.S. residents, then, further liberalization amounts to moving Canadian regulatory policies closer to those of the U.S. system. Harry Freeman of American Express has already called for "some measure of bilateral convergence of...supervisory and regulatory policies." Such suggestions carry broad implications for Canadian public policy as Canadian taxpayers could bear the cost of institutional failures and bad debts extended across the border.

Financial services disputes are to be resolved by a formal consultative process between the Canadian Department of Finance and the U.S. Department of the Treasury. This means that the U.S. Department of the Treasury will have the right to challenge all large and small Canadian regulatory initiatives (administrative rules or policy changes), thus curtailing the independence of Canadian agencies like the Office of the Superintendent of Financial Institutions. When Canadian and American supervisors disagree about the behaviour or stability of a specific U.S.-controlled institution, Canada will be obliged to let the U.S. participate in national decision-making.

Taken together, the financial services provisions of the trade pact are likely to lead to increased American takeovers of Canadian financial institutions and an expanded American presence in financial markets. Once Canadian deregulation is in place, American institutions and investors will be able to plunge into activities denied them even at home. With American subsidiaries growing, individuals and groups of investors buying Canadian financial enterprises, and both American banks and non-banks using their financial depth and technological advancements to obtain a market niche in Canada, a large and formidable American presence in the Canadian financial system is all but certain. With respect to banking markets alone, Canadian financial analyst and former Bankers Association economist Solomon Sarpkaya has predicted that, by the year 2000, American banks will have obtained about one-third control. Of the remaining two-thirds, says Mr. Sarpkaya, one-third would be held by other foreign banks and one-third by those that are Canadian-controlled. For reasons of fierce competition and slow regulatory change in the U.S., the Canadian banks' share of the American banking market, on the other hand, should remain about the same as at present — 1.5 per cent.

Conclusion

It is in the interest of American financial institutions to take advantage of their new freedoms in the Canadian market. Federal Reserve Board Chairman Alan Greenspan and senior officials at the U.S. Department of Treasury recently endorsed regulatory reform proposals to encourage American bank growth as a prerequisite to more intense global competition. While in the 1950s all fifteen of the world's largest banks were American, today Japanese banks constitute the world's top nine banks and dominate the international field. The extent of the American decline in this regard is further demonstrated by the fact that only two American banks, Citicorp of New York and BankAmerica of San Francisco, now rank among the twenty-five largest institutions. The American strategy is to eliminate barriers to financial and commercial cross-ownership, and create five to ten "superbanks" that are strong enough to compete with the Japanese and Europeans. In North America, this strategy would include use of American subsidiaries as vehicles for growth, perhaps through a series of acquisitions and takeovers of Canadian-controlled institutions. For instance, with the aid of its $193 billion parent, Citibank would be in an excellent position to initiate the drive to a North American common market in financial services, dominated, of course, by the United States.

A trend towards more foreign participation in Canada's financial sector has grave consequences for the economy, particularly in

Canada's underdeveloped regions. Those sectors that traditionally contribute to jobs in the regions and that need funds for investment — small business, junior resource companies, farmers — generally have not been customers of foreign-owned Schedule B banks. As the Porter Commission pointed out, foreign banks serve non-resident shareholders; their first allegiance is not to the communities in which business is located. Furthermore, regions such as Atlantic Canada have already suffered from an outflow of capital as aggregate personal savings entrusted to financial institutions have been used to fund bank projects in other areas. In this way, a region's savings have not always been put to work at home. This situation is not likely to improve with a greater foreign presence in our financial system, especially during times of economic downturn when funds get transferred out of the country at an alarming rate. Because of its substantial investment needs, and its cyclical, resource-based regional economies, Canada could become, as is said in the industry, "red-circled" as a source of low and diminishing returns.

Rather than becoming a junior partner of American finance, Canada should consider alternatives at the multilateral level. Since 1961, the Organisation for Economic Co-operation and Development (OECD) has developed twin Codes of Liberalization: the Code of Current Invisible Operations and the Code of Capital Movements. These codes aim to cover a large portion of international transactions and payments other than trade in goods. The Capital Movements Code was recently broadened to include issues of non-resident ownership in financial institutions. The OECD codes frown on expedient, bilateral agreements that emphasize reciprocity and national treatment as opposed to a multilateral approach. The codes have made good progress over the years and Canada would have been well-served to have promoted that route to an open international environment, in addition to other multilateral efforts that recognize the need to manage and direct changes brought about by financial innovation and deregulation. Instead, the Mulroney government opted for continental financial integration that, in time, will surrender Canadian sovereignty over our most important economic sector.

15

Agriculture and the Food Industry

John W. Warnock

Trade in agricultural products between Canada and the United States is substantial. The United States is a major market for Canadian producers of live animals, beef and pork, while Canada is an important market for American producers of fruits, vegetables and oilseeds. Traditionally, the United States has maintained a favourable balance of trade with Canada in food and agricultural products, but this changed in 1985. It is widely agreed that the shift was due almost entirely to the 25 per cent devaluation of the Canadian dollar.

Both Canada and the United States have long traditions of protection and support for agriculture. But the approaches are very different. Canada has relied heavily on the marketing-board system, the general approach used in the British Commonwealth. In contrast, the United States depends more on direct financial aid to producers. It should also be remembered that farm income supports in the United States are among the highest in the world; on average, they are much higher than Canadian income supports. In 1986 the American government provided farmers with over $25 billion in the form of direct deficiency payments, price supports, quota protections, and so on. A list of American support payments to the grain industry is found in Schedule 1 of Annex 705.4 of the free-trade agreement.

Many observers were surprised that agriculture ended up being covered by the free-trade agreement. The difference between government programmes in the two countries, the seemingly intractable problems facing American and Canadian farmers and the fact that agricultural problems are international in scope argued against including this sector in the trade deal. But agricultural issues were on the table, despite the belief of many in the farming community that divergent views could not be resolved in the talks.

The Goals of the Two Governments

In the bilateral free-trade negotiations, the Mulroney government listed three main objectives: to gain more secure access to the American market for Canadian exporters, to liberalize trade rules in order to improve the existing access for both agricultural and food products, and to preserve Canada's traditional agricultural programmes, both federal and provincial.

Both the Mulroney government and the Reagan administration agreed that agriculture should be included in any free-trade agreement in order to provide a precedent for the current round of negotiations at the General Agreement on Tariffs and Trade (GATT). Currently, agriculture is excluded from GATT trade regulations and codes.

American objectives in the area of food and agriculture can only be understood in the context of the overall policy goals of the Reagan administration. The United States has a major balance of payments deficit which it is under tremendous pressure to reduce. In the agricultural sector in particular, the decline of American exports in recent years has been a serious domestic problem — between 1980 and 1985, American agricultural exports fell from $47 billion to $31 billion. The American government expects to help redress the problems of the agricultural sector, as well as the larger problem of its balance of payments deficit, by expanding the opportunities for increasing food and agricultural exports to Canada.

The goals of the American government in the bilateral trade talks were well known and appeared in a number of official publications. First, it wished to remove all tariffs in the food and agricultural area. Even after the GATT tariff reductions negotiated internationally during the Kennedy and Tokyo rounds in the 1960s and 1970s, the remaining Canadian tariffs in the area of processed foods range from 5 per cent to 17.5 per cent, roughly twice as high as American tariffs. The Americans were particularly anxious to see the removal of duties on potatoes and onions and seasonal tariffs on fresh fruits and vegetables.

The second major goal was the removal of non-tariff barriers to trade, both federal and provincial. Some of these are protections for the wine and brewing industries, provincial procurement policies and provincial marketing boards for agricultural products. The Americans placed a high priority on the removal of import quotas from the Canadian supply management boards — the Canadian Wheat Board, the Canadian Dairy Commission and the poultry and egg marketing boards.

Third, the American government demanded an end to various federal and provincial subsidies for agriculture and processed foods. These included provincial farm subsidy programmes, assistance to food processing plants, and freight subsidies under the Western Grain Transportation Act and the Feed Freight Assistance Act.

Finally, there was the question of the foreign exchange rate. A number of American farm organizations insisted that there had to be a return to parity in the two currencies. American farm experts were proposing a currency parity system similar to that which exists in the European Community, where agricultural prices are automatically adjusted when a national currency appreciates or is devalued. Politically, this issue proved to be too explosive. It was decided to put it off until the next round of negotiations, after the free-trade agreement had been implemented.

From the beginning, most Canadian farm organizations were sceptical about a free-trade agreement with the United States. There seemed little to be gained in the American market and there was the possibility of losing much of the Canadian market to greater American imports. Following the recommendation of the Macdonald Royal Commission, most farm organizations urged the Mulroney government to exclude agriculture from the agreement. Many of the individual commodity organizations asked that their product be specifically removed from the negotiations. The notable exceptions were the beef and hog producers who believed that they could gain a market share in the U.S. if the application of American trade laws could be softened as the result of an accord.

The Terms of the Agreement

The Mulroney government argues that the free-trade agreement meets all three of their objectives. That interpretation has been challenged by most of the farm organizations in Canada. In addition, *The Financial Times of Canada* and the investment firm of McLeod, Young, Weir both concluded that agriculture and the food industry were "major losers" in the free-trade agreement. This view can be supported by a closer examination of the specific provisions of the agreement.

First, it should be noted that the dairy industry has been excluded from the agreement. This is not surprising, as the income support systems in the two countries are extensive and politically very sensitive. Furthermore, in the short time-frame for the negotiations imposed by the 1984 U.S. Trade and Tariff Act, it was not possible to reach an agreement in this sector. However, the Dairy Farmers of Canada have asked that the Mulroney government expand the import control list to include products like yogurt, ice cream and liquid milk, currently protected only by tariffs.

Pork and hogs were specifically excluded from the agreement. The Canadian negotiators were unsuccessful in getting the American government to remove its countervailing duty on the export of Canadian hogs. Farm organizations and marketing boards representing Canadian pork producers have expressed disappointment that there was no real change in the trade dispute-settlement mechanism. All Canadian exporters will still have to face the long and expensive process of defending their industry against trade actions initiated by their American competitors.

There is widespread agreement that the central benefit to Canada in the area of agriculture and food is the mutual exemption from restrictions for beef and veal under meat import laws (Article 704). However, the agreement does not prevent the American industry from seeking countervailing duties on the export of beef from Canada. Western Canadian packing plants, including Intercontinental Packers, Gainers, Canada Packers, Fletcher's Springhill Farms and now Cargill, have all received substantial government subsidies. In many cases the purpose was to expand capacity specifically to serve the American market. This industry remains extremely vulnerable to countervailing action by the United States.

The Mulroney government pledged that the free-trade agreement would not adversely affect Canada's supply management marketing boards. Unfortunately, this is not entirely the case. While milk was excluded from the agreement, under Article 706 import quotas for poultry and eggs were slightly increased and so the ability of the boards to control supply and price for these commodities has been affected. Further, domestic pricing for wheat has been eliminated, and, under certain conditions, the Canadian Wheat Board could be stripped of its control over import licensing for wheat, barley and oats. Yet, despite these changes, the Mulroney government and the Trade Negotiator's Office argue that marketing boards are protected by the Agreement because of Article 710. This article states that both parties retain their rights and obligations under GATT Article XI, which permits the imposition of import quotas on agricultural products where there are government-supported supply management programmes. But in contrast, Article 703 pledges both governments to "work together to improve access to each other's markets through the elimination or reduction of import barriers." The American government has long taken the position that supply management marketing boards are "import barriers." At the annual U.S. Department of Agriculture Outlook Conference in December 1987, the U.S. Trade Representative, Clayton Yeutter, noted that they did not get everything they wanted in this first round of negotiations on agriculture. He singled out "state trading systems" such as the Canadian Wheat Board. Yeutter pledged that these "unresolved irritants" would be raised during the current GATT negotiations and at the next round of the Canada-U.S. free-trade negotiations.

At the recent round of GATT negotiations in Geneva, the Mulroney government chose not to ask for protection of supply management marketing boards. Indeed, the Canadian delegation has been supporting the Reagan administration's efforts to *remove* Article XI from GATT and its codes. At the Canadian Agricultural Outlook Conference in Ottawa in December 1987, Aart de Zeeuw, Chairman of the GATT negotiating group on agriculture, told the gathering that the Canadian delegation is openly "part of the group that want to completely eliminate the exceptions which...have been created for agriculture concerning quantitative import restrictions." There is certainly a fundamental contradiction between the position that the Mulroney government takes on the Canada-U.S. free-trade agreement and its negotiating position at GATT.

The big loser in the free-trade agreement is the horticultural industry. The removal of all tariffs on agriculture and food products includes the 10 per cent seasonal tariff on fruits and vegetables (Article 702). This industry, despite the 25 per cent devaluation of the Canadian dollar, is struggling to survive the low prices of the 1980s. The Mulroney government stresses that under the agreement (Article 702.1), for the next twenty years the government may reinstate the 10 per cent seasonal tariff if prices fall below 90 per cent of the average monthly import price as calculated over the preceding three years, and provided that there has been no increase in total acreage planted to the specific crop. This is the so-called "snap-back" provision. But it can only be instituted after five consecutive working days of low import prices and after two days of consultations. As the growers have pointed out, a day or two of low prices is all that is needed to break the market, and this provision offers no real protection.

The unilateral removal of all provincial supports for the Canadian wine industry (Articles 801-4) most likely means the end of the grape-growing industry in Ontario and British Columbia. The only hope for the survival of the wine industry is to import grapes and to reduce labour costs to levels as low as those in the United States. It should be noted that this sacrifice of the horticultural industry in Canada undermines the efforts by the federal and provincial governments to preserve our high quality agricultural land which is capable of growing high-value horticultural crops. Much of this land is close to urban centres and could well be lost to food production forever if it is turned over for real estate development.

The agreement also removes the subsidies under the Western Grain Transportation Act for all agricultural products going to the United States through British Columbia ports. This is the first time that the Canadian government has accepted the definition of a transportation subsidy in Canada as an export subsidy. The entire transportation support programme is now opened up to U.S. countervailing actions and similar action under GATT.

In a lot of ways, the most surprising part of the agricultural section of the free-trade agreement is contained in Article 708, which covers technical regulations and standards. The two countries have created a series of working groups to "harmonize" or "make equivalent" all standards in the area of animal and plant health, standards of inspections for the food industry, veterinary drugs and feeds, pesticides, food and beverage additives and contaminants, and packaging and labelling. The treaty defines harmonization as "making identical."

Many Canadians have questioned whose standards will prevail in the harmonization process. The fear is that higher Canadian standards will be sacrificed to meet the existing standards of the dominant party, the United States. Under the Reagan administration and its deregulation policies, American standards in many areas have been eased. For example, Canadian safety requirements for new pesticides are now more stringent, as are standards on unwanted residues in foods. The Saskatchewan Pork Producers Association has insisted that health regulations must not be relaxed in order to prevent the import of pseudorabies, a disease found in American hogs. But Annex 708.1, Schedule 4 (3) states that "Canada shall permit the direct importation, without quarantine...in the case of pseudorabies, live swine from the United States of America for immediate slaughter." This could be an indication of what we can expect from the working groups. Furthermore, once these standards are harmonized, they can only be changed by mutual agreement. This is an enormous surrender of sovereignty on the part of the Mulroney government. It supports the argument by former Secretary of State for External Affairs Mitchell Sharp and others that this bilateral free-trade agreement is just the first step towards a North American common market.

The Impact on the Food Processing Industry

In 1986 the Grocery Products Manufacturers of Canada and the Canadian Food Processors Associations surveyed their member companies on the possible impact of a free-trade agreement with the United States. The vast majority of the managers responded that they feared they could not compete because they had higher labour costs, higher energy costs, and they had to pay more for Canadian farm products. They predicted that under free trade there would be a net loss of jobs in Canada and that many American branch-plants would pull back across the border. Their members indicated that future expansion by Canadian-based food corporations would probably be in the United States. If they were to survive, they concluded that the Canadian dollar had to be fixed at $.75 (U.S.), interprovincial barriers to trade had to be abolished, and the Canadian food processing industry had to have the right to purchase farm goods from across the border.

Since the release of the text of the proposed free-trade agreement, numerous representatives of food corporations have been quoted as saying that they will be in trouble if input costs are not equalized with those in the United States. The plants most threatened by increased American competition will be the smaller, Canadian-owned plants in the more outlying regions of Canada. The large conglomerate food companies, concentrated in central Canada, have the best chance of surviving. The majority of these are American-owned.

As Jon Grant, president of Quaker Oats of Canada, points out, "there will be tremendous pressure on the Canadian agricultural community to reduce prices to compete against American products." The logic of the free-trade agreement is to pit farmers against food processors. As tariffs come down, farmers will lose control over sales to the food industry, and marketing boards will inevitably lose their ability to set prices as cheaper American imports move into Canada. At this point, with the income supports from the board in danger, the viability of the Canadian farming community is compromised. Indeed, this explains why the American Farm Bureau, the largest American farm organization, strongly supports the free-trade agreement. It believes that when Canadian tariffs are eliminated on processed goods, then baked goods, chicken, turkey, egg or milk-based products can enter Canada more freely from the U.S. and Canadian supply management will be effectively undermined, leaving the Canadian farmer to rely on the "mercy" of market forces.

Conclusion

The agricultural section of the proposed free-trade agreement with the United States conforms to the general direction of the agreement — continental integration. The overall aim of the negotiations in the agricultural area was to create a "level playing field," eliminating or harmonizing government programmes and income-support systems. However, agriculture and the food industry in Canada can never compete on an equal footing with their American counterparts because of the shorter growing season, lower levels of population density, greater distances for transportation, higher construction costs, and higher energy costs.

The experience of World War II demonstrated the need for any country to retain the basic ability to feed its own people. Canadian governments have recognized that the maintenance of viable farm communities and a food and beverage industry requires considerable support and protection. Furthermore, all provinces have recognized the importance of agriculture and the food and beverage industries to regional development and employment. While the bulk of manufacturing in general is concentrated in central Canada, the food and beverage industry is more evenly distributed across Canada, more or less following population patterns. These industries also provide many relatively well-paying jobs for women workers. The free-trade agreement, and greater reliance on the "free market," threaten this historic tradition. In the long run, free trade with the United States in the area of agriculture and the food industry can only result in greater concentration of production in central Canada and greater regional disparities.

PART III

Beyond Trade

16

Free Trade and Continental Integration

Mary Beth Montcalm

The Canada-U.S. free-trade agreement is seen by many Canadians as precipitating continental economic and political integration. And this view is correct. The deal will, indeed, hasten integration of the Canadian and American economies and, contrary to the Mulroney government's rhetoric, reduce Canadian political sovereignty. For example, it will severely limit, if not eliminate, subsidies aimed at alleviating regional disparities within Canada since, under the terms of the agreement, these can still be viewed as "unfair" trade practices and thus subject to retaliation.

Yet it is incorrect to regard the free-trade agreement as somehow *initiating* continental economic and political integration. This accord is the latest stage of an historical process underway for most of the twentieth century and especially since World War II, when postwar Liberal policies actively encouraged economic growth through reliance on American investment in Canada. To be understood, the free-trade deal should be viewed as part of the restructuring of international capital which, for the last fifty years, has simultaneously fostered continental integration and Canadian disintegration.

The End of a Dream

From the outset, Canada's existence was tied to the notion of an integrated economy based on an east-west axis and linked to a British metropolis. The political framework established in 1867 coincided with this early east-west strategy. The federal government, crucial to the dream of an east-west economy, was given the lion's share of constitutional powers and placed in charge of national economic ambitions. Virtually all important commercial and trade activities, such as railways, banking and wheat, were placed under federal authority. Montreal, possessing a port and strategically located for exports to Britain, was Canada's largest city and undisputed metropolis. The 1879 National Policy, similarly, envisioned a regionally complementary economy based on industrialization in central Canada, resource extraction in the hinterlands — especially the west — and export of staple commodities via an all-Canadian railway built to link the east and west of the country.

Over the twentieth century, however, the attempt to forge an east-west economy has not withstood changing international patterns. Early in this century, Britain began its decline as a world economic power as the United States became increasingly dominant. Especially since World War II, ties with the former British metropolis have lessened and Canada has been drawn into the American economic orbit, as the following Table indicates. Whereas in its early years, the Canadian economy emphasized staples (such as furs, grain and wood) bound for Great Britain, new staples (like oil and gas, iron ore, nickel and hydro-electricity) are oriented to the needs of the American market, and Canada's economic connections have shifted to the United States.

Economic continentalization has weakened the dream of an east-west economy. Today, provinces have extensive trade ties with the United States. Indeed, in some parts of the country, trade ties with contiguous American states are growing more dynamically than trade ties with neighbouring Canadian provinces. Western provinces have become associated with American interests through the oil and gas industries. The Columbia River Treaty and the Auto Pact strengthened economic ties between British Columbia, Ontario and adjacent states. Manitoba and Quebec have become interdependent with their

American neighbours through the export of power south. British Columbia relies heavily on the export of lumber and natural gas to Pacific states, and imports food and manufactured goods from them. Alberta's trade, reliant upon the export of oil and natural gas, is linked to the American midwest and western interior. The Ontario economy is highly integrated with those of New York and Michigan, and Quebec and the Maritime provinces have close economic ties with the New England states.

Canadian Commercial Exchanges (in percentages)

	Exports to			Imports from		
	Great Britain	U.S.	Others	Great Britain	U.S.	Others
1870	38.1	51.4	10.5	56.1	32.4	11.5
1880	48.3	40.6	11.1	48.3	40.3	11.4
1890	48.7	42.5	8.8	38.8	46.0	15.2
1900	57.1	34.2	8.7	25.7	59.2	15.1
1910	50.0	37.3	12.7	25.8	58.9	15.3
1920	39.5	37.4	23.1	11.9	75.3	12.8
1930	25.1	46.0	28.9	15.2	67.9	16.9
1940	43.1	37.6	19.3	14.9	68.8	16.3
1950	15.1	64.8	20.1	12.7	67.1	20.2
1960	17.4	55.7	26.9	10.7	67.2	22.1
1970	8.9	64.7	26.4	5.3	71.1	23.5
1975	5.4	65.3	26.3	3.5	68.1	28.4
1980	4.3	63.3	32.4	2.8	70.2	27.0
1981	4.0	66.2	29.8	3.0	68.6	28.4
1982	3.2	68.7	28.6	2.9	70.5	26.7
1983	2.8	73.1	24.3	2.4	72.1	26.0
1984	2.2	75.8	22.0	2.5	72.0	25.5
1985	2.0	78.5	19.5	3.0	71.6	25.4
1986	2.3	77.6	20.1	3.3	69.5	27.2

Source: *Canada Year Books*

The Price of Continentalism

The geographic restructuring implied by continentalism has meant that Canada has relied increasingly on investment by U.S.-based multinationals for manufacturing infrastructure and overall economic dynamism. Multinational manufacturers, however, disproportionately locate in the "golden horseshoe," close to the American manufacturing core. As early as 1960, 70 per cent of American subsidiaries were located in southern Ontario, and this concentration has led to the economic marginalization of formerly vital regions. It has also produced regional strains that have been particularly evident in Quebec and the west.

In consolidating Toronto as the overwhelming Canadian metropolis, and peripheralizing the once predominant Montreal economy, continentalism has seriously weakened the position of Quebec in Confederation. The consequences have included an increasing determination on the part of Quebec governments to ensure economic vitality in Quebec, not to mention separatist agitation in the province. In fact, Quebec nationalism during the 1960s and 1970s was far more the result of business departures to Toronto than the cause of this trend, as is popularly believed. Similarly, economic concentration in southern Ontario has strengthened the western view that the federal level is ineffectual, if not downright discriminatory toward the west. Investment decisions made by American-based multinationals, such as emphasis on the export of unprocessed resources, have worsened the sense of vulnerability in the resource hinterland since they leave it exposed to fluctuations in world prices for resources. Not surprisingly, these provinces increasingly have resorted to provincially-based economic strategies aimed at ensuring greater regional economic prosperity.

In addition to encouraging economic concentration in southern Ontario, and thereby fostering resentment in other regions, continentalism has provided provincial governments with the scope for individually-based economic strategies by expanding the economic sphere falling under provincial jurisdiction. Whereas in early Canadian history the preponderance of economic activity fell under federal authority, the post-war linking of the Canadian and American economies has expanded the provincial role in economic policy-making. Canada's new staples, such as oil and gas, mining, and hydro-electricity, fall largely under provincial rather than federal jurisdiction, a power strengthened in the 1982 constitutional revisions. This sig-nifies Canada's move away from a national economic strategy towards economic policies directed by individual provinces. Realignment of the Canadian economy on a north-south axis and integration with the American economy have both diminished the importance of the federal level and fostered pursuit of essentially provincial and competitive economic strategies. Provinces have not hesitated to use their jurisdic-tional scope to attain provincial economic objectives, even to the detri-ment of both neighbouring provinces and, in the long-term, the Canadian economic union as a whole.

In fostering their own economies, provincial governments have used a wide range of tools. Provincial Crown corporations established for and oriented toward the stimulation of provincial economies, legis-lation discriminating against the economic interests of now competi-tive neighbouring provinces, and interprovincial barriers to trade have proliferated. Most provinces have preferential government purchasing policies that discriminate against products from other provinces and they frequently get into bidding wars (using guarantees of infrastruc-ture, government grants, loans or tax advantages) in order to attract private investment to their own province. This is a process in which the only real winner is the corporate, and often multinational, inves-tor; the major losers are the "have-not-provinces" which cannot com-pete effectively with wealthier provinces. Provinces also frequently export resources to American corporations at rates cheaper than they export them to neighbouring provinces.

Ironically, now that the National Policy has been abandoned and the balkanized Canadian economy is seemingly irrevocably linked to that of the U.S., the American economy itself is faltering. American industries are becoming less competitive in world markets, talk of American "deindustrialization" is widespread, several economic sec-tors are in obvious decline, the U.S. has become the world's largest debtor nation, and dynamism within the world economy has shifted to Pacific Rim countries. The American response to this situation has been to protect itself through the erection of trade barriers. Despite a rhetorical commitment to "free and fair trade," the U.S. has increasingly resisted its economic decline through retaliatory trade legislation. Canada has been both a direct and indirect target for an array of protectionist legislation emerging from the U.S. Congress. This trend poses a serious threat to the Canadian economy because of the degree of continental integration and Canada's dependence on trade with the United States.

While continentalism has involved balkanization and disintegration within Canada, it also has expanded the scope of activity of both the American and Canadian business classes. Although American penetration of the Canadian scene has long been noted, and in fact has, since the 1960s, been the subject of considerable debate within Canada, in recent years continental integration has involved more than American investment in Canada. In fact, during the past decade this aspect of continental integration has declined. Canadian companies in pursuit of the larger markets that changing international conditions necessitate have increasingly focused their attention on the United States. To circumvent the effect of growing American protectionism and as part of the continentalization of the capitalist class, Canadian businesses have become major investors in the United States. Canadians are, in fact, net exporters of capital to the U. S. and Canadian companies have become the largest foreign investors in the American economy. Today, Canadian multinationals are highly involved in activities such as real estate, construction, manufacturing and retail sales within the United States. While this dimension of continental integration has not altered the problems posed for the Canadian economy by continentalist trends, it reveals that many Canadian companies have become major actors in the continental economy.

The Road Ahead

To a great extent, federal and provincial stands on the free-trade agreement reflect the conflicting interests of, on one hand, the Canadian business class as a whole, and the regional elements of that class on the other. It is no surprise, for example, that Ontario, which historically has benefitted most from the protectionist wall erected in the nineteenth century, should be the most vocal provincial critic of the pact. Nor is it surprising that Ontario and Quebec should differ on the free-trade agreement since the Quebec economy, with continentalism, has become highly dependent on hydro-electric exports to the American market.

While not initiating continental integration, the free-trade agreement constitutes a further stage in this process and will worsen many of the problems already posed by the political and economic balkanization it has spurred. Furthermore, have-not provinces and Canada's labouring classes in particular, will be especially vulnerable in an environment subject to American definition of what constitutes a "level playing field." Traditional Canadian efforts to overcome regional disparities and existing social welfare programmes, for example, may well fall before pressures on the American Congress to protect American industries disadvantaged by Canadian competition. Yet continental integration is now so overwhelming that Canada's extraction from this context, and the loss of political and economic cohesion and sovereignty that it implies, will not be easy. Only a concerted political will to challenge market forces through greater economic regulation and planning, and a determination to preserve distinctive Canadian values, could support the scope of the task at hand. Nevertheless, the long-term existence of Canada depends precisely on this kind of determination.

17

Regional Disparities

Scott Sinclair and Michael Clow

The federal Conservative government has suggested that free trade will reduce regional disparities and usher in a new era of prosperity in the west and Atlantic Canada. But, in fact, the Mulroney-Reagan deal threatens the core of the economic well-being of the most "have-not" regions. The trade deal will hurt, not help, the great majority of people in the most disadvantaged region of the country, Atlantic Canada. There, it offers only minimal gains for the owners of a handful of resource-exporting companies. Understanding why this is so requires us to examine both the causes of disparities in Atlantic Canada and the nature of the economic deal with the United States.

The roots of Maritime economic underdevelopment and poverty are not located in the collapse of the pre-Confederation Golden Age of wood, wind and water. They lie in the combined effects of the takeovers of Maritime banks and manufacturing industry by central Canadian firms, and of the emigration of the region's most successful industries and banks to Montreal following the region's rapid post-Confederation industrial development. Maritime branch-plant industries, and the local factories of corporations who moved to Montreal, were run into the ground and closed down following the First World War. Meanwhile, the takeover of local banks and the exodus of the Bank of Nova Scotia and the Royal Bank to Montreal deprived the region of investment.

Incredible conditions of poverty and emigration were eased only by the federal government's decision, under public pressure, to establish the nationally-funded systems of unemployment insurance, medicare, welfare and other transfers of money to provincial governments for public services. Today, unemployment insurance is the basis of jobs in fishing, forestry and farming. "Good jobs" are those in government and public services like education and health. The private sector is largely a service sector dependent on government spending, while the vaunted resource sector provides a decent living for only a small, and declining, group of unionized workers. The Maritimes is still a land of poverty and hard times.

Newfoundland is a special case. The poverty of this island can be traced to the grip of St. John's merchants, such as the Bowrings and the Crosbies, who long held Newfoundland fishers in debt bondage and reaped the bounty of the sea for their own benefit. The later development of Newfoundland's mineral and forest resources relied on the pool of poor fishers eager for work. Again, the wealth was commanded by local elites or foreign corporations; nowhere did enough "trickle down" to ameliorate chronic poverty and unemployment. Only the inclusion of Newfoundland in the national system of unemployment insurance and the federally-funded expansion of services and government employment has staved off more miserable economic and social conditions.

When one realistically appraises the current state of the Atlantic Canadian economy, specifically the weakness of the private sector and the reliance on transfers and public services, it is easy to see that the promised benefits of the market-driven, free-trade strategy for economic growth have been wildly exaggerated. Worse, at the same time, the government programmes and policies which have made social and economic conditions tolerable in Atlantic Canada are seriously threatened by the agreement. Finally, the experience of the Maritimes in the first fifty years of Confederation is an historical precedent for expecting that the free-trade agreement will lead to a comparable concentration of ownership and centralization of industrial production — this time in the United States and at the expense of Canada as a whole.

Free Trade: A Market Panacea?

Free trade has historically been more popular in the hinterlands than in central Canada. The protective tariffs first established by the National Policy of John A. Macdonald in 1879 were fiercely resented outside Ontario and Quebec. While serving central Canada manufacturing, they disadvantaged the Atlantic and western Canadian economies. But it was the concentration of industrial and financial wealth in Canada, not the national tariff, that caused the collapse of the Maritime economy.

Free-trade supporters have been quick to capitalize on the divisive legacy of the National Policy and the pattern of economic development it engendered. "It is probable," the Macdonald Royal Commission concluded, "that the most significant long term effect of free trade would be...the removal of the most persistent and corrosive sources of regional alienation in Canada's political history...Canadians elsewhere in the country still believe strongly that the manufacturing economy of central Canada is being maintained at their expense." Business leaders such as Thomas d'Aquino and John Bulloch have echoed this sentiment. The prime minister, rising in the House to debate free trade, denounced the existence of "two Canadas, one which is rich and promising and one which is underdeveloped and underemployed."[1]

The prime minister's boast that free trade will allow the poorer regions to "trade their way to prosperity" through expanded resource exports to the United States is contradicted by the results of even partisan studies. The most recent analysis by the Finance Department estimates a very modest national gain of 24,000 jobs a year for the next five years and a once-only 2.5 per cent increase in national income. The federal government has quoted widely from a now discredited Economic Council of Canada report predicting a net gain of 350,000 jobs by 1995. But the council chair, Judith Maxwell, admitted recently to the parliamentary finance committee that new analysis based on the text of the actual agreement foresees only a minor boost to the national economy. All in all, even supporters' hopes for expanded "free-trade" with the U.S. are unimpressive.[2]

The predicted regional benefits of the agreement are smaller still. Maxwell concluded that there would likely be no "quantitative impact on regional disparities in this country." Earlier, the author of a wildly optimistic estimate of free-trade's impact, Queen's University economist Richard Harris, dismissed the prime minister's contention that free trade will redress Canada's regional problems as "bunk!" Indeed, the federal government itself argued at the outset of negotiations that "all studies confirm that Ontario will be the greatest net beneficiary" of Canada-U.S. free trade.[3]

The thinness of the evidence betrays free-trade supporters' appeals to regional grievances as patently political. Mulroney, d'Aquino, Premier Grant Devine, and former premier Peter Lougheed all paint "fat-cat" Ontario as the potential free-trade spoiler, frustrating the aspirations of the outlying regions. This baiting of Premier David Peterson conveniently ignores the fact that another provincial premier, Joe Ghiz of P.E.I., also opposes the trade, as do the two major federal opposition parties. And public opinion, though it reflects some regional differences, is more evenly divided across the country than on other divisive issues.

It is to be hoped that all parties to the free-trade debate will soon be candid enough to admit that opportunities for economic growth in the poorer regions of the country represented by the Mulroney trade deal are hypothetical and scant. In return, Canada has conceded control over many policy instruments important to regional development. Because of these concessions, poorer regions like Atlantic Canada stand to lose far more than they can hope to gain.

Even if they fare well, the resource-exporting industries of the region are too capital-intensive to provide many additional jobs. According to Statistics Canada, national employment in the resource industries fell by 10 percent between 1981 and 1986. And even if you believe (as the present federal government appears to do) that sound resource policy means to dig it, cut it, dam it, pump it, and ship it south as fast as possible, the free-trade agreement still doesn't make much sense. Most resource exports already enter the U.S. at low tariff rates or tariff-free. It is U.S. trade-remedy laws, especially countervailing duties, that have been used to harass Canadian resource exports. These laws have in fact been incorporated into the agreement (see chapter four).

Truly sound resource policy involves more than accelerated exports. Resource exploitation must be sustainable and benefits to the local and regional economies should be maximized. Currently, key sectors like forestry are already facing medium-term shortages of their raw materials. Furthermore, resource exports tend to follow the typical boom-cycle. The real challenge in the resource sectors is not to secure access to an already open American market, but to cope with the damaging effects of this cycle by retaining a larger share of resource rents during the boom and ensuring appropriate, sustainable management of renewable and non-renewable resources throughout the cycle.

This deal, by surrendering many important policy instruments — including the right to review most foreign investment, the right to impose local content and local employment requirements on American investors, the right to restrict the repatriation of the profits of U.S.-based trans-nationals, and the right to independent resource and energy pricing — greatly reduces the ability of Canadian governments and communities to challenge terms dictated by trans-national resource corporations and to ensure fairer returns to regional economies.

At best, the present deal can be expected, by eliminating remaining tariffs, to provide incentives for further processing of certain resources prior to export to the United States. This advantage will go disproportionately to large firms with the sophisticated marketing structure required to crack the American market for consumer goods. National Sea Products, a trans-national fish company owned by a consortium of Nova Scotia's wealthiest families, is often touted as a regional company poised to profit from further sales in the American market. Its president, Gordon Cummings, is a vocal promoter of the free-trade deal. It has somehow been overlooked that a few years ago this "lean and mean" international competitor faced bankruptcy. Only the infusion of tens of millions of dollars of public money allowed it to survive.[4]

The 1984 restructuring of the fishing industry was the principal irritant which led to the U.S. countervailing duty action against fresh Atlantic groundfish. In the end not only the Transitional Programs for the Atlantic fishery, designed to save the big companies like NatSea, but a total of fifty-one federal and provincial programmes, many of them important to the small inshore fisheries, where subject to countervailing duties. Special unemployment insurance rules for fishers narrowly escaped countervail.

As new rules regulating subsidies are negotiated over the next five to seven years, these sensitive issues will be reopened. The Atlantic fishery is an export-led industry and New England has always been an important market. But beyond eliminating already low tariffs this agreement provides no secure access. The best protection for Atlantic fish exports remains a high-quality, competitively priced product. Despite fear of American protectionism, fish exports have grown steadily over the last several years. This is because heightened health awareness has resulted in a sharp increase in per capita U.S. consumption of fish and poor resource management has meant that American domestic production cannot meet American needs. But the deal gives the Canadian fishing industry no greater clout in the American market. The leverage is all the other way, as the American government and producers are better able to pressure Canada to eliminate programmes to assist the domestic fisheries.

At worst, trans-national firms could decide, even in the absence of tariffs, to ship raw materials south for further processing closer to American markets. It is to prevent this that Canadian controls on exports of unprocessed fish, logs, and uranium exist. Restrictions on saw logs and Atlantic (but not Pacific) groundfish have, for the time being, survived the negotiations, but in most other areas, no new measures can now be put in place. Atlantic Canadian jobs will depend entirely on the investment strategies of trans-national corporations like National Sea, which already has processing plants in the United States. Once this agreement is implemented, Canadian governments will be unable to respond to disinvestment and capital flight.

Meanwhile, smaller Canadian manufacturing firms, like New Brunswick's Ganong or Nova Scotia's Stanfield, will face heightened American competition in their home markets. Not all the manufacturing jobs lost as tariffs are removed will be in Quebec and Ontario. Some of the most vulnerable industries, such as food processing, are quite decentralized and among the country's biggest employers. By eroding the already tenuous manufacturing base of the regions, the trade deal will increase regional resource dependence and dim hopes for diversification.

The deal also greatly restricts the abilities of both federal and provincial governments to regulate the service sector in ways which restrict American ownership or control (see chapter thirteen). In fact, services represent a greater proportion of economic activity in regions like Atlantic Canada (80 per cent) than in Ontario (68 per cent). It is in the service industries that most new jobs are created: national employment in the service sector grew by nearly 11 per cent between 1981 and 1986.

New advances in information, telecommunications, and computer technology make geographical decentralization of service industries an attractive possibility, but there is little reason to assume that this will happen automatically because of market forces. Public regulation and community direction will be required. Because this agreement ties the hands of governments in the service sector, any potential for decentralization and regionally balanced economic growth represented by the new technology will likely be forfeited.

If, as seems likely, the market benefits promised by free-trade supporters don't materialize, the poorest regions of the country, such as Atlantic Canada, will find themselves deprived of the benefits of many useful public policies without any compensating advantages.[5] The limiting of public intervention extends beyond resource management to investment, services, energy, agricultural support programmes, social programmes, and more. The effort to maintain national standards for public services has, arguably, been one of the most important achievements of Canadian regional policy. Much remains to be done, but free trade threatens progress to date. Greater mobility of capital within North America will give business greater clout in its effort to decrease its tax burdens and to curb social programmes and public spending. The poorer regions will feel the squeeze most.

Extending Equality in Canada

In a series of legal challenges the United States has clearly demonstrated that it rejects the legitimacy of Canadian regional development programmes. In two recent countervailing duty cases (against softwood lumber and fresh Atlantic groundfish) monies spent under virtually the entire gamut of Canadian regional development programmes were judged to be illegal subsidies under American trade law. Among those programmes countervailed were Industrial and Regional Development Programs (IRDP), Regional Development In-

centives, Agricultural and Rural Development Agreements, the P.E.I.
Comprehensive Development Plan, Economic and Regional Development Agreements, and the Community Industrial Adjustment Program.
The history of American objections goes back to the early 1970s when
regional development assistance to Nova Scotia's Michelin Tire operations resulted in countervailing duties.

Even before the current negotiations, federal policy-makers
reacted to American criticism. American trade law distinguishes between "generally available" and "specific" subsidies. Although the application of trade law is ad hoc and discretionary, the former
programmes are viewed more favourably than the latter. In 1982, when
the Department of Regional Economic Expansion (DREE) was
abolished, the industrial incentives system was overhauled to try to
conform to American trade law. One result is that, since that time, the
lion's share of incentives has gone to the industrial heartland of the
country. In 1984 to 1985, the Department of Regional Industrial Expansion, DREE's successor, directed 41.8 per cent of the IRDP budget
to Ontario while the four Atlantic provinces combined were allocated
just 17.8 per cent.[6]

Canadian federal officials' response to the threat of U.S. countervail reduced the effectiveness of Canadian regional development
policy. Generally available programmes — that is, programmes open
to all eligible applicants — are poor tools for regional development.
Most assistance goes to the most highly developed regions, simply because that is where the greatest number of applicants will be found.
Ironically, the effort to escape U.S. countervail was unsuccessful. In
April 1986 the U.S. Department of Commerce ruled that monies spent
under the Industrial and Regional Development Programs were
countervailable subsidies.

According to provincial officials, the federal Conservative government is very reluctant to approve regional development spending in
sectors that it considers sensitive to Canada-U.S. trade relations. It will
not, for example, readily approve programmes which would increase
existing Canadian capacity in forestry or the fishery. The free-trade
thrust ties Canadian policy-makers even more closely to American
concerns, even where such concerns handicap regional economic
development policy. One wonders what recently created agencies, like

the Atlantic Canada Opportunities Agency, will be safe to do within such a constricting framework.

Given the strength of American objections, it is hard to agree with the federal government's contention, as noted in the agreement, that "Canada's capacity to pursue regional development and social programmes remains unimpaired. Indeed, it has been strengthened." Regional development programmes are not protected in this deal, and the possibility that they can be protected in ongoing negotiations with the U.S. is remote.

The agreement does not deal specifically with regional development programmes. Instead, Article 1907 calls for the two countries to develop, over the next five to seven years, a new system of rules and disciplines concerning the use of government subsidies. If Canada and the U.S. fail to reach agreement on a substitute system within seven years, Article 1906 provides that either party can terminate the agreement on six-months notice.

The Mulroney government is trying to convince the Canadian public that the bilateral review of U.S. trade laws is an improvement over unilateral action by the United States. The problem, however, is not the application of U.S. trade laws, but the laws themselves. Unfair laws, even if "impartially applied," remain unfair.

Supposedly, one of the main objectives of the Canadian government in entering free-trade negotiations was to arrive at a common, legally binding definition of subsidy which would protect Canadian regional development, as well as social, cultural, and other programmes described by the prime minister as the "essence of Canada." The American side stuck to proposals that would have effectively eliminated Canadian regional development programmes. Since no acceptable agreement could be reached, the whole question of subsidies was put off.

There is no reason to believe that the American position on regional development programmes will change during future negotiations on subsidies. Because Canada has already given up so much on energy, investment, and services, the Canadian bargaining position will be even weaker. In addition, Canada is required under the agreement to participate in binational panels limited merely to reviewing the application of U.S. trade laws. This will implicate Canada in the enforcement of these unfair laws. Canada's representatives will be, in effect, putting a stamp of approval on U.S. trade laws. These rulings will be rendered even as negotiations regarding subsidies proceed. The interaction between binational dispute settlement, which limits Canadian representatives to enforcing U.S. law, and ongoing negotiations, which pit us against a power ten times Canada's size, will further undermine Canada's defence of its distinctive regional development, social, and other public programmes.

To date, the actual financial impact of U.S. countervailing duties against Canadian regional development programmes has been slight. For example, in the groundfish case the total countervailing duty attributable to explicit regional development programmes was just 0.882 per cent, only a small portion of the 5.82 per cent total duty levied. It is principles that are at stake. The U.S. does not accept the legitimacy of these programmes which are part of the fabric of the Canadian way of life. The possibility that the Canadian government might in the near future accept, or be compelled to accept, a bilateral agreement on subsidies that would strictly limit regional development programmes is a more serious threat to these programmes than U.S. countervail itself.

Because it was an American priority, one of the few areas where Canada and the U.S. agreed on rules governing subsidies concerned military spending. Governments will be free to intervene as they wish where public spending can be justified on national security grounds. Article 2003 exempts direct or indirect military spending from the agreement. As other avenues are closed off, the risk is that Canadian governments will resort increasingly to military spending as an instrument of regional policy. The agreement gives the Canadian government considerable latitude to increase directed defence procurement and to subsidize defence-related production as it implements the ambitious military buildup set forth in the recent White Paper on Defence.[7]

Prior to the signing of the agreement, Donald Macdonald and other prominent supporters of free trade argued that Canadian regional development programmes could be protected through a trade-off recognizing the U.S. right to subsidize the military and Canada's right to promote regional development. Not all American military procurement is subject to open bidding procedures. A significant portion of U.S. military purchases and contracts are reserved for minorities and small business interests through so-called "set asides." These programmes are used to develop new industry and promote minority rights. Though the deal is silent about Canadian regional development programmes, set asides on behalf of American and minority and small businesses are explicitly exempted (Annex 1304.3, General Notes).

The goals of the American set asides and Canadian regional development programmes — to create employment for the jobless and to stimulate economic growth in disadvantaged areas — are not dissimilar. But the means certainly are. Because military spending is capital-intensive, it creates far fewer jobs than investment in civilian sectors of the economy. Initially, many companies that take advantage of government financial assistance may be filling Canadian national defence contracts. But if these plants are to sustain production and employment they must turn to the export market. In the last three years, Canadian arms exports have tripled as the federal government promoted foreign sales more vigorously, loosened export restrictions, and changed procurement policies to encourage the manufacture of more marketable, complete weapons system.[8] As military production becomes more established, workers in areas of high unemployment will be confronted with an unsavory choice between joblessness and deepening involvement in the global arms race.

The freedom that Canadian governments will have to pour money into military programmes contrasts starkly with the discipline to be imposed on all other aspects of industrial policy by a free-trade pact. The federal government's Defence White Paper extols the potential regional development virtues of defence spending. There are already signs that military spending is being directed increasingly to Quebec and Atlantic Canada, traditionally the two largest recipients of regional development assistance. Litton Industries, part of a consortium constructing a low-level air defence system, fled from P.E.I. in the face of government scepticism about industrial benefits and strong public opposition to arms production. It found a home alongside Pratt and Whitney, another military contractor, in the new aerospace technology park near Halifax, N.S. Proposals to lure Thyssen to Cape Breton, where the company plans to build armoured cars for Saudi Arabia, have resurfaced. It is very likely that free trade will encourage Canada to rely more heavily on wasteful and destructive military spending as a tool of regional development.

There are serious problems with the regional development programmes which Canada has built up over the last twenty-five years. Industrial incentives to locate firms in economically depressed regions of the country have not proven particularly effective. More often than not, they have simply subsidized firms which were not linked sufficiently to the local economy and were consequently short-lived, or which were interested mostly in cheap labour or low-cost raw materials. But transfers from infrastructure, health, higher education and other purposes have ameliorated the lot of Atlantic Canadians even where they did not address the root causes of the region's economic malaise.

The U.S. has no comparable tradition of public policy to narrow regional disparities. The nearest it comes is with its military industrial strategy. The free-trade deal will give freer rein to long-standing American attacks on Canadian regional development policy. As the negotiations and increasing vulnerability to U.S. retaliation whittle down Canada's distinctive approach to regional development, an insidious result will be the militarization of our regional policy. We will move toward the American pattern.

Conclusion

Over the past century, competition within the framework of Canadian economic union between central Canadian and Maritime industry and finance has led to a concentration and centralization of wealth and jobs in central Canada. Competition and the market de-industrialized and underdeveloped the Maritimes. In the period following World War Two, demands by many ordinary Canadians to share in national economic prosperity resulted in a national system of social measures and public services that was particularly important for impoverished regions like the Maritimes and Newfoundland. Public sector jobs, welfare, medicare, and unemployment insurance became the basis of a regional economy that the resource sector alone cannot support.

The free-trade deal will encourage concentration and centralization of wealth similar to that which produced Canadian regions deprived of major industry and finance. Canada as a whole may well become a have-not region in the American economy as a result of the

Mulroney-Reagan accord. Shrinking employment will decimate the small and medium-sized business sectors, as happened in the Maritimes earlier this century. The Canadian economy will be "Maritimized." Without the need for Atlantic Canadian labour, or the means to pay for regional support programmes, the newly Maritimized central Canadian economy will no longer be healthy enough to finance the support measures that have stimulated the Atlantic economy.

Over the past decade regional support programmes have been eroded. Even prior to the free-trade initiative, Canadian regional development policy was in disarray. Despite twenty years of regional development efforts, regional disparities in earned income per capita have not been significantly reduced. Fiscal conservatism and ideological hostility to state involvement in the economy were reinforced by sensitivity to the threat of U.S. countervail. Funding levels declined. Much of what money remained was wasted on "fly-by-night" entrepreneurs or political favourites.

On the other hand, the political demand for regional equality and economic justice has not diminished. The commitment to equalize regional economic opportunities was recently entrenched in the Canadian Constitution. It is widely accepted that Canadians, whatever region they come from, deserve the same high quality of health care, education and other public services.

It is these sentiments, coupled with resentment of the relative prosperity of the Ontario economy, that free-trade supporters have tried to exploit. Upon examination, however, the argument that this trade deal is good for Canada's poorer regions does not hold water. Leaving economic decisions to the logic of the market, and the large corporations that dominate that market, will not redress regional disparities.

To question free trade is not to defend the economic status quo; there is need for change and especially for new approaches to economic problems. But it is equally important that in reaching a new economic consensus Canadians reserve the right to use whatever policy instruments are necessary to combat effectively regional inequalities. The resource-dependent regions need a balanced economic strategy that uses returns from the resource sector to diversify the manufacturing sector and strengthen public services. Renewable and non-renewable resources must be better managed for a sustainable future. This means a more, not a less, active public sector and stronger support for community-based and co-operative enterprise. The free-trade agreement heads in the opposite direction, reorganizing society and the economy around corporate bottom lines. It is a triumph of corporate logic over political democracy. The people of the poorest regions, like Atlantic Canada, stand to lose the most. To renew their commitment to redress regional disparities, Canadians must reject this agreement.

18

Free Trading the Environment

Frank James Tester

Asked by a reporter on October 8, 1987 if the environment had ever been discussed during the free-trade negotiations, federal Environment Minister Tom Macmillan made his answer clear: "...in the months that it took to negotiate the free-trade agreement, the environment wasn't raised." He added that the pact with Washington was simply a trade agreement and that it didn't really concern environmental matters. But this is a surprising statement, considering what many Canadians do for a living. Despite the Auto Pact and the industrialization of southern Ontario, Canadians elsewhere rely overwhelmingly for their livelihood on the exploitation and export of natural resources: timber, wheat, minerals, oil, gas, and increasingly, electricity. Resource exploitation of this magnitude has a significant impact on the environment.

The United States also had, at one time, natural resources in abundance. However, as the world's largest consumer nation, the United States has seriously depleted its own reserves of oil, gas, some minerals, available hydro sites and fresh water, and it is looking to Canada for new supplies. In the past, we have been only too willing to comply — water is the only natural resource that we have not yet exported to any significant extent.

Economic growth, based on increased exploitation of Canada's natural environment, obviously has considerable benefits for some Canadian and American interests. However, the costs fall on all

Canadians through effects on the health of the Canadian population, loss of property values, loss of access to and quality of recreational opportunities, and increasing costs for environmental regulation and control, borne through a tax system heavily dependent on personal income taxes. By fostering a market-driven approach to development at any cost, the free-trade agreement poses a serious threat to the environment which sustains us.

Standards and Emission Controls

The trade deal calls for a harmonization of standards, testing procedures and regulations between the two countries. Despite the minister of the environment's beliefs, these provisions directly affect measures to control environmental hazards and pollution. Chapter 6 of the agreement applies to technical standards. These include "technical specifications, technical regulations, standards and rules for certification systems that apply to goods, and processes and production methods..." (Article 609).

In some cases, U.S. federal air and water quality standards are higher than those of Canada. However, it is not merely higher standards that are important. It is also their enforcement. This requires both political will and the necessary resources, both of which are now lacking in the United States — the cuts to the budget of the U.S. Environmental Protection Agency (EPA) under the Reagan administration have not augured well for environmental protection in that country. There are also logical reasons for believing that harmonization between Canada and the United States will not produce higher standards. The creation of a larger market and increased competition will put additional pressure on the private sector to reduce production costs, including the costs of meeting environmental standards. The implications of free trade for public policy have already been shown by the Ontario Chamber of Commerce which, in December 1985, suggested that Ontario might have to relax tough new acid rain rules and other pollution laws to help local businesses compete with their American counterparts under a free-trade agreement.

It is true that the American courts are more lenient when it comes to allowing public interest groups to appear before them on environmental issues. This right, known as "standing," has been granted to American groups — and even Canadian ones in the case of cross-border disputes — even when the participants have not necessarily been directly and personally affected by the pollution in question. In addition, American law does allow individuals to sue polluters without fear of being saddled with the defendant's legal fees. Moreover, many Canadian environmentalists feel that the U.S. Freedom of Information Act is superior to our own.

Can it then be suggested that the Canadian environment might benefit from a harmonization of rules, regulations and procedures under the agreement? Will free trade help Canadian environmentalists acquire the same rights and privileges before the courts, and the same access to information, as American citizens? This is unlikely. There is no reason to believe that the Canadian legal system will change its position on the question of who can appear before the courts because of a free-trade agreement; this question of standing needs to be addressed by Canadian law. Canadian environmentalists also need vastly improved freedom of information legislation, but it is hard to see how a free-trade agreement will bring this about.

For too long, environmentalists have ignored the realities of the larger system within which the courts are located. Action in the courts concerning environmental matters often has more political value, in that it brings public attention to issues, than it does practical value in actually resolving the issue in question. Pitted against high-priced corporate lawyers within a system which emphasizes monetary values and property rights, American courts have been as reluctant to protect the environment as Canadian ones. While Canadians have, in some cases, been successful in using American courts to address issues of cross-border pollution, the results are mixed and the financial costs are considerable.[1]

Canadian environmental groups have some experience with American courts which should caution environmentalists against putting too much faith in the court system. For example, in 1981, Toronto's Pollution Probe joined in an action to force the Occidental Chemical Company and municipal, federal and state governments in the United States to excavate the Hyde Park dump site along the Niagara River. The dump leaks chemical waste into the Niagara River. They lost. In another case, the Ontario Government lost an attempt to address pollution from another Niagara River location — the "S" site dump.

Clearly, the results of trying to protect the drinking water of a majority of Ontario residents through the American court system have not been entirely satisfying. While standing can be obtained, the results of litigation and of participation in administrative or policy hearings are mixed. Free trade will do nothing to change this situation. In fact, it will make a bad situation worse.

In Ontario, where air-quality standards are a major concern, the Ontario government has recently moved to overhaul the province's air pollution regulations. This significant initiative, and new legislation to cut back on the discharge of waste into the province's waterways, are both jeopardized by the competitive, market-oriented approach of the agreement. Similarly, recent changes in taxation which address the amortization period for pollution control equipment could be threatened by the agreement (Article 603, especially (b)). In September 1987, Premier Peterson of Ontario announced $150 million in provincial loans which would cover up to 40 per cent of a company's costs in meeting pollution control regulations. Both of these measures could be regarded as an unfair government subsidy and grievable under the free-trade agreement.

In addition, Schedule 7 of Chapter 7, which deals with agriculture, commits the parties to work toward equivalent guidelines, technical regulations, standards, and test methods. Of particular importance is clause (f)i which calls for equivalence in the process for risk-benefit assessment — that is, comparing the monetary benefits to the monetary risks. This is a game which is stacked against the environment. The assumption behind the approach is that price equals value. But it can be argued that prices are set, not by society as a whole, but rather by those with the power and influence to mould and shape the market through advertising and control of the inputs to production. Market prices are, therefore, unrelated to intrinsic value. In risk-benefit analysis, values which are not central to a market (the content of which is determined by narrow business interests) are diminished.

The risk-benefit clause has important implications in the area of pesticides. The current Canadian system for approving herbicides, pesticides and agricultural chemicals is already far from ideal. A 1987 report by the Law Reform Commission of Canada called on the federal government to clean up its approach to the registration of herbicides and pesticides. It noted that, in 1976, Canada imported 117 million pounds of pesticide from the U.S. — as much as all of western Europe. It called for greater public access to information as well as a Canadian testing laboratory, and pointed to the need to re-evaluate pesticides previously approved on the basis of faulty research. In the United States, the EPA relies heavily on American manufacturers for the data it uses in approving herbicides and pesticides. Falsified data, questionable research methods and fraud have all characterized this approval system. For example, Anne Burford, President Reagan's first appointed director of the EPA, resigned after having been charged with, among other things, accepting falsified data which was then used in regulatory processes. Under free trade, Canadians could end up with the worst of two systems: a risk-benefit approach to product approval and no automatic right (and limited financial means) to be heard before American hearings approving chemicals which will affect the Canadian environment.

The harmonization suggested by the free-trade agreement does nothing to address the concerns expressed by the Law Reform Commission. Free trade makes it unnecessary for the Canadian government to establish a Canadian lab for product testing and toxicological research. In 1984, the Mulroney government ended funding for the Environmental Secretariat of the National Research Council, the only programme in Canada that produced internationally recognized, publicly available research on toxic substances. Yet the effects of many chemicals can be unique to the Canadian environment. In this matter, the free-trade agreement surrenders Canadian sovereignty to American corporate interests, with major implications for the Canadian environment.

While there are many serious problems with the Canadian system, it is underpinned by a concern for human health. Theoretically, pesticides and chemicals which can be shown to be detrimental to human health are not to be approved. The system is not without flaws. In 1987, for example, the lifting of a federal ban on 2,4-D while health data were being reviewed allowed the province of Ontario to approve new products containing the controversial weed-killer. On the other hand, a recently extended Canadian ban on the use of alachlor — an agricultural herbicide — despite arguments that the economics of the ban warranted reconsidering the chemical's use, illustrates the point that health criteria, in the Canadian system, can count more than supposed "economic" benefits.

However, in the American system, such substances could be approved if it could be shown that the benefits of doing so outweighed the costs. In fact, at the alachlor hearing, the manufacturer argued that the decision should be made on the basis of risk-benefit analysis. Obviously the multinational chemical company believed it had something to gain from adopting the American approach. And, unfortunately, Canadians appear to be moving in the direction of risk-benefit analysis. The University of Waterloo has in place an Institute for Risk Research which researches and does risk-benefit analysis. Sponsors of the Institute's work have included the Department of Health and Welfare, the Department of Transport, the Mining Association of Canada and Procor Ltd. of Canada, a chemical firm. The federal government has also withdrawn financial support for a toxicology research centre at the University of Guelph. Under free trade, the move from health-based assessment to the flawed risk-benefit analysis could be further promoted, with disastrous consequences for human health and the Canadian environment.

Toxic-Waste Disposal

Perhaps the most significant problem faced by modern industrial society is the disposal of waste. Not surprisingly, industrial and domestic wastes have grown in volume and complexity parallel to the growth of North American economies since World War II. New products and technologies have produced new and increasingly hazardous wastes. The United States currently faces major problems in the disposal of domestic and industrial waste — including wastes created by the nuclear fuel cycle. The free-trade agreement does not address this issue directly. However, with the continentalism it promotes, Canada runs the risk of becoming a major dumping ground for American toxic wastes.

The reasons are straightforward. Since the American government implemented tough new waste-control measures, the costs of handling toxic and other wastes have increased and the options available to

American firms have decreased. Canada is seen as having vast, uninhabited areas where wastes can be processed, buried or stored without engendering the wrath, or endangering the health, of Americans. The result, since 1980, has been a tenfold increase in bids by American companies wishing to dump waste in Canada.[2] For nuclear wastes, the geology of the Canadian Shield is regarded by many Canadian and American experts as being ideally suited to the disposal of these materials. A role as a major disposer of nuclear wastes is one possibility for Eldorado Nuclear Ltd., given the desire of the federal government to privatize it and the need for the corporation to diversify to a firmer economic base. Finally, the volumes of some wastes generated in Canada are too small to make the development of toxic-waste disposal facilities economical. However, with the addition of American wastes, economy of scale can be achieved. Free trade encourages the development and use of Canadian facilities for the disposal of American wastes.

American attempts to handle its nuclear waste by-products have been beset with problems. Located at Carlsbad, New Mexico, the first American underground nuclear-waste site, costing $700 million, has developed leaks that likely make it inoperable. The site was designed to store plutonium from the manufacture of bombs, but leaking water could result in the contamination of aquifers and rivers in the area. These recent developments, and the continentalism encouraged by free trade, are likely to increase joint ventures between Canadian nuclear concerns and the U.S. Department of Energy, with an eye to finding alternative possibilities for disposal in the Canadian Shield.

The province of Ontario is already a net importer of hazardous wastes, according to the Ontario Environment Ministry. In the first half of 1987, Ontario imported nearly three times the weight of hazardous waste that it exported to the United States. While current bilateral arrangements allow the Canadian government to stop shipment of any wastes to which it objects, few applications are opposed. The EPA has indicated that most companies apply to ship wastes to Canada because it is economically beneficial to them. Under free trade, Canada cannot place a surtax on hazardous materials being imported into the country.

An American company which currently operates an offshore incinerator ship in Europe — Chemical Waste Management Inc. of Illinois — applied to the Canadian government in 1987 for a permit to incinerate wastes off Maritime coasts in Canadian waters. The off-shore incineration of waste in Europe and the United States has met with considerable opposition and American companies are clearly looking to Canada as a possible alternative. Canada does have wastes that could be disposed of by off-shore incineration, notably oils containing PCBs. It is likely that American companies regard the Canadian offshore waters as having real potential for this form of waste disposal. Much of Canada's maritime coastline is thinly populated and opposition is likely to be much less than from the considerable populations of coastal regions in Europe and the United States.

Water

On November 5, 1987, federal Environment Minister Tom Macmillan announced that large-scale exports of Canadian water would not be government policy. This announcement was intended to address growing fears that Americans are looking to Canada as a potential source of badly needed fresh water. But the policy announcement was not accompanied by any specific suggestions for legislative change. Without legislation to back up this policy, there is little to stop the government from changing the policy once the free-trade deal is secured.

Canadian environmentalists have good reason to fear that American interests are eyeing Canadian water.[3] Policies come and policies go. Simon Reisman, prior to being appointed the government's free-trade negotiator, was associated with GRANDCO. This consortium has in place a fantastic scheme for exploiting the fresh water pouring into James Bay. The consortium is made up of Bechtel Canada Ltd.; Underwood McLellan; the UMA Group of Calgary; two Montreal companies, SNC and Rousseau; and Sauvé and Warren Inc. These companies include principals who are, or who represent, some of the most powerful industrial leaders in the country, with excellent connections to the Conservative Party. The $100 billion GRANDCO scheme involves building a coffer dam 160 kilometres across James Bay, flooding it with fresh water and using 10,000 megawatts of power generated by Atomic Energy of Canada reactors to pump it 650 kilometres to Georgian Bay. Merely listing the possible environmental implications of such a scheme is a significant undertaking. Such a project would change the climate of northeastern North America and the ecosystems of James and Hudson Bays.

But the GRANDCO scheme is not the only possibility for transferring water to the United States. During the 1970s, the Alberta government built a number of dams on rivers flowing east from the Alberta foothills, including a dam on the Red Deer River. It is currently constructing a controversial dam on the Oldman River in the southern part of the province. Documents leaked to the Alberta NDP opposition make it clear that these dams could become part of a scheme to transfer water from the Peace-Athabasca system in northern Alberta to the south, and ultimately to the United States. The Peace-Athabasca delta is one of the most significant and sensitive biological areas in North America.

In British Columbia, schemes to turn part of the Rocky Mountain trench into a huge lake, with the water being sent south to arid regions of the American south and midwest, have a long history. The most recent scheme is a project proposed by the American engineering firm of Ralph M. Parsons of Pasadena, California. It calls for water to be diverted from the Yukon, Laird, Peace, Fraser and Columbia Rivers into an 800-kilometre-long trench and then diverted east to the Great Lakes and to the American southwest.

The Americans do need our water. The population of the American sun belt has more than doubled in the past twenty years. The resulting demand for fresh water has seriously depleted traditional sources. Houston, Texas, has depleted underground aquifers to the point where ground surface levels have dropped, taking parts of the city with them. In southern California, disputes have developed with neighbouring Arizona over rights to divert the Colorado River. All across the southern states, underground fresh water supplies have been drying up. States like Texas, Arizona, New Mexico and California have all come into conflict over dwindling supplies.

One other major problem suggests the likelihood of considerable pressure being put on Canada to export water to the United States. The states of Oklahoma, Nebraska, Kansas and west Texas overlie the Ogallala aquifer, a huge reservoir of water covering an area of about 22,000 square kilometres. Huge, that is, until recently. Years of intensive irrigation to grow some of the richest crops in the United States, coupled with other domestic and industrial uses, have left this massive freshwater aquifer in sorry shape. The U.S. Army Corps of Engineers has recommended that it be recharged with water from the Great Lakes. And the water-diversion schemes of the U.S. Army Corps of Engineers are legendary. The Central Utah and Central Arizona projects — the latter of which connects Phoenix with the Colorado River — involve hundreds of kilometres of canals and tunnels, many pumping stations and dozens of reservoirs.

Canadians sometimes think that schemes to divert Canadian waters are too grand, too costly and too far beyond belief to be taken seriously. However, the size, complexity and cost of already completed American schemes make one thing clear. Size, complexity and cost are not insurmountable barriers to Americans where demand for fresh water is concerned.

It is clear that, on both sides of the border, water is increasingly looked upon as just another resource. And despite Tom Macmillan's diversionary tactics, the GRANDCO scheme remains a favourite of Premier Robert Bourassa, who included a chapter about it in his book, *Power from the North*. The premier is clear. Water, like anything else, is an exportable commodity. While water is not specifically mentioned in the deal, it is not excluded either. And it would have been a simple matter to exclude it. Saying "no" to American demands for water will be difficult in the face of an agreement designed to promote a continental approach to resource exploitation. Given the tremendous need developing south of the border, it is unlikely that Tom Macmillan's much heralded policy will stay in place once the deal is concluded.

Forestry and Agriculture

For some time, American lumber interests have claimed that Canadian lumber competes unfairly with American lumber because Canadian provincial governments sell timber rights to forestry companies at rates which are too low. In other words, stumpage fees in Canada are inadequate. This is a claim with which Canadian environmentalists would agree.[4]

Forestry is Canada's largest earner of foreign exchange. The influence that forest companies have on government policy is therefore, considerable. Since Confederation, Canadian governments have been aiding lumber barons and the forest industry by practically giving them the country's forest resources. Canadians, unlike Americans, have never had a process for assessing the environmental implications of current forest practices. Only the province of Ontario has recently taken any steps in this direction. In British Columbia, the rape of the landscape continues without regard to environmental damage.

When the American government, pushed by the American lumber lobby, moved to place a countervailing duty on Canadian softwood lumber exports to the United States, its interests were not in ensuring that Canadian companies increase the amount of money and effort invested in proper environmental management. Their only concern was that Canadian lumber prices not undercut American prices. Unlike the United States, Canadian provincial governments subsidize the Canadian lumber industry by giving grants to forest companies for replanting. This is both a practice which amounts to a public subsidy of the private sector — a long-standing Canadian tradition — and a way of ensuring that some replanting of the depleted resource takes place.

In place of the American duty, the Canadian federal government agreed to levy a 15 per cent export tax on softwood lumber exports to the United States. In order to get the export tax removed, the government of British Columbia recently struck a deal with the American government, changing the provincial forest regulations. To get Washington's approval, the B.C. government agreed to end subsidies to the forest industry for replanting. Thus, the responsibility for replanting B.C. forests now falls on the forest companies. If the previous situation for replanting and environmental management was bad, the new situation is worse.

On another front, the number of farms in Canada has been dropping steadily since the 1940s while the number of hectares under cultivation has risen. In Alberta, the number of farms has dropped by about 40 per cent in this period while the number across the country has declined by roughly 25 per cent. The explanation is simple. Farms have become bigger and, increasingly, a corporate style of farming, intended to take advantage of economics of scale, has replaced the family farm. An attitude toward land and resources which, in the presence of market forces, concentrates on maximizing production has been encouraged. The result is a national environmental disaster. Soil erosion, the indiscriminate use of increasing volumes of herbicides, pesticides and chemical fertilizers and the misuse and pollution of precious water resources have all been the result of a national farm policy which focuses on maximum production and which "mines" Canadian soils and water resources.[5]

The Senate Standing Committee on Agriculture, Fisheries and Forestry, in a 1984 report entitled *Soil at Risk, Canada's Eroding Future*, estimated that soil erosion costs Canadian farmers $1 billion a year.[6] A recent Science Council of Canada report confirms this figure, estimating that all forms of soil degradation, including erosion, salinity, acidity, compaction and loss of organic matter, cost $3 million a day or $1.3 billion annually. This figure represents an astonishing 38 per cent of current net Canadian farm income.[7]

Free trade encourages an intensified form of this type of farming by further subjecting agriculture to market forces. The methods and practices which are encouraged by the "logic" of the free-trade agreement include the use of more herbicides, pesticides and chemical fertilizers, lack of crop rotation and the fostering of an image of the farmer as a producer of raw materials rather than a husbander of the land and a provider of our domestic food supply.

It can be argued that the most environmentally wise form of social organization for Canadian agriculture is the family farm. Historically, the attitude concerning family farms was that they were to be passed on to sons or daughters as the means by which they might make a living. The attitude to land and resources was not that they were simply to be mined for profit in the short term, but rather that they were to be treated in such a way as to maintain their viability as a productive unit for future generations. That said, however, agricultural policies in this country have undermined the family farm since the late 1950s, when we became a major trader on international agricultural markets and federal policy increasingly treated Canadian wheat as a major export crop which would contribute to a rising standard of living. Free trade accelerates these trends. It encourages a form of agricultural production which is destructive of the environment and which is, ultimately, not sustainable.

And, finally, there is another free-trade related development which should worry Canadian farmers and those concerned about the Canadian environment. Bill 107, introduced in the House of Commons in early 1988, will give American multinational corporations effective control over the right to distribute seed in Canada. The proposed legislation helps them consolidate their control of the patents of strains of seed for important cash crops. These strains often require large amounts of pesticides and fertilizers to grow and it is not hard to guess who supplies them — large multinationals. The result will be an increased vertical integration of the production of food in this country and the promotion of a form of agriculture which, as is increasingly obvious, has disastrous implications for the environment. In this respect, too, free trade and a harmonization of the rules affecting multinational corporations like Shell, Union Carbide and Ciba-Geigy, spell slow but ultimate ruin for Canadian soils, water resources and Canadian farmers.

Energy

In western and northern Canada, as well as off the east coast, free trade is likely to be a stimulus for the development of energy "mega-projects" such as the Athabasca tar sands and frontier oil and gas. That this is the government's intention was made clear by federal energy minister Marcel Masse in a November 1987 speech to a Toronto energy conference sponsored by the American Stock Exchange. These mega-projects have serious environmental consequences, including profound consequences for air quality and ground water as well as disturbances of terrain that affect wildlife and waterfowl. In the case of offshore oil and gas exploration, the serious threat of spills or blowouts to marine ecosystems is a major concern — especially in the Beaufort Sea.

Article 906 of the free-trade deal enshrines government incentives to companies wishing to undertake large-scale projects. Though energy conservation may be the best way to address supply problems, the free-trade agreement provides impetus for a pattern of conventional energy development. Under free trade, the energy sector of the Canadian economy will be able to treat the government like an insurance policy, benefitting from market rules during good times without sacrificing access to government support when and if needed.

Along the eastern slopes of Alberta, free trade, coupled with increasing American demand for petroleum, provides incentive for increased exploration and drilling in environmentally sensitive areas. This is likely to threaten recreational land use and protection of watersheds vital to all of western Canada.

Environmentalists can expect an increasing number of conflicts like the most recent battle between the Alberta Wilderness Association and Shell Canada. The company recently launched a gas-well drilling programme in the spectacular Corner Mountain area near Waterton National Park. Once part of the park, this area had been designated a prime protection area. On the east coast, renewed exploration will intensify conflicts between fishers and the oil industry, such as those currently evident as Texaco Canada Resources attempts to drill on Georges Bank. In general, across the country, free trade promises to contribute to conflicts among Canadians about whether to conserve or exploit our renewable and non-renewable resources.

Chapter 9 of the agreement also covers uranium and electricity. Under the Canadian Uranium Upgrading Policy announced by the minister of state for mines in 1985, uranium ore must be upgraded before it is exported. The free-trade agreement eliminates this provision. The United States has also agreed to end its prohibition against the import of Canadian enriched uranium (Annex 902.5(1)).

Canada has the world's richest uranium deposits. For example, ore from the Cigar Lake mine in Saskatchewan is about 10 per cent uranium. By comparison, most U.S. ores contain about 0.1 per cent. While there is currently a glut of uranium on the world market, the quality of Canadian ore makes it particularly attractive to processors. Uranium mining and processing now add about $800 million per year to the Canadian economy. The most significant Canadian reserves are in Saskatchewan and the Northwest Territories.

One of the dirtiest and most hazardous facilities for the processing of uranium ore is the Kerr-McGee facility in Oklahoma. Uranium yellowcake from Canada, processed by this plant, contributes directly to the unusually high rate of cancer of local residents. Groundwater supplies have been contaminated with radiation, there have been serious leaks in retaining ponds and the company currently wants to dump over 100,000 kilograms of toxic uranium waste into the Arkansas River. In fact, all of Canada's uranium export contracts contribute to cancer rates which are rising, not only in Canada, but globally. The United Nations Scientific Committee on the Effects of Atomic Radiation — a very conservative body — has said that in the United States, every year of nuclear-power generation at 1980 levels condemns 1,300 people to death from low-level radiation. Other estimates are much higher. A free-trade agreement which encourages the Canadian mining of uranium for use by the United States endangers the health of Canadian and American citizens and contributes to one of the most insidious and deadly forms of pollution on the planet.

Article 907(c) of the agreement states that Canada can restrict imports or exports of an "energy good" — including uranium — if it is necessary to implement national policies or international agreements relating to the non-proliferation of nuclear weapons or other nuclear explosive devices. The agreement does not cover the use of uranium or other energy goods for other military purposes. The United States Navy is currently concerned that it may, in future, not be able to secure necessary supplies of uranium for its nuclear propulsion reactors. While Canada's current nuclear non-proliferation requirements prohibit the use of Canadian uranium to fuel military equipment, it is clear from the wording of the text that the United States holds out the hope that, in future, Canadian uranium may be used to propel American nuclear submarines and warships. Furthermore, this possibility must be linked to the current government's intention of acquiring nuclear-powered submarines for the Canadian armed forces. In this case, Canada's nuclear non-proliferation commitments are likely to change.

A third source of energy covered by this section of the agreement is electricity. Annex 905.2 of the agreement commits Canada to removing the "least cost alternative test" currently administered by the National Energy Board (see chapter nine). The environmental implications of Annex 905.2 — which will result in yet more hydro-electric projects — are awesome. The James Bay project, at a cost of $25 billion, was one of the largest construction projects Canada has ever seen. Initiated by Robert Bourassa in the early 1970s, it resulted in the diversion of major river systems, the flooding of an area the size of the province of Nova Scotia and major changes for the James Bay Cree which have affected hunting, trapping and fishing. Further, the construction of dams on the Canadian Shield appears, from recent research, to be associated with the presence of mercury in fish populations. In Manitoba, government scientists recently concluded that the harnessing of water is responsible for mercury levels in fish populations which are four times higher than the limits allowed by Canadian authorities and double the levels permitted in the United States. We remain largely ignorant about the long-term effects of dams and harnessed water in subarctic climates.

More dams on the Canadian Shield and the advent of James Bay II can only result in a dramatic increase in all of the environmental effects normally associated with hydro dam construction. The destruction of shore-line ecosystems threatens the survival of wildlife populations. Clearing for construction camps, access and corridors for transmission lines destroys hundreds of square kilometres of wildlife habitat. Roads provide access and open vast areas to non-native hunting and forestry operations. Large-scale harnessing of water changes local climates by producing the evaporation of water from the surfaces of large reservoirs. The weight of these newly-created bodies of water also changes local seismic activity.

Meanwhile, Robert Bourassa has been negotiating contracts with American buyers and recently concluded the sale of five hundred megawatts of power to Vermont. This power sale, and others, facilitated by a free-trade agreement, will allow Quebec to expand its hydro-electric system in the northern parts of Quebec. Similarly, there is reason to believe that more environmentally destructive hydro projects in British Columbia and northern Alberta will be given a boost by this agreement.

In eastern Canada, much electricity is generated by nuclear plants. In the United States, the construction of nuclear plants has ground to a halt, partly in response to the public opposition generated following the Three Mile Island disaster, but more directly, by costs. In the United States, the insurance costs for atomic reactors have soared and this consideration alone seriously undermines the viability of nuclear generation. In Canada, the federal Nuclear Liability Act, passed in 1976, limits the liability of nuclear power plant operators to a paltry $75 million. Meanwhile, Atomic Energy Canada Ltd. needs sales. In the Maritime provinces, the persistent need to boost the regional economy and proximity to the eastern seaboard of the United States suggests the strong possibility of nuclear plants being built on the Canadian side of the border to supply power to the American market. In Nova Scotia, the province's coal reserves could be put to use to supply generating plants built to meet American electricity demands.

For years, environmentalists in the U.S. have blocked attempts by Boston Edison Co. to build nuclear power plants on the American side. A $3 billion undersea cable was recently considered by the utility to import power generated from coal by the Nova Scotia Power Corporation. While the project appears to be foundering because of technical and economic problems, the intent is clear. Americans get the power. Canadians — in the name of construction jobs to replace those lost through the collapse of agricultural, food processing and some manufacturing industries — get air pollution, acid rain, spoiled landscapes and, in the case of nuclear plants, all of the hazards associated with the nuclear fuel cycle.

Ontario Hydro has recently been calling for the construction of more plants to meet what it claims is a growing provincial demand for electricity. Projecting demand has always been a risky business. But with access to an American market facilitated by a free-trade agreement, the risk of committing to additional power facilities — nuclear power facilities are favoured by Ontario Hydro — is diminished. The Canadian nuclear industry has been strangely quiet about how it feels about free trade. Canadians should be suspicious.

Conclusion

Ultimately, Canadian economic and social relations are tied to the environment. Our relationship to the environment provides employment opportunities and the resources necessary to construct social programmes and the quality of life Canadians enjoy. Free trade promotes a philosophy of economic growth and development which is ultimately doomed. We cannot continue to exploit the earth's resources in a never-ending binge of growth and development and expect the planet to survive. Even the United Nations World Commission on Environment and Development, composed of some of the world's most prominent politicians, forward-looking business leaders and advisors on environmental and economic affairs, was wise enough to recognize this fact.[8]

Free trade promotes a form of increased resource exploitation which is desperate, short-sighted and antiquated. It promotes a market-oriented approach to the organization of Canadian society which, as the past one hundred years have demonstrated, has dire consequences for the environment of Canada and the world. One can only conclude that the Canada-U.S. free-trade agreement, in comparison to the recommendations for just and sustainable economic development made by the United Nations World Commission on Environment and Development, is a giant backward leap in the dark.

19

The Impact of the Free Trade Deal on Work

Patricia Lane

Prime Minister Mulroney justified his free-trade initiative as part of his electoral promise of "jobs, jobs, jobs." But in January 1988, after the release of the actual text of the deal, the minister of finance could only claim that free trade would create 24,000 jobs in each of the next five years. This figure is less than 5 per cent of the 487,000 jobs which were created in 1987 in Canada. It is, in fact, smaller than the error factor in Statistics Canada's annual survey of the labour force. In other words, 24,000 jobs could be created or lost and Statistics Canada would not know about it, let alone be able to identify free trade as the cause.

The Mulroney government is now saying that the deal should be supported, even without significant job creation, because it will bring great economic opportunities for Canadians. This chapter will explore the nature of those "opportunities" and the effect that the free-trade agreement will have on the workplace.

A Changing World

From the 1930s to the 1970s a kind of social contract was in place in Canada. This social contract rested on a national consensus in favour of full employment, social programmes and a limited but legally protected right to free collective bargaining. The right to strike when a collective agreement expired was tolerated in exchange for prohibition of strikes during the term of an agreement; workers also gave management undisputed authority over production and investment decisions. Not all workers agreed that the trade-off was a good one, but it was the deal that prevailed.

In the late 1970s things began to change. Full employment became a thing of the past, as did constantly rising real wages. Conservative governments across the country cut back social services, and baby boomers gradually came to the realization that they were the first-ever generation of Canadians unable to predict with some certainty that their children's education would be better than their own. It became clear that, at least in the minds of business and conservative governments, the old social contract was dead.

The terms for a new social contract have since become the subject of a great debate in Canada. In the balance hangs the nature of work, and what it will mean for future generations to work for a living in this country.

Business argues that, in order to profit from global economic restructuring, it must increase its freedom to move capital from one location to another. In the workplace, this may mean contracting-out, or worse. Even profitable plants like Firestone in Hamilton shut down as business takes advantage of opportunities to maximize profits elsewhere. Corporations use capital-intensive technology to displace people, and defend the layoffs by citing the need to compete against low-wage goods from other countries. The same argument is made to justify demands for wage concessions and resistance to improved pension and benefit packages. Employers blame increasing surveillance and supervision of workers on globally induced demands for greater efficiency. Business groups pressure governments to privatize public services. The corporate lobby attacks existing social programmes because they cost too much. Corporations want lower taxes, period. In a word, there is a desire to complete the withdrawal of capital from the old social contract. This desire is manifested in reduced job security, higher unemployment levels, declining real wages, and a corresponding unwillingness to make investment commitments for a particular regional or national economy, unless encouraged to do so by tax breaks, tariffs, or other performance requirements set by government.

Workers have responded to these trends in unsurprising ways. Unions have sought more job security and layoff protection.

Employees have fought for retirement income security by demanding pensions indexed to inflation. Demands for substantial wage increases are being made across the country. Some workers have also begun to ask for a degree of control over investment decisions and greater industrial democracy. Among unionized employees, there is a national drive for a shorter work week.

Concern over the status of women in the workplace is also increasing. Workers are negotiating for pay equity, paid parental leave and real child-care options. As capital moves more freely around the globe, workers focus on their communities and their families. Men, too, seek parental leave. Employers are growing used to hearing demands for more time off in the form of vacations, leaves of absence for travel and education, flexible working hours and job-sharing options.

Government responses to this debate have taken two fairly distinct forms in Canada. Some governments have greeted capital's withdrawal from the "contract" with measures to head off a corresponding disintegration of labour's promise of industrial peace. British Columbia's Social Credit Party has led the way in designing a programme of legislative intervention which combines privatization and cuts in social spending with laws intended to weaken unions and promote the corporate agenda. Provincial governments in Nova Scotia, Ontario, Quebec, and Alberta, have also passed labour legislation which the International Labour Organization, an organ of the United Nations, has declared to be contrary to international standards regarding rights to free collective bargaining and freedom of association.

Federally, the Mulroney government is second only to the Vander Zalm government in its privatization efforts. It has placed a damper on wage increases by accepting high unemployment outside southern Ontario, and has attacked social programmes like indexed pensions. Its deregulation programme is well under way in the financial sector, where it promotes increased mobility of capital (see chapter fourteen).

There are also examples of a different governmental response. Some legislatures have assisted workers to negotiate on a more equal footing with employers. In Manitoba, the Pawley government introduced pay-equity legislation. In the Yukon, the New Democrats are on the verge of implementing "Yukon 2000," a programme for economic renewal based on local control, sustainable development and enhanced working conditions. In Ontario, legislated pension indexing is at least up for discussion while pay-equity legislation is a reality.

The governments in the first group share both a neo-conservative ideology and support for the free-trade deal. Those in the latter category strongly reject both neo-conservatism and free trade.

Profits Over People

The free-trade agreement will have an impact on this debate. First, it will continue the neo-conservative programme of neglecting employment issues. The "national treatment" provisions of the agreement will increase foreign ownership, buy-outs, takeovers, mergers and the number of large corporations. Recent Statistics Canada data suggest that this strategy is more likely to result in further layoffs than in job creation: between 1978 and 1985, employment in U.S.-owned firms declined and all the new jobs in Canada were created by small Canadian-owned firms, most of which had little or no export potential.

Not only has the federal government had to concede, in effect, that the free-trade deal will not create significant new employment, but it has also failed to address fears about major new job losses. On October 13, 1987, Finance Minister Michael Wilson predicted "displacements" of up to 500,000 Canadian workers. While he claims that workers who lose their jobs will only be unemployed for a short time, Wilson has not told us where the new jobs will be.

Many of the jobs to be "displaced" from agriculture, for example, are held by people living in rural areas, who are not perfectly fluent in either official language and who have few other marketable skills. At a recent forum, one industry representative who supports the deal declared that there is nothing to worry about, that new jobs will be created — perhaps in designing computer software. This seems an unlikely career change for a fifty-year-old Chinese or Indo-Canadian woman who now supports her family by harvesting broccoli.

Employment fields traditionally occupied by women will be disproportionately at risk. American firms supporting the deal are particularly anxious to have guaranteed access to our service sector which currently employs 90 per cent of women who work outside the home (see chapter thirteen). Women's jobs will be lost should American companies make the desired inroads, and the jobs that remain in this sector will be less desirable.

An Ontario study of the effect on workers of the 1980-1982 recession tells us that while 62 per cent of the men who lost their jobs were able to find new ones, only 38 per cent of the women were able to do so. When women did find jobs, it took them longer than it did men; while 43 per cent of the men had new jobs within five months, only 22 per cent of the women did. The study also reports that while men on average found new jobs at higher wages, new jobs for women paid less. Women tended to be further concentrated in traditionally female job ghettoes.[1]

Women, and the families they support (most single parents are women), have a lot to lose when an economic restructuring takes place. The federal government has made it clear that it does not plan to improve the safety net into which these women will fall, and that it is not prepared to expand existing under-funded retraining and relocation programmes. Women, older workers, those who live outside the major urban centres and those who lack fluency in English will have very little access to retraining possibilities. Their "displacement" may be very long-term, certainly longer than unemployment insurance benefits in many cases.

The problem of finding adequate replacement employment is compounded by the deal's underlying assumption that people should move to where the jobs are. In the United States, regional economies have generally been allowed to rise and fall according to the dictates of the market. In Canada, by contrast, we have often intervened with regional development policies designed to prevent the erosion of a community's economic base when it is threatened by market forces. Under the free-trade deal, the only form of government employment assistance to regions which will not be an unfair subsidy, and therefore illegal, will be military production spending.

Many workers who do not actually lose their jobs will feel the negative impact of free trade in depressed working conditions and wages. Once American corporations are freed of "produce in Canada" requirements — which brought their branch-plants here in the first place — they will have no reason to stay unless they can persuade their employees to make it worth their while economically. These operations will threaten to fly south if employees do not take benefit rollbacks in order to reduce the cost of doing business in Canada. For the same reason, workers will be hesitant to enforce safety regulations, even where they remain in place; and the most well-intentioned governments will be loath to beef-up existing regulations. Pay equity, industrial democracy, mandatory child-care, the right to scrutinize investment decisions, shorter work weeks, longer layoff notice — in short, all the issues now being raised by workers in the debate over the future of work — will take second place to the threat of capital flight.

Proponents of free trade argue that the deal will leave our resource industries untouched because we have had free trade in these products since 1912. They say the deal will benefit Canada because it will provide for security of access to American markets; but others, who approach the issue from the perspective of its impact on workers and communities, believe more of the same is not necessarily a good thing.

Forestry in B.C. is controlled by five large multinational corporations. In the last ten years they have laid off thousands of workers, polluted salmon streams, and been totally negligent in the management of the resource. Bitter strikes have been fought over contracting-out, wages have been depressed, and being a forest worker is still the most dangerous occupation in the province. One might expect a major government initiative like the free-trade deal to address some of these problems rather than to encourage companies to carry on as they have in the past.

The business side of the debate will also have its position enhanced by governments striving to design a legislative programme which makes the most of the deal. Article 102 of the agreement commits the parties to "eliminate all barriers to trade." Government actions or policies will be judged by their effect, not by their purpose or intent. What constitutes a "barrier to trade"? As Marjorie Cohen notes in her book, *Free Trade and the Future of Women's Work*, the president of the International Trade Commission in the U.S. claims that the public sector in Canada accounts for about 40 per cent of all economic activity, and that "such active involvement in the private sector has few parallels in the United States and consequently has been viewed by certain American companies as an unfair trade practice." This perspective calls into question virtually the entire spectrum of government programmes related to labour, employment and regional development which differ from those in the U.S. The analogy of the elephant sleeping with the mouse (ironically, first used by Mulroney) is an apt one. We do not hear Ottawa arguing that Alabama's right-to-work laws are an unfair subsidy. Nor did Simon Reisman complain of labyrinthine legal procedures, which keep most of the American labour force non-union, as an unfair government gift to industry. Anti-union laws, like B.C.'s Industrial Relations Act or Nova Scotia's Michelin Bill, may become a practical requirement of the "level playing field."

The management of health-care facilities is specifically included in Annex 1408 of the agreement. American corporations like Humana Inc. will be able to bid on administration contracts for hospitals, long-term care facilities and other care-giving organizations. Faced with an increased funding squeeze, governments will be hard pressed not to award the contract to the lowest bidder. We can therefore expect increased privatization, depression of wages, more part-time work in place of full-time employment, and an undermining of delivery standards in the health-care sector.

Medical laboratories are also eligible for national treatment under the deal. There are already serious public policy concerns about profit-taking at the expense of government-run medical insurance plans, which occurs when medical labs are run by the private sector. CBC's "Sunday Morning" recently documented the deterioration in California and Washington of the quality of cervical cancer pap smear tests caused by private sector competition. The pap smear is a safe, simple procedure for the early detection of cervical cancer, administered annually to most Canadian women of childbearing age. Early detection of the cancer virtually assures successful treatment; without it, infertility or death may result. In the United States, pap smears are screened in a variety of ways. Some are done in public hospitals where salaried workers take a high degree of care with each tissue specimen. However, companies like American Cytogenics Inc. operate huge "pap mills" like the one in North Hollywood which pays workers 80 cents a slide to process as many as 160 slides a day. (The State of California recommends a maximum of 75 a day for reasons of quality control.) Piecework and double shifts characterise the industry. Error rates are as high as 25 per cent.

What does this mean for Canada? Simply, if American companies can operate freely in Canada, public labs will be under great pressure to decrease their costs, resulting in depressed wages and poor working conditions for lab employees and a threat to the health of millions of women.

Conclusion

Working people in Canada are engaged in a discussion with each other and with their employers and governments about what their workplaces should look like in the future. Issues like provision of decent living standards for retired seniors, the creation of real child-care options, and the development of resources for the constant learning that a society in transition requires, are being raised by workers and discussed and debated in lunchrooms, legislative assemblies and at bargaining tables across this country. Corporations, too, are raising issues. Their agenda would enable them to respond to the global economic restructuring by playing off one government against another and would permit them to operate in Canada with many fewer obligations to workers or communities than they now have. The Mulroney-Reagan free-trade deal will give the microphone, the platform, the podium and the auditorium to the business side of the debate for years to come.

20

Reading Between the Lies: Culture and the Free-Trade Agreement

Susan Crean

For something that was not supposed to be part of the free-trade deal at all, culture has a large and pervasive presence in the text of the final agreement between Canada and the United States. It has been given special treatment and is mentioned mainly by way of exceptions to the new rules, but it most assuredly has not been left out. This is not surprising. Anyone who has been following the trade talks attentively, or is aware of the history of Canada-U.S. cultural relations, knows that the Americans are intensely interested in culture — always have been — and will not be persuaded to set it aside. Moreover, they have a number of scores to settle with Canada, and so far as their negotiators were concerned, these were always on the agenda and part of the talks. Only the Canadian representatives were willing to pretend otherwise.

The Deal

From the outset of the free-trade talks, the concern about the effects of the deal on the cultural sector, and its impact on our freedom to make cultural policy for ourselves, has been answered by the Mulroney government in two ways: with protestations that Canadian cultural sovereignty will remain inviolate, and, when that failed to convince the cultural community, with an undertaking to keep the cultural industries off the bargaining table. Had either promise been kept there would presumably be nothing to say on the matter, and no interpretation necessary. This chapter could begin and end with a recitation of Article 2005 which reads:

> 1. Cultural industries are exempt from the provisions of this Agreement except as specifically provided in Article 401 (Tariff Elimination), paragraph 4 of Article 1607 (divestiture of an indirect acquisition) and Articles 2006 and 2007 of this chapter.

> 2. Notwithstanding any other provision of the Agreement, a Party may take measure of equivalent commercial effect in response to action that would have been inconsistent with this Agreement but for paragraph 1.

Leaving aside, for the moment, the question of how exempt the exemption is, we can begin with the exceptions, which are fourfold. First, the cultural industries — defined as book, magazine and newspaper publishing, film and video, audio and video recording, music publication and radio and television broadcasting — will be subject in the same way as other industries to tariff elimination. This means that the last remaining duties on recordings and printed matter imported into Canada will be removed. Second, in the event that a cultural enterprise located in Canada is acquired indirectly by American interests, and following a review under the Investment Canada Act a divestiture is requested by the Canadian government, the agreement states that Canada must offer to purchase the company from its American owners "at a fair, open market value, as determined by an independent, impartial assessment." Third, Canada has agreed to recognize copyright in the retransmission of television programming by cable, something the Americans have been agitating for since amending their Copyright Act in 1978. Whether the original transmission was intended for free, over-the-air reception by the general public or not (as in the case of pay television and other specialty service channels), permission must be sought and payment made to the copyright holders. Canada has undertaken to make the necessary legislative amendments and to have a repayment scheme in place by 1990. Fourth, the Print-in-Canada requirement of the Income Tax Act will be repealed so it will no longer be necessary for publications to be printed in this country in order for advertisers to claim legitimately the cost of advertising space as a deduction against income.

These exemptions are significant and revealing. By the first, the tariff protection — which along with the 30 per cent Canadian content ruling for AM radio allowed the Canadian recording industry to take root in a hostile environment — will be abolished seven years ahead of the gradual phasing-out that is already underway. In addition to the immediate effect the loss of the 11.8 per cent tariff will have on jobs and original production in this sector, there is the principle to consider. Although few tariffs now remain in the cultural area they are never-theless a standard means for a country to ensure indigenous produc-tion (especially critical when the "products" are works of the collective imagination). Without a backward glance — and with no forward thinking about what our culture, including the cultural industries, may need in the future — we have renounced tariffs as an instrument of public policy.

This makes the next exception all the more curious, for it suggests that the Canadian government is preparing to move in a completely new direction, breaking ground in policy terms and, for that matter, ap-parently breaking its own commitment to privatization by introducing public ownership in the mass media. Outside of the CBC and Nation-al Film Board (and more recently, provincial educational broadcast-ing), public ownership has not been pursued in this country as a means of Canadianizing the media. Public subsidy and regulation have been the options preferred, partly because they maintain a hands-off relationship between the state and culture. It is hard to believe that the Mulroney government is serious here, and we will have to wait for the other Gucci loafer to drop to discover what it intends to do with the cultural firms acquired in this manner, if indeed it envisages making such acquisitions at all, for it is entirely possible that divestiture will never be requested — as it was not in the case of the much publicized Prentice-Hall takeover in 1985. Pretexts can be found again, and this provision could be a powerful incentive to hunt for them diligently.

The retransmission right, while costly to Canada, is legitimate and desirable, and is supported by the cultural community as a matter of principle. Moreover, one of that community's long-standing criticisms of Canadian television has been that broadcasters and cable companies have never had to pay the full price for the American programming that fills their schedules to the marginalization of Canadian content. Abundantly available, cheap American shows have historically stifled original Canadian production. But if there is a good side to this article, there is also a hidden razor-blade — an agreement to establish a joint advisory committee "comprised of government and private sector experts to review outstanding issues related to retransmission rights in both countries and to make recommendations to the Parties within twelve months." In other words, the tough issues which would not submit to resolution in the talks are being referred to a new round of negotiations, and both countries have bound themselves to a time limit. Furthermore, underneath the term "retransmission right" lie most of our broadcasting, informatics (information technology) and telecommunications activity, and it would appear that the U.S. has just acquired the right to oversee the formulation of Canadian broadcasting policy.

The fourth exemption, like the third, only tells part of the story. The Print-in-Canada requirements are contained in Section 19 of the Income Tax Act which defines a Canadian magazine using quite stringent criteria of ownership, residency, editorial content as well as typesetting and printing. These provisions were introduced by Bill C-58, the famous *Time-Reader's Digest* bill. Since the late 1950s, it had been apparent that, so long as these two American magazines were allowed to soak up 50-60 per cent of advertising revenues in Canada, a viable Canadian magazine industry could not develop. In the early 1960s, the Canadian government got as far as drafting legislation to correct the situation. It was envisaged that only advertising placed in *Canadian* magazines would qualify as a tax-deductible business expense, thus making American magazines with Canadian editions a less attractive vehicle for advertisers. But the Auto Pact was then under discussion, and the White House had only to make a few veiled threats to get the Diefenbaker cabinet to recant. *Time* and *Readers' Digest* were made honorary Canadian citizens and the Auto Pact became reality. Thirteen years later the Liberals took another swing at the problem, and amid howls of protest from across the border Bill C-58 — which had the same provisions as the earlier legislation — was passed into law in 1976. In the intervening decade, a domestic magazine industry has, indeed, been built on that legislative foundation; the predictions for C-58 were proven accurate. However, the U.S. has never accepted our law as the final word. American magazine publishers, printers as well as broadcasters (U.S. border television stations were also affected by the law), have been lobbying Congress without rest for a decade; the issue has remained near the top of the American list of "irritants." So it was obvious from the outset of the talks that the Americans would insist that C-58 be on the table. Only innocents or charlatans could deny this history, maintaining that C-58 would be kept out of play.

And C-58 is not alone. The American negotiators are also after the postal subsidy programme which is a vital element of support for Canadian magazines, and the draft agreement actually included a commitment to equalize postal rates for some publications. To the surprise of many, this was dropped from the final text, apparently because the two sides were so far apart on the issue (Canada was talking about letting *Time* and *Newsweek* in; the U.S. was talking about all publications with a circulation over one thousand). According to the Canadian Periodical Publishers Association (CPPA), the Americans have simply decided to change tactics, figuring they will have better success taking their complaint to the General Agreement on Tariffs and Trade (GATT). Moreover, they have a longer-term goal, which is to clear the way for American printers to expand their business into Canada.

Since eliminating the manufacturing clause in American copyright law, thereby dropping the requirement that foreign publications be printed in the U.S. if more than 1,500 copies are to be distributed, American printers have been lobbying for access to the Canadian market. The agreement gives them two important concessions. Besides the removal of the Print-in-Canada part of C-58, printing and typesetting have been omitted from the definition of the cultural industries and are therefore are not exempt from the agreement. This leaves just two regulations in their path. First, item 99221-1 of Schedule C of the Customs Tariff, which prevents the importation of magazines in which more than 5 per cent of the advertising is directed to Canadians (this would mean that if Canadian magazines were printed in the U.S. they could not re-enter Canada). Second, there are the postal regulations which stipulate that periodicals qualifying as Second Class mail must be printed in Canada. The CPPA does not believe repealing the Print-in-Canada requirement will by itself be harmful, for the remaining definition is still very strict. But read in the long-term context, these two concessions are less innocuous than they seem. Canadian magazine publishers regard them as the thin end of a wedge which will guarantee the intensification of pressure for the removal of other programmes designed to assist the industry. And, when all the ramifications of the agreement are played out, our magazine industry could be severely damaged.

Although there are many intangibles in Clause 1 of the agreement's Article 2005, it is actually crystal clear when compared to the second clause. This so-called "Notwithstanding clause" is the conundrum, though on the surface it too seems straightforward. Both countries, it says, can go right ahead promoting their cultural industries, but both risk retaliatory action from the other in response to anything which would be inconsistent with the agreement but for the exemption. Translation: the cultural industries are not part of the agreement unless they involve actions which are not otherwise permitted.

There is, of course, good reason why double negatives are considered bad grammar; being indirect statements, they inject imprecision into the discussion and open the door to multiple meanings. This clause will probably keep several dozen lawyers warm through many winters trying to divine its meaning and it will be years more before any definitive interpretation is possible. For, by its vagueness, the clause raises a host of questions and none of these can be answered by the government with any degree of assurance. For example, though tariffs are now being eliminated in the cultural industries, can they be reintroduced as a "measure of equivalent commercial effect"? What limitations, if any, are there on the scope of retaliatory action? Since the article as a whole ostensibly removes the cultural industries from the body of the agreement, does this preclude recourse to the disputes-settlement mechanism? If one side takes retaliatory action to recoup the commercial effects of cultural policy, and the other side considers this illegitimate or excessive, what recourse is there? Who decides what a "measurable commercial effect" is and how that effect is to be calculated? If the compensatory commercial action taken by one country falls within the definition of dumping or countervailing duties, is there an argument to be made that would give the other country access to the disputes-settlement mechanism? Or, as the prevailing legal opinion has it at the moment, does the Notwithstanding clause amount to prior agreement giving the United States a free shot at any part of the Canadian economy?

Despite its murky legal implications, the main thrust of Article 2005 is perfectly clear. The first clause obviously came from the Canadian side and represents an attempt to live up to the government's promise to protect Canadian cultural sovereignty. The second constitutes the price exacted by the Americans. Canada can make whatever cultural policies it wants, but if in doing so the commercial status quo of American interests is affected, the U.S. has the right to extract its pound of flesh. That much at least is clear: the deal gives the U.S. the right, (leave in advance, as it were), to retaliate. Such a concession, it can be argued, actually leaves the cultural industries with less protection than the other sectors of the economy included in the deal. Certainly it is the kind of special treatment that makes you pine for ordinary dispensation.

Cultural Surrender

The most disturbing and probably the most far-reaching aspect of the Notwithstanding clause is the precedent it sets by accepting the American definition of culture. Early on in the trade talks External Affairs Minister Joe Clark was heard ruminating on the differences between Canadian and American approaches to book publishing. He said: "To us it's culture; to them it's business." Clark was right, there is a difference. And true, in the United States, culture does mean business — the biggest, in fact, if you include the entire information sector. He also correctly acknowledged that, in Canada, we have historically reserved economic judgment on culture, recognizing that there are justifications, besides monetary gain, for making our own films, writing our own books and gathering our own news. But it would be most accurate to say that culture and business are inextricably intertwined and interdependent. As innumerable commentators around the world have noted, American entertainment functions as publicity for the products and services of American industry. Just as the function of the programmes on American commercial television is to supply advertisers with an audience (appropriately skewed as to age, income, sex etc.), so the American media can be viewed as delivering consumers and devotees to the American way of life. To imagine that these activities can be separated, that culture and economics can be carved into discrete compartments where they will not impinge on other aspects of life in the body politic, is one of the reigning conceits of our time. The idea that the economy operates entire of itself, that it is even possible to make a "purely economic" decision, is an idea which is loaded with cultural values.

In the past two decades, Canadian society has experienced a cultural expansion of epic proportions which has repeatedly found access to the mass media barred from without. Driven by the determination of a generation of creators who decided to flaunt convention and work in Canada for Canadian audiences, the movement has succeeded in establishing a Canadian presence and voice in the media and the arts where one did not really exist before. This has been achieved by prodigious personal effort, but without access to the Canadian marketplace through the national systems of communication, the Canadian voice has mostly been heard in local and regional registers. It is still not easy to address a national audience.

The essential dilemma which cultural policy has been grappling with since it was invented in the early 1970s is how to break into the mainstream of popular culture which, in this country, is mostly American. Governments have introduced all sorts of programmes to subsidize the development of the cultural industries over the years, but these have been directed almost exclusively to production. Time and again, secretaries of state and ministers of communications, revved up by the demands of the cultural community and convinced by their own industry studies, have gone to Cabinet to get a policy that would do something about distribution. Time and again, as one wag put it, the minister went in with a tiger of a policy and came out with kitty litter, as Cabinet shied away from action and buckled under pressure from the Americans. As a result, the structural changes which are absolutely necessary if Canadian culture is ever to have a national presence in this country, have never materialized.

The figures tell the tale: 3-5 per cent of the screen time in Canadian movies houses is devoted to Canadian films; 2-4 per cent of videocasettes sold are Canadian; 20 per cent of books sold are published by Canadian-owned firms which publish 80 per cent of the Canadian-authored titles; 97 per cent of film revenues leave the country, 95 per cent headed for the U.S.; 85 per cent of records and tapes sold in

Canada are non-Canadian; 77 per cent of the magazines sold are foreign; 95 per cent of the drama aired on television is non-Canadian.

So American culture remains the one cultural common denominator for all Canadians. And the cultural industries, far from being made an exception to prove the rule, ought to be read as an object lesson. There are no barriers now preventing Canadian producers from selling in the United States — except American attitudes. Though Canadian policy-makers rarely stop to notice the fact, Americans are loath to purchase culture from abroad. They import almost no television programming (except for PBS), very few books, fewer feature films, and only a smattering of music since most foreign artists are either produced on American labels or distributed by them. It is highly unlikely that this will be changed by a free-trade deal with Canada, even though we are their biggest cultural customer. The one-way flow across the forty-ninth parallel will not be reversed or modified by the agreement; there will not be new revenues for original Canadian film production, and in the cultural sector as a whole the most we can hope for is 20 per cent of our own market. With no plans, real or rhetorical, for adjusting this picture, we have to conclude that as little as 3 per cent of the domestic market is just fine for the Tories, and to them an acceptable definition of cultural sovereignty. Perversely, then, C-58 — the one and only stake the Liberals ever made on the marketplace on behalf of Canadian culture — was one of the first offerings made by Ottawa to lure the slyly diffident Americans to the bargaining table.

By the terms of the free-trade agreement it will now become harder to do anything about American domination of our mass media. Whatever we do try will elicit immediate retaliation, which means that whatever is accomplished will have to be paid for twice — over and above the cost of the programme itself, we will have to pay off the Americans. The agreement therefore dramatically raises the political odds against any affirmative action for Canadian culture, for now we will not just have to convince the politicians about the rightness of such action, we will have to convince them it will be worth it even if other Canadians in other sectors will be penalized. This pits Canadian workers and artists against each other and forces us all into a situation of having to "choose" between bread and books. Very adroitly, the

American negotiators set the cat among the Canadian chickens and have settled back to watch us self-destruct.

Notwithstanding the exemption, this agreement will irrevocably change Canadian cultural policy. Contrary to the government's claim, the agreement does not retain our full capacity to support the cultural industries. It commits us to pursuing culture as a business, the American way. And it signifies a renunciation of Canadian efforts to modify American presence in our media. Not bad for one sentence and thirty-two words.

Loopholes

Culture adds up to more than the cultural industries. Likewise, the cultural industries are greater than the definitions given them in an agreement which leaves out a great deal — all the creative professions which are the well-spring of any cultural industry, for example, as well as printing and typesetting and bookselling. The arts are not mentioned either, presumably because they are non-profit and non-profitable. Yet there are pockets of profitability in the arts (commercial theatre, for instance) and all sorts of arts-related professions and services which support Canadian art by providing artists with freelance incomes. There is nothing in the agreement to suggest that the arts will be protected from the indirect effects of the deal as it applies to these subsections of the economy. By the same token, artists will have no recourse to the Notwithstanding provision of Article 2005 should their commercial position be adversely affected by American actions. Artists who make a living typesetting (and I do know several who do just that), who fall victim to American competition and have to close down their studios and go out of business, are out of luck. There is no way for Canada to extract repayment for that kind of loss.

Just formulating that observation, however, lights up other quirks in the thinking behind the agreement. The wording of Article 2005 indicates that the trigger for retaliatory measures is government action, as is the case under GATT agreements. Damage caused by private enterprise in the marketplace, which is, after all, the kind of damage Canadian cultural industries are most likely to face, is untouchable and designated fair game. Yet, so far, no one in authority seems to have wondered whether the Notwithstanding clause works in reverse or even if it is meant to. When, and under what sort of circumstances, would Canada be in a position to extract a little "equivalent commercial" compensation of our own? The fact is that it has been designed for American retaliation, not Canadian, as the American summary of the text makes explicit: "Canada faces no constraints on its ability to promote the development of Canadian culture through economic measures. The United States can take measures of equivalent economic effect to respond to actions taken by Canada in the cultural area. The U.S. recognizes the importance to Canada of maintaining its cultural identity. At the same time, however, the U.S. wants to ensure that Canadian cultural policies do not constitute an unnecessary barrier to U.S. trade."

In sum, then, Article 2005 adds up to this: some cultural industries have been exempted, but on the understanding that we will not do anything about the status quo of American media in our marketplace; the U.S. is guaranteed continued access to the billions of dollars its cultural industries extract annually from the Canadian economy; and Canada has acceded to conditions which will make it impossible for us to fashion policies that will shape the content of our own mass media.

Realizing that the bulk of Canadian cultural activity is not exempted or dealt with comprehensively inevitably sends us off on a fishing trip through the text, searching for places where culture may be implicated. The service sector is an obvious place to look as many cultural activities fall into this category. There is nothing in Chapter 14 which would prevent the growth of U.S.-based design, publicity and management services in the cultural sector — cultural industries included. Indeed, private American firms have already been contracted to run some university bookstores, though publishers and booksellers vociferously protested the move and in one case forced a retreat. Under the free-trade agreement, however, this will be allowed to continue and expand. It is not impossible to imagine such private sector services, including exhibition, design and management, being brought into public museums and art galleries. But the exact status of sectors not specifically named will only be determined by invoking the disputes-settlement mechanism.

There are two places where the arts are specifically mentioned in Chapter 14 of the agreement, although the first one is stated in code, (literally, it is identified only by a Standard Industrial Classification number), and thus in such a way that most people (maybe even our negotiators) missed it. Among non-university, post-secondary educational institutions included in the deal are schools of art and the performing arts which will be open to the private sector and American competition in management and all commercial services. And in Annex 1404, architecture is singled out for special treatment and Canada has therein agreed to the development of mutually acceptable professional standards and criteria regarding education, examination, experience, conduct and ethics, and professional development, and has undertaken to harmonize provincial licencing practices so that the profession will operate on a smooth and level continental playing field.

And then there is the tricky little question of subsidy, left to further negotiations to be worked out. How will the subsidy to the cultural industries be regarded — particularly the support provided to those sections not exempted or otherwise covered in the agreement? What will prevent American cultural firms operating in Canada from demanding equal treatment and access to Canada Council support for, say, writers and book promotion tours? And in the investment section, there are, likewise, implications for culture which are difficult to forecast. There, neither the cultural industries nor the arts are exempted from direct investment; whatever money wants in, is apparently welcome. Databanks, information processing and the software side of informatics governed by copyright law are all open to foreign involvement and exploitation. Although these represent the growth industries of the future, they have been renounced as instruments of cultural development, or as strategic sites for Canadian job creation and Canadian content. (And has anyone thought through the legal implications for the privacy of Canadian citizens now that our data can be processed in a foreign country under foreign law?)

The only concession to Canadian cultural tradition — and in reality more a concession to the political sensitivity of the moment — is the special rule regarding indirect takeovers. As previously noted, this is a extraordinary rule. Not only does the government seem to be agreeing in advance to purchase cultural firms affected by a takeover at a price to be determined by independent assessment, it is conceding to the rule of North American rather than Canadian market forces. It also appears to be agreeing to public ownership in the cultural sector, or at least to public participation in the purchase of certain American branch-plants which, most likely, would not remain in government hands but be turned over to private owners for a subsidized price.

Down the Road

It is not easy to predict what the ultimate effect of the free-trade agreement will be on the cultural life of the country, or even the cultural industries. Change there will be, without doubt, even if it will occur only slowly and subtly. However, for the sake of trying to understand the phenomenon, to at least give it a face and some dimensions, let's try to imagine.

Take the business of book publishing. Of all the mass media in Canada, book publishing has arguably developed the most distinctively Canadian voice. Canadians know and read Canadian writers, (and so do a growing number of people in other countries), and the majority of them are published by Canadian-owned firms. Some Canadian writers have even acquired celebrity status; so have a few publishers — Jack McClelland, Mel Hurtig, Anna Porter and Adrienne Clarkson among them. Moreover, these people are not just famous for being famous. They have had a lot to say over the years about the political issues of our time and are quite likely to turn up on "The Journal," or at public hearings to deliver their considered opinions about free trade, the Meech Lake Accord or pornography legislation. In short, it is possible to talk about a Canadian book publishing culture, and one of its most remarkable qualities is its regional character. However inept book distribution and publishing policy may have been, they have been premised on the idea that literature is regionally bound and that regional presses ought to feed into a nation-wide system. Regional, in Canadian English, refers to cultural as well as geographic location.

By comparison, American book publishing, which also has a regional side to it, is organized more in the direction of specialization, and the division of intellectual labour is done according to categories and markets. The definition, therefore, is primarily economic. The clue is in the way the printing industry is structured. According to Willy

Cooper, president of the Canadian Printing Industries Association, the difference can be described as follows: "Large American undertakings tend to have fewer manufacturing locations than do Canadian companies. Typically, in the United States, such facilities are dedicated to the production of huge quantities of a limited number of product lines. The Canadian situation, reflecting the linguistic and geographic reality of this nation, is altogether different. Canadian printing firms often have a large number of plants located across the country, producing a wider variety of products for local or regional distribution."

Life after free trade will immerse Canadian book publishing in a business milieu ever more powerfully driven by the beat of American enterprise. This suggests that the single most important change will be the sea-change of attitudes and habits which will engulf the business community at large as it reorients itself to regional and cross-border markets. The full force of American commercialism will thereby be unleashed and it will feel like a steroid injection. In such an environment, some Canadian publishers may actually do very well, and all sorts of new players will appear with new ideas and wheels to deal. The literary presses will likely survive, with public funding, but only for show; the concept of their participating in a genuine national market probably will not. McClelland & Stewart will not disappear overnight; yet when next its bottom line crashes, the cultural imperative *cum* political will to bail it out with public money may just not be there. In short, the transformation of Canadian book publishing will not be a case of the immediate demise of the Canadian-owned sector but the reorientation of the industry as a whole so that it ceases to have much meaning or weight in the culture that surrounds it. As it is by-passed it will become marginalized.

The Canadian negotiators, however, have not understood this; they seem to be able to contemplate the complete transformation of economic and trading relations between our two countries, and among the regions of our two countries, and still imagine that culture is off the table. And by inaccurately gauging the American agenda, they have failed to achieve what they set out to achieve in the cultural sector and do not even recognize their own error. The text may say that the cultural industries are exempted — but that is not what it means. Culture is about values, and cultural policy is about ensuring that our values have a voice in the commercial hubbub that explicitly celebrates

American values. With the free-trade agreement, the Mulroney government has completely abandoned the project of a national market for Canadian culture. All of our cultural industries will, by coercion or force of commercial circumstance, eventually rationalize and reorganize themselves to harmonize with the patterns of American enterprise. They may survive, but only as specialty producers.

In this sense, the agreement is a monumental statement of failure and surrender. The failure of the central government and central Canada to live up to its rhetoric of nation-building and cultural and regional development. Ontarians cannot blame Westerners or Maritimers or Northerners for opting to do business for a time with their neighbours to the south. It cannot be any worse than trying to extract a decent arrangement out of Ontario, and they will not be made to feel inferior to Seattle or Dallas or Baltimore, as they are now to Toronto. (The irony of ironies is that Toronto is likely to become an important North American city, but it will have decreasing importance, in every way that matters, to other Canadians.) The free-trade advocates may then be, pathetically, looking at the wrong thing. The issue is not who is braver or stronger or more confident about taking on the Americans and winning; the issue is who are we cosying up to, and how far we want to let the vast pulsing dynamo of American consumerism rule our lives. The issue is not access to the American market for Canadian culture, but access to our own.

To say that cultural sovereignty has been protected because the cultural industries (or parts of them) have been exempted (sort of) from certain aspects of the agreement is sheer duplicity. In thirty-two words the Mulroney government has committed us forever to asking, first, what the Americans will let us have, and, second, what we want and need as Canadians. If that is not a violation of cultural sovereignty, what is?

21

Undermining Canada's Constitution

Deborah Coyne

Canada is a difficult country to govern at the best of times. Yet
throughout history it has achieved social and economic progress while
accommodating linguistic, cultural and regional diversity. Such success is directly related to the division of legislative powers between
two jurisdictions — federal and provincial. The dynamic, creative ten-
sion and competition between the two orders of government in key
areas of public policy has led to progressive action that has helped to
shape a diverse yet compassionate society. But all this is contingent on
strong national leadership and the recognition that the federal government plays a critical role: it must build the bonds that strengthen a sense
of community and of national identity. This means promoting basic
rights and freedoms now guaranteed under the Charter, and protecting
the interests of weaker provinces and regions. Reaching national goals
requires, among other things, social programmes, economic development strategies and regional initiatives.

On this score, it is important to reflect on the impact of the Canada-
U.S. trade deal on national leadership capacity. Does the deal affect
the balance of power between the provinces and the federal government? Is the ability to maintain a distinct Canadian identity compromised by the accord with the United States?

How We Are Different

Contrary to what is often believed, differences between the two countries are significant. For instance, the Canadian approach to domestic issues is less doctrinaire or ideological than that of the United States. Canadians generally believe that the government can and should play an active role in society and the economy to reduce inequality and promote justice. This country does not subscribe to the "magic of the marketplace" approach to policy, nor does it draw sharp lines between the public and private sectors. Canadians are less individualistic and materialistic than Americans. Emphasizing community values and sharing, Canada tries to be a bilingual, multicultural nation and to sustain a diverse yet compassionate society.

This vision of the role of government and the relationship between the individual, state and society is clearly reflected in the Charter of Rights and Freedoms. The Charter blends an emphasis on individual freedom with respect for community values. It requires that cultural, religious and linguistic communities be taken into account in interpreting the rights guaranteed to individuals. In sharp contrast to the American Bill of Rights, the Charter also reflects the belief that there need not be any contradiction between state regulation and individual liberty, and that freedom is enhanced by our public institutions. This is most obvious in the Charter's commitment to multiculturalism and in its broad guarantees of equality, minority language education, and mobility rights, all of which are subject "only to such reasonable limits prescribed by law as can be demonstrably justified in a free and democratic society." In addition, the Canadian Constitution now entrenches the principle of equalization payments to have-not provinces and the commitment of governments to promote equal opportunities for all citizens.

In the area of foreign policy, Canadians are more accurately described as internationalists, rather than as nationalists or continentalists. In other words, Canada defines itself through participation in the international arena. Whether it be peace and security, international development, human rights, environmental protection or trade and financial affairs, Canada sustains an international tradition.

Unlike Americans, for whom the world is effectively North American and who still exhibit a strong isolationist streak in their international outlook, Canadians have always looked beyond North America, not only to foster economic well-being through international trade but also to resist absorption into the giant neighbour to the south. Maintaining a distance from the United States has been the key to playing an important role on the world stage. Though Canada belongs to the industrialized world and participates in NATO, the Organisation for Economic Co-operation and Development and the Group of Seven, it is perceived by other middle-powers, and by developing countries, as a nation that shares many of their values and aspirations and that can understand their fears and sense of vulnerability. In foreign policy, it is expected that Canada will act as an interlocutor both between the developing and developed worlds and between East and West, and as a facilitator of peaceful international change.

Free Trade and Canada's Future

According to the federal government, the bilateral trade agreement will have little, if any, impact on the shape of the Canadian federal system or on Canada's international personality. They say that the agreement deals overwhelmingly with matters under federal jurisdiction, notably international trade, and that it does not affect the distribution of legislative powers between the federal and provincial levels of government. It is simply a limited economic arrangement to secure access to the American market for Canadian exporters. The federal government, therefore, asserts the constitutional right to sign and implement the agreement unilaterally. (Only the provisions dealing with wine are acknowledged to be subject to provincial jurisdiction, thereby requiring provincial implementation.)

In sharp contrast to this view, opponents of the bilateral trade deal argue that it will alter the shape of the Canadian federation and the balance of power between the federal and provincial governments. The deal, they say, sets us on a course of economic development that deliberately weakens political authorities at all levels and shifts power to private economic actors. It reflects the assumption that we should minimize government intervention and instead rely on impersonal market forces to ensure an efficient allocation of national resources.

According to Ontario's attorney-general, Ian Scott, the deal is nothing short of a constitutional document. "Like a Constitution, the scope of the agreement is all embracing. It touches on virtually all aspects of governmental activity....The agreement imposes new constraints on what Canadian governments can do for people in the future, and the erosion of our ability to govern ourselves will be difficult to reverse." Thus the free-trade debate is about people and to whom, if anyone, they may look for the social and economic policy they require. Scott emphasizes that the trade deal restricts the ability of Canadians to call on *any* government for action in the public interest.

From this perspective, the bilateral trade deal draws Canada towards further economic integration with the United States. Creating a so-called "level playing field" for Canadian and American businesses means the harmonization of key policies. When this is combined with the substantial weakening of both the federal and provincial governments that results from the constraints set out in the agreement, the clear implication is that the future course of economic and social development will be orchestrated south of the forty-ninth parallel. This will erode Canada's distinctive international personality, weaken Canadian identity and perhaps lead to the eventual absorption of Canada by the United States.

These very different views of the impact of the trade deal on the shape of the Canadian federation reveal competing visions of Canada that reflect different assumptions about our future evolution as a nation, the role of government and the relationship between the individual and the state within our federal structure. The deal cannot, then, be considered as simply an economic arrangement that should be judged primarily by whether or not it makes Canada stronger economically. It is not simply a matter of trading more securely with the United States. Rather, as long-time cabinet minister Mitchell Sharp has pointed out, the widespread misgivings about the trade agreement relate not to its economic consequences, but to its significant impact on Canada's sovereignty. In other words, it is a question of whether Canadians maintain control over the very institutions of government that sustain nationhood.

In assessing the impact of the trade deal on the federal-provincial balance and our capacity for national leadership and independent action, it is important to assess its relationship to the government's key constitutional initiative — the Meech Lake Accord. In this respect, as Raymond Breton of the University of Toronto has observed, the Meech Lake Accord places the provinces in a position to determine the social agenda within their own boundaries, while the bilateral trade agreement with the United States promotes and bolsters institutional development at the continental level. The danger is that Canadian social development on a distinctly national level will be neglected. Further, the combined impact of the bilateral trade deal and the Meech Lake Accord is likely to result in provincial governments playing more prominent roles both in national policy and in international affairs. Critical policies on national and international issues would then be reduced to the lowest common denominator of rival provincial interests.

Richard Simeon of Queen's University, a leading authority on federal-provincial relations, has highlighted the profoundly decentralizing impact of the bilateral trade deal on the structure of Canadian federalism. The deal not only weakens political authorities by shifting power to private economic actors, but also constrains federal economic powers — such as fiscal and monetary policy instruments and tariffs — without equal constraints on the provinces. Ottawa will simply become less important both for the provinces and for the private sector. It will become difficult to think coherently about an economic entity called Canada, much less one whose destiny could be guided by a central government. "Free trade is a national strategy all right, but it is one that denies the federal government the power to mount one, even if it could be defined."

Equally disturbing for Canada's ability to direct its future course of economic and social development is the failure of our leaders to recognize that the implementation of viable and effective programmes to improve our national economic performance depends increasingly on the co-ordination of policies for which the provinces are at least in part responsible. These policies include education, social assistance, child-care, parental leave — all critical to society and to human development. They include an effective national telecommunications policy to assist in the transition to the global electronic society, and national environmental protection programmes to set out a course of sustainable economic development.

Effective national leadership is clearly critical in guiding the necessary federal-provincial negotiations and ensuring meaningful progress on all these fronts. Only a strong federal government is able to insist on minimum national standards for new social and economic programmes. Without national leadership, groups that generally prefer the status quo will be able to stalemate federal-provincial negotiations by playing off the provinces against the federal government. Equally, it will be difficult to argue for greater equity and justice internationally if Canada's domestic situation deteriorates.

Major changes to our social support system will be effectively precluded by the trade deal. For instance, it will be impossible to implement a national comprehensive disability insurance scheme.

Without going into detail, one effective way to implement such a scheme is for the federal government to encourage all provinces to move to publicly-administered automobile insurance and then integrate it with the already publicly-administered workers' compensation systems, as has already been successfully accomplished in Quebec. Eventually, the appropriate national shared-cost programme would be established with national standards similar to those in the Canada Health Act, and compensation would be extended beyond accident-related disability to any disability, however caused.

This is where the trade deal comes in. The investment provisions of the agreement, specifically Article 1605, make the creation of any such public scheme subject to the requirement to provide "prompt, adequate and effective compensation" to the privately-owned companies which might be affected. This will be determined ultimately by a binational tribunal where the provinces that would be responsible for initiating the public action will not have the right to participate in the process. In addition, affected American firms can protest that such public schemes contravene the two key principles in the services section of the agreement: the right of establishment and the right of commercial presence. Finally, challenges can also be mounted under the monopolies provision in Article 2010 and the "nullification and impairment clause" in Article 2011.

Thus, the free-trade agreement will constrain the policy options open to both levels of government and deter public action in a whole range of social policy areas. When this is combined with the provisions of the Meech Lake Accord — particularly the constitutional limitations on the federal spending power and the ability of provinces to opt out of national programmes with financial compensation — Canada could wind up balkanized. Inequalities of wealth and opportunity among Canadians may become the norm. The sense of national community that comes through a commitment to sharing and to pursuing greater social justice for all Canadians may be lost.

Nor is this all. As the former head of the Science Council of Canada, Stuart Smith, has observed, Canada already has too many foreign-owned branch-plants that have no mandate to export and that rarely develop or design higher technology goods. And yet, strategic support for domestic investment and for research-intensive and export-oriented business requires powers that are abandoned by the deal. The irony is that under Article 103, it is the federal government that undertakes to ensure that the provinces observe the terms of the trade deal, including those provisions that effectively limit the ability of government to direct industrial policy. Thus, the federal government ends ups being assigned a role under free trade that serves to deny the provinces the right to intervene in favour of Canadian industry!

Government action is needed to bring about change in the Canadian economy. Yet under the trade agreement, such action will be open to challenge if it appears to favour Canadian enterprise over American. Moreover, this serious undermining of government's capacity for industrial leadership is compounded by the way in which the trade deal opens up the financial sector to American companies. Under the deal, provincial authority to regulate trust companies is undermined by federal fiat. This means that the provinces lose control over the channels through which critical financial resources are allocated. Financial flows, left alone, go to finance real estate and mines, not high technology and research and development.

A Loss of Vision

As a sort of economic constitution, the bilateral trade agreement fundamentally changes the shape of the Canadian federation and precludes the national leadership required to meet the challenges of the twenty-first century. And yet at the international level, Canadians face the challenges of adapting to the global technological revolution, shifting away from our reliance on natural resources and certain traditional manufacturing sectors, and improving productivity and competitiveness. The international agenda also includes such global issues as arms control, international development and environmental protection. At the domestic level, we face the challenges of devastating levels of poverty and unemployment, inadequate training and education, stark regional disparities and a widening gap between affluent and poorer Canadians.

To overcome these challenges successfully requires something more than the inadequate patchwork of federal and provincial responses that has been seen to date. Government leaders have failed to articulate a national strategy to ensure that Canada will remain in the front ranks of the developed world, notwithstanding the intense global rivalry generated by the technological revolution. Instead, the federal government seems consumed with brokerage politics and dominated by narrow business interests. A patchwork of ad hoc accords with different regions, deregulation in telecommunications and financial services, and the fixation on bilateral relations with the Unites States characterize the confused policy agenda. Most alarmingly, two key government initiatives — the bilateral trade deal and the Meech Lake constitutional accord — are being undertaken without a mandate from the people of Canada and in a fundamentally undemocratic way. At worst, they may well extinguish Canada as a single, sovereign nation.

22

The Canadian Public and Free Trade

Donna Dasko

Canadian history is filled with failed attempts to create a free-trade zone between Canada and the United States. The current free-trade initiative has crossed some major hurdles toward this goal, but several more remain — the American Congress must approve the negotiated agreement and the Canadian Senate and the provinces must pass enabling legislation. Finally, for the current free-trade agreement to be implemented, Brian Mulroney's Conservatives must win majority or near-majority support in the next federal election.

For free trade to succeed, Canadians must support it as well. Public opinion research suggests that the current initiative does have the support of Canadians in most regions. At the onset of 1988, support for free trade was up across the country with a slim, but not overwhelming, majority of Canadians favouring the idea.

Support for the free-trade agreement itself, however, is lower than support for the idea of free trade. The Canadian public is clearly divided about whether or not they favour the deal struck in October 1987, and the specific provisions of the deal are viewed even more critically.

The public debate about free trade in the period after the October agreement moved in two directions. Proponents of free trade, particularly some premiers, concentrated their arguments on the benefits of free trade for their provinces. At the same time, free-trade opponents shifted their criticisms away from free trade as a concept and toward criticism of the deal itself.

The efforts of both sides have had an effect on public opinion, but by 1988 the pro-free-trade forces seemed to have gained momentum. The provisions of the deal have not received wide public discussion, while the argument of some premiers that free trade would help their provinces achieve economic equality with Ontario has captured the attention of western Canadians in particular, and put the opponents of free trade on the defensive.

Survey data suggest that opponents of free trade have had an effect, and will continue to be effective as Canadians hear more about the deal. But they must also address the regional concerns which the free-trade debate has heightened.

Free Trade: The Initiative

National polls conducted by Environics began tracking Canadian attitudes toward free trade in April 1984 when the idea was one of many trade initiatives being discussed within the federal government and the business community.

Free trade with the U.S. had little meaning to the public at that time but it did imply a closer economic relationship with the United States. In the final days of Pierre Trudeau's years in power, Canadians had grown weary of the regime and its perceived anti-American thrust, and the climate was right for a different approach to Canada-U.S. relations. Canadians responded positively to the notion of free trade, with 78 per cent agreeing that there should be free trade in an April 1984 Environics survey. Although free trade was not an issue in the 1984 federal election, both the new Liberal leader, John Turner, and Conservative leader Brian Mulroney held out the promise of closer Canada-U.S. ties.

As free trade entered the public realm in 1985, support for the idea dropped to the 65 per cent level in mid-year. With the prime minister's announcement in September that the government intended to seek a free-trade deal with the United States, support for free trade fell to 58 per cent by November and 54 per cent by February 1986.

The falling support for free trade was the unintended result of a strategy on the part of the federal government not to make the issue highly visible lest it raise expectations among Canadians which might not be met. Free trade could not be promoted without risk until negotiations were at least initiated, and the American response could not be guaranteed until the Senate gave the go-ahead.

The low profile given free trade by the government during the critical period after September 1985 allowed opponents of the initiative to seize the moment and to state their objections forcefully to Canadians. Support for free trade fell to 52 per cent — a bare majority — by June 1986, and opposition increased to 36 per cent from only 17 per cent in 1984. Canadians, for the first time, began to consider the possible effects of free trade on Canada's cultural sovereignty, political independence and vulnerable industries.

The launch of the Canada-U.S. negotiations in mid-1986 led to a long period of debate about the benefits and problems of free trade and what might or might not be on the negotiating table. The provincial governments were drawn into the national discussion for the first time, but the focus then was largely on the question of the federal government's authority to implement a treaty without provincial support.

Support for free trade received a boost from increasing protectionist activity on the part of the Americans. By December 1986, the American tariff on cedar shakes and shingles, and especially the countervailing duty on softwood lumber, had the effect of increasing support for free trade among Canadians back up to the 58 per cent level. But the temporary resolution of these events, along with the increasing criticism of the prime minister and his government throughout 1987, led to softening support for what had become, in the public's mind at least, the government's major policy goal. The Ontario election in September, with its strong anti-free-trade tone, also proved to be a key factor in eroding support for the initiative.

By October 1987, federal Conservative support had dropped to 24 per cent of the decided electorate — a modern-day low for a governing party in Canada. Support for free trade dropped with it, falling to the 49 per cent mark. The announcement of the deal did nothing initially to boost support for either free trade or the federal Conservative Party.

Interestingly, strong and moderate opposition to free trade peaked in June 1986 at 36 per cent, then fell slightly and returned to the 34 per

Table 1
Support For Free Trade
Environics' National Surveys
(N = approximately 2,000)

"Please tell me whether you strongly agree, somewhat agree, somewhat disagree or strongly disagree that there should be free trade between Canada and the U.S.?"

	Apr '84	June '85	Nov '85	Feb '86	June '86	Oct '86	Dec '86	Mar '87	June '87	Oct '87	Dec '87
Agree	78%	65%	58%	54%	52%	57%	58%	57%	56%	49%	57%
Disagree	17	30	31	35	36	33	31	28	34	34	32
No opinion	5	5	11	12	12	10	12	14	10	17	10
Strongly agree	46	34	28	20	19	22	25	22	23	18	22
Somewhat agree	32	31	30	34	33	35	33	35	33	31	35
Somewhat disagree	12	20	16	16	17	17	15	13	16	18	16
Strongly disagree	5	10	15	19	19	16	16	15	18	16	16

cent level. Neither strong opposition nor strong support were building during this period; rather there were continuous small shifts between levels of support and opposition.

Free Trade: The Agreement

The October announcement that a free-trade agreement had been struck finally put an end to the "phony war" phase of the debate and provided a concrete focus for the national discussion.

In the days and months following the announcement of the deal, free trade gained some prominent opponents, notably Liberal leader John Turner and most of the federal Liberal caucus. Free trade also gained some prominent and vocal supporters, notably Premiers Robert Bourassa, Grant Devine, and Bill Vander Zalm. In addition, chief negotiator Simon Reisman embarked on a public campaign to sell the deal, lending his authority as a trade negotiator to the government's cause. Just as important, free trade had gained the support of a clear majority of newspaper editorial boards across the country, according to a press analysis by the publication *Political Alerts*. The threat of American protectionism was again having an effect, this time on newspaper editors who shifted their commentary about free trade away from political and cultural sovereignty issues and toward a concern with economic issues, particularly the need to protect Canada from American trade actions.

In the period following the agreement, some supporters of free trade feared that the "rational" economic arguments for free trade would be drowned out by the more "emotional" arguments of free trade's opponents who continued to argue that Canada's cultural and political sovereignty would be eroded. But a number of provincial premiers themselves turned the rational into the emotional by arguing that Ontario's opposition to free trade was an attempt to deny their provinces the economic prosperity that Ontario enjoyed. This heightened regionalism proved to be a key factor in consolidating and building support for free trade in western Canada and other regions.

By December, support for free trade among Canadians climbed from the low point of 49 per cent in October to 57 per cent. Opposition to free trade had hardened at 34 per cent in October and fell only two points to 32 per cent by December. It was the undecided Canadians who shifted toward free trade; indecision fell from 17 per cent in October down to ten per cent in December.

The December survey shows that regional differences remain a key determinant of attitudes toward free trade. Support for the concept remains highest in western Canada with 66 per cent in favour, followed by Quebec with 58 per cent, Atlantic Canada with 57 per cent and Ontario with 50 per cent. Overall opposition is almost identical in the West, Ontario, and Quebec, but strong opposition is highest, at 21 per cent, in Ontario.

However, support for free trade today is even more strongly related to political party affiliation than it was two years earlier. On the one hand, 80 per cent of those intending to vote Progressive Conservative federally support the initiative and only 13 per cent oppose it, while only 44 per cent of federal New Democrats support the idea and 48 per cent are opposed.

The importance of political party affiliation for understanding free-trade support is revealed in a significant finding: support for free trade among federal Conservatives is higher than that found in any other demographic, regional or political segment of the Canadian public, and opposition to free trade on the part of federal New Democrat supporters is also the highest found among any group of Canadians.

Support for free trade among other groups has also shifted. Age has become less of a factor today, as younger Canadians have become less enthusiastic about the initiative and older Canadians more so. Education and income have now emerged as more important than occupation, with high-income Canadians, in particular, strongly supportive. A gender gap has also emerged, with women, especially those in the labour force, more opposed to free trade than men.

Although a majority of Canadians supports the idea of free trade, the public is clearly divided in its support of the agreement itself. 40 per cent of Canadians say they favour the October free-trade agreement while 39 per cent oppose the deal. A significant number — 21 per cent — are undecided. The gap between support for free trade as a concept and support for the October agreement is a substantial 17 points.

The debate since the signing of the deal has taken its toll on "national reconciliation." Ontario is the only region where opposition is

TABLE 2
Support For Free Trade, December, 1987

"Please tell me whether you strongly agree, somewhat agree, somewhat disagree or strongly disagree that there should be free trade between Canada and the U.S.?"

	Overall	West	Quebec	Atlantic	Ontario	PC Supporters	NDP Supporters	Liberal Supporters
Strongly agree	22%	30%	18%	20%	19%	42%	13%	17%
Somewhat agree	35	36	40	37	31	38	31	38
Somewhat disagree	16	15	18	19	16	9	21	18
Strongly disagree	16	13	14	9	21	4	27	18
No opinion	10	6	9	15	13	8	8	10

TABLE 3
The Free Trade Agreement, December, 1987

"Do you strongly favour, somewhat favour, somewhat oppose or strongly oppose the free-trade agreement that has been negotiated between Canada and the United States?"

	Overall	Quebec	Atlantic	West	Ontario	PC Supporters	NDP Supporters	Liberal Supporters
Strongly favour	9%	8%	10%	11%	8%	19%	4%	6%
Somewhat favour	31	39	35	31	24	41	24	31
Somewhat oppose	20	21	20	18	21	13	24	22
Strongly oppose	19	14	13	18	25	6	33	23
No opinion	21	18	22	22	23	22	15	18

greater than support, with 32 per cent in favour of the agreement and 46 per cent opposed. The opposite is true in other regions. Support for the deal is highest in Quebec at 47 per cent, with 45 per cent in Atlantic Canada favouring it and 42 per cent in western Canada. Opposition to the deal in these regions is highest in the West, at 36 per cent, followed by Quebec at 35 per cent and the Atlantic provinces at 33 per cent.

Reaction to the free-trade deal elicits a response among supporters of federal political parties which is similar to that for the concept of free trade — Conservatives favour the deal and New Democrats oppose it.

A gender gap also appears in support for the agreement, with men favouring the deal more than women. However, highly-educated and high income groups, who show strong support for the concept, are divided in their perceptions of the deal. Perhaps most significantly, a plurality of union members, especially those in public sector unions, opposes the agreement.

Further probing of public opinion concerning the perceived effects of the free-trade agreement shows the public divided about whether Canada's cultural identity and political independence will be eroded. But public opinion has not moved on these issues since the October agreement, and levels of concern about cultural sovereignty and political independence in December 1987 remain unchanged from earlier in the year, and indeed are unchanged since early 1986.

Instead, the public has responded to the economic debates about free trade. Canadians believe that free trade will lead to lower consumer prices but they also show increasing concern about unemployment. And in Ontario, most people (44 per cent) believe the agreement will erode the Auto Pact. Only 23 per cent do not think it will.

The survey research suggests that the more detailed and specific the questions are, the more negative Canadians become about free trade. For example, the specific provisions of the agreement are a concern to Canadians, with the majority disapproving of the energy pricing, the energy access, and the foreign ownership provisions of the deal.

Still, by the end of 1987, a majority of Quebecers and western Canadians and a plurality of Atlantic Canadians were prepared to say that free trade would be good for their province's economy. Only in Ontario did a plurality believe otherwise.

Free Trade: Into The Future

Canadians have been looking to, and listening to, opinion leaders in the free-trade debate since that debate began. The signing of a free-trade agreement in October 1987 gave concreteness to the federal initiative, but it also allowed the national discussion to go in many different directions. The concept of free trade has gained support, and it has also given a boost to the federal Conservatives, particularly in western Canada. Credit for both is due in no small measure to the vigorous support of free trade by many provincial premiers. The free-trade initiative is finally proving to be beneficial to the federal Conservatives, as even the opposition parties concede. By early 1988, both Liberal leader John Turner and New Democrat leader Ed Broadbent were insisting that free trade would not be the only issue in the next election.

The public opinion research suggests that the most effective opposition to free trade lies in focusing on the provisions of the deal and the agreement itself. But this will be difficult, particularly when attention shifts periodically to the American Congress and how it deals with free-trade issues. As the survey findings suggest, heightened perceptions of American protectionism among Canadians give rise to increased support for free trade. And with seven of Canada's premiers now firmly on the side of free trade, opposition will be more difficult than ever. Opponents of free trade will have to respond to the fact that the free-trade debate has given rise to new regional awareness and expectations.

Endnotes

Chapter 3

1. I am indebted to Professor Robert Young of the University of Western Ontario for the meticulous reading and helpful suggestions he made on this chapter's earlier drafts.
2. For two economists' critique of the inefficiencies caused by U.S. trade policy see Alan M. Rugman and Alain Verbeke, "American Trade Policy and Corporate Strategy," mimeo, June 1987. For the considered wisdom of the legal profession, see American Bar Association and Canadian Bar Association, *Settlement of International Disputes Between Canada and the United States of America: Resolutions Adopted by the American Bar Association on August 15, 1979 and the Canadian Bar Association on August 30, 1979 with Accompanying Reports and Recommendations*, 1979. For a classic statement of two professional diplomats' managerial approach see Livingston T. Merchant and A.D.P. Heeney, "Canada and the United States — Principles for Partnership," *Department of State Bulletin*, August 2, 1965.
3. *Royal Commission on the Economic Union and Development Prospects for Canada*, Vol. I, p. 321.
4. Denis Stairs, "A Pig in a Poke," *Policy Options*, January 1988, Vol. 9. No. 1, p.10.

Chapter 6

1. The Canadian legislation to be amended includes the following statutes: Bank Act, Canada Grain Act, Canadian and British Insurance Companies Act, Canadian Wheat Board Act, Copyright Act, Customs Act, Customs Tariff, Department of Supply and Services Act, Federal Court Act, Importation of Intoxicating Liquors Act, Income Tax Act, Investment Canada Act, Investment Companies Act, Loan Companies Act, Special Import Measures Act, Standards Council of Canada Act, Trust Companies Act, Western Grain Transportation Act. As well, Ottawa has promised to amend the Plywood Standards regulation of the Canada Mortgage and Housing Corporation
2. U.S. legislation to be amended includes only the following: Section 301 of the Customs Act of 1980; Section 902.5 Atomic Energy Act Section 161 v.; 902.5 Export Administration Act of 1979. As well, the U.S. has agreed to amend 905.2 Bomeville Power Intertie Access policy; the Commodity Credit Corporation and support payments as found in the Agriculture Act 1949.
3. J. Grunwald and Kenneth Flamm, *The Global Factory: Foreign Assembly in International Trade*, (Washington D.C.: Brookings Institution, 1985), p.12.
4. Ibid., p.13.
5. For a detailed examination of American subsidization practices, see Ira C. Magaziner and Robert Reich, *Minding America's Business*, (New York: Vintage Books, 1983).
6. Paul Sevigny, *Constant Market Shares and Competitiveness: An Analysis of Canada's Export Growth 1970-1982*, Special Projects and Policy Analysis Division, Department of Finance, August 1984.
7. Peter Drucker, "Japan's Choices," *Foreign Affairs* 65:5 Summer 1987, p.928.
8. See, Robert Z. Lawrence and Robert E. Litan, *Saving Free Trade: A Pragmatic Approach*, (Washington: Brookings Institution, 1986), pp.6-7.

9. For a powerful critique of the new world order and its impact on a country's commercial policy, see Robert W. Cox, *Production Power and World Order: Social Forces in the Making of History*, (New York: Columbia University Press, 1987). Part III Production Forces and the Making of the Future is particularly relevant to the making of Canadian foreign policy.

10. The figure is taken from a paper prepared for the Ministry of State for Economic and Regional Development, "The Rocky Road to 1990" and is cited in the presentation of the Quebec Teachers Federation to the Macdonald Commission. See Chap. 11 in Daniel Drache and Duncan Cameron (eds.), *The Other Macdonald Report*, (Toronto: Lorimer, 1985).

11. Robert Kuttner, *The Economic Illusion: False Choices Between Prosperity and Social Justice*, (Boston: Houghton Mifflin Company, 1984), p.92.

Chapter 13

1. Congress of the United States, Office of Technology Assessment, *International Competition in Services* (Washington: July 1987).

2. Ibid., p. 9.

3. For examples of the impact on specific industries, see Marjorie Cohen, "Americanizing Services," in Ed Finn. ed., *The Facts on Free Trade*, (Toronto: James Lorimer & Co., 1988) pp. 63-67.

4. For an analysis of U.S. House of Representatives and Senate bills designed to remedy U.S. trade problems in telecommunications [H.R. 3 and S.1420] see Daniel Roseman, "Telecommunications Trade: Exporting Deregulation," *International Economic Issues* (Halifax: The Institute for Research on Public Policy, 1987), pp. 27-34.

5. Canada, *Report of the Consultative Committee on the Implications of Telecommunications for Canadian Sovereignty* (Ottawa, March 1979), p. 57.

6. Ibid., p. 64.

7. For more information on the impact of free trade on data processing see, Marjorie Griffin Cohen, *Free Trade and the Future of Women's Work: Manufacturing and Service Industries* (Toronto: Garamond Press, 1987), pp. 70-74.

8. *Inside U.S. Trade*, October 9, 1987.

Chapter 16

This article is adapted and developed from "The Costs of Continentalism," *Compass*, 5, 4, November, 1987.

Chapter 17

1. See *Report of the Royal Commission on the Economic Union and Development Prospects for Canada*, Vol. III, (Toronto: University of Toronto Press, 1985); Thomas D'Aquino (President and Chief Executive Officer Business Council on National Issues) and John Bulloch (President, Canadian Federation of Independent Business), "The Canada-United States Trade Initiative: A Joint Statement," Ottawa, June 26, 1986, p. 5; and *Hansard*, Monday, March 16, 1987.

2. *Economic Benefits from the Canada-U.S. Free Trade Agreement*, (Ottawa: Department of Finance, January 1988); Magan S., Someshwar, R. and Lodh, B., "Impact of Canada-US Free Trade on the Canadian Economy," Discussion paper no. 331, (Ottawa: Economic Council of Canada, August 1987); and "Trade deal only a minor boost, MPs told," *Toronto Star*, Feb. 3, 1988.

3. *Toronto Star*, ibid.; Martin Cohn, "Few regional benefits in free trade, economists say,"; James Kelleher, *Trade Negotiations*, (Ottawa: Dept. of External Affairs, 1985), p. 30.

4. Parker Barss Donham, "The making of a free enterprise myth," July 15, 1987.

5. See Barry Lesser, "The Frying Pan and the Fire," *Policy Options*, November, 1985. p. 32.

6. Donald Savoie, "Establishing the Atlantic Canada Opportunities Agency," May, 1987, p. 14.
7. Department of National Defence, *Challenge and Commitment: A Defence Policy for Canada.* (Ottawa, Supply and Services, 1987), p. 76.
8. Ernie Regehr, *Arms Canada: The Deadly Business of Military Exports,* (Toronto: Lorimer, 1987).

Chapter 18

1. Readers are referred to Paul Muldoon, David Scriven and James Olson, *Cross-Border Litigation, Environmental Rights in the Great Lakes Ecosystem,* (Toronto: Carswell, 1986), for a complete review of cases affecting the Great Lakes and considerations relevant to these arguments.
2. This information is available through the U.S. Freedom of Information Act. It is not uncommon for Canadians to get more through the American Act than they can get from the Canadian system.
3. Further details about U.S. interests in Canadian water can be found in Michael Keating, *To The Last Drop: Canada and the World's Water Crisis,* (Toronto: Macmillan, 1986).
4. Readers interested in the problems cur-

rently facing the Canadian forest industry are referred to Patricia Marchak, *Green Gold: The Forest Industry in British Columbia,* (Vancouver: UBC Press, 1986); Jamie Swift, *Cut and Run,* (Toronto, Between the Lines, 1983); and Ken Drushka, *Stumped,* (Toronto: Douglas and MacIntyre, 1985).
5. A readable article on the Canadian farm crisis can be found in *Harrowsmith Magazine,* Vol.9, No.4, 1984, entitled "Thorns of Plenty," by E. Alden and M. Vescera.
6. Standing Senate Committee on Agriculture, Fisheries and Forestry, *Soil at Risk, Canada's Eroding Future,* (Ottawa: 1984), p.2.
7. The Science Council of Canada, *A Growing Concern: Soil Degradation in Canada,* (Ottawa, 1986), p.7.
8. United Nations World Commission on Environment and Development, *Our Common Future,* (Oxford and New York: Oxford University Press, 1987).

Chapter 19

1. For an analysis of this study see: Marjorie Griffin Cohen, *Free Trade and the Future of Women's Work,* (Toronto: Garamond Press, 1987).

Index

Africa, 80

Agreement on an International Energy Program (IEP), 112

Agricultural and Rural Development Agreements, 190

Agriculture, 3, 22, 53, 73, 166-174, 207-209; American exports to Canada, 167-168; and General Agreement on Tariffs and Trade, 167, 170-171; beef and veal, 169; Canadian exports, 169; competition with American producers, 173-174; dairy industry, 169-170; dispute-settlement mechanism, 169; food processing industry, 172-173; health regulations, 172; horticulture, 171; marketing boards, 166, 168, 170; nontariff barriers, 168; pork producers, 169; subsidies to, 11, 166, 168-170; tariffs, 167-168, 171, 173; technical regulations and standards, 172; wine industry, 171

Air Canada, 121

Aitken, Max, 90

Alberta, 95, 205, 207, 210, 212, 217

Alberta Heritage Fund, 95

Alberta Wilderness Association, 210

American Express, 141, 163

American Farm Bureau, 173

American International Group, 141

American Telephone and Telegraph, 141

Amoco Corporation, 112

Asia, 80

Atlantic Canada Opportunities Agency, 191

Atomic Energy of Canada, 204, 212

Austria, 120

Auto industry, 43, 53, 89, 125-130 (See also Auto Pact)

Auto Pact (Canada-U.S. Automotive Trade Agreement), 14, 22, 73, 106, 125-130, 177, 197, 253; domestic content requirements, 86, 127-128; obligations under, 125-130; qualification for, 125-130; safeguards of, 126

Baker, James, 8, 88

Bank Act, 158, 162

Bank of British Columbia, acquisition of, 158-159

Bank of International Settlements, 157

Bank of Nova Scotia, 74, 90, 159, 183

BankAmerica, 164

B.C. Petroleum Corporation, 95

Bentsen, Lloyd, 6, 7

Bill of Rights (U.S.), 239

Block, John, 9

Bourassa, Robert, 114, 206, 211-212; *Power from the North*, 114, 206, 250

Brazil, 67, 74

Breton, Raymond, 242

Britain, 72, 176

British Columbia: and forestry, 93, 207, 220; and hydro-electricity, 212; and transport, 171; and water, 205; and wine industry, 171; government, 217

Broadbent, Ed, 254

Bronfman, Edward, 157

Bronfman, Peter, 157

Bulloch, John, 185

Burford, Anne, 201

Business Council on National Issues, 31, 51

Canada: access to American markets, 4, 46-58, 81, 92, 117, 120, 167, 188, 220; access to international markets, 66; agricultural industry, 166-174, 207-209; and Atlantic groundfish dispute, 47, 187, 192; and cedar shakes and shingles dispute, 49, 248; and Constitution, 24, 195, 238-245; and continental policy, 22, 72-82, 176-182; and Crown corporations, 31, 75, 87, 121, 132-133, 180; and cultural industries, 36, 223-237; and CUSTER, 31-33, 36, 38-41, 43-45; and financial services industry, 27, 156-165, 244; and General Agreement on Tariffs and Trade, 19-21, 33, 47-49, 56-58, 151, 170-171; and international policy, 22, 80-81, 239-240; and national industrial development, 72, 79-82, 121; and national sovereignty, 73-79, 90, 95, 103, 139, 165, 176-182, 236-237, 238, 241-245; and softwood lumber dispute, 33, 97, 207; and tariffs, 47, 64-

Canadian Dairy Commission, 168
Canadian Food Processors Association, 172
Canadian Grain Commission, 42
Canadian Periodical Publishers Association (CPPA), 227
Canadian Petroleum Association (CPA), 105
Canadian Petroleum Monitoring Agency, 108
Canadian Printing Industries Association, 236
Canadian Radio-television and Telecommunications Commission (CRTC), 73, 121
Canadian regional disparities, 81, 92, 138-139, 165, 173-174, 182, 183-196, 245; Atlantic Canada, 90, 183-184, 186-187, 190-191, 193-196; military spending, 193-194; regional development programmes and subsidies, 189-194, 219, 221; unemployment, 188
Canadian Standards Association, 29
Canadian Transport Commission, 73, 121
Canadian Uranium Upgrading Policy, 210
Canadian Wheat Board, 73, 168, 170
Charter of Rights and Freedoms, 238-239
Chemical Waste Management Inc., 203-204
Chrysler, government aid to, 76
Citibank, 141, 164
Citicorp, 164
Clark, Joe, 229
Clarkson, Adrienne, 235
Clyne Commission, 149
Cohen, Marjorie, 220; *Free Trade and the Future of Women's Work*, 220
Columbia River Treaty, 177
Cultural industries, 223-237; arts, 232, 234; Bill C-58, the *Time-Reader's Digest* controversy, 226-227, 231; book publishing, 224, 231, 235-236; Canadian public ownership of media, 225; Canadian vs. American definition of culture, 229-230; competition with American television programming, 226; copyright and broadcast retransmission right, 224-226; cultural subsidies, 234; divestiture, 224; film production, 231; film recording, 224; foreign investment, 224, 234-235; magazine publishing, 224, 227-228; music publication, 224; newspaper publishing, 224; "Notwithstanding" clause, 228-229, 232-233; postal subsidies, 227; Print-in-Canada require-ments, 224-227; radio and television broadcasting, 224; sound recording, 224; tariffs, 224-225; video recording, 224; vulnerability to American media, 230-232
Community Industrial Adjustment Program, 190
Comprehensive Development Plan (P.E.I.), 190
Conservative Party of Canada, 246, 254
Continental Bank, acquisition of, 158
Cooper, Willy, 235-236
Copyright Act (U.S.) (1978), 224, 227; manufacturing clause, 227
Cummings, Gordon, 187
D'Aquino, Thomas, 185-186
Dairy Farmers of Canada, 169
Danforth, Jack, 6
De Havilland, government purchase of, 76
De Zeeuw, Aart, 170
Defence White Paper, 193
Defense Production Sharing Agreement, 132
Department of Agriculture Outlook Conference (U.S.) (1987), 170
Department of Commerce (U.S.), 3
Department of Defense (U.S.), 9
Department of Energy (U.S.), 203
Department of Energy, Mines and Resources, 113
Department of External Affairs, 31-32, 43, 69
Department of Finance, 42, 59-61, 64, 66-67, 69, 163, 185; "An Economic Assessment," 59-61
Department of Health and Welfare, 202
Department of Regional Economic Expansion (DREE), 190
Department of Regional Industrial Expansion (DRIE), 31, 190
Department of State (U.S.), 3, 43
Department of Supply and Services, 136, 139
Department of the Treasury (U.S.), 42, 43, 163-164
Department of Transport, 202
Desmarais, Paul, 157
Devine, Grant, 186, 250
Dole, Robert, 10
Dome Petroleum, 112
Economic Council of Canada, 185
Eldorado Nuclear Ltd., 203
Employment Equity Program, 136
Energy: 2, 24, 27, 53, 73, 75, 77, 94-96, 105-116, 209-213; and national treat-

ing practices, 6-8, 47, 53, 144-145,
176, 189, 220; exports to Canada, 47,
56-57; investment in Canada, 22, 51-
52, 66, 83-90, 224, 234-235; objectives for free-trade agreement, 2;
ownership of banks in Canada, 160-
164; trade deficit, 3, 7, 47, 53, 56-58,
167; trade harassment, 5, 6, 47, 92,
181; military spending and "set
asides," 132, 138-139, 192-194
United States Trade Representative
(USTR), 3, 11, 36
Vancouver City Savings Credit Union,
159
Vander Zalm, Bill, 217, 250
Victoria and Grey Trust, 162

West Germany, 72
Westcoast Transmission Company, 113-
114
Western Accord, 104-107
Western Grain Transportation Act, 168,
171
Wilson, Michael, 218
Work, 215-222; collective bargaining,
215; demands of employees, 216-217;
effects of movement of capital, 216-
217; labour legislation, 217-218; right
to strike, 215-216; right-to-work legislation, 221; status of women, 217-219;
unions, 217
Yeutter, Clayton, 5, 10, 15, 36, 88, 170
Yukon, 217; "Yukon 2000," 217-218